THE LOG BOOKS

TASH WALKER ADAM ZMITH

THE LOG BOOKS

**VOICES FROM QUEER BRITAIN
AND THE HELPLINE THAT LISTENED**

faber

First published in 2026
by Faber & Faber Limited
The Bindery, 51 Hatton Garden
London EC1N 8HN

Typeset by Typo•glyphix, Burton-on-Trent, DE14 3HE
Printed and bound by CPI Group (UK) Ltd, Croydon, CR0 4YY

All rights reserved
© Tash Walker and Adam Zmith, 2026

The right of Tash Walker and Adam Zmith to be identified
as authors of this work has been asserted in accordance with
Section 77 of the Copyright, Designs and Patents Act 1988

A CIP record for this book
is available from the British Library

ISBN 978–0–571–38833–2

Printed and bound in the UK on FSC® certified paper in line with our continuing
commitment to ethical business practices, sustainability and the environment.
For further information see faber.co.uk/environmental-policy

Our authorised representative in the EU for product safety is
Easy Access System Europe, Mustamäe tee 50, 10621 Tallinn, Estonia
gpsr.requests@easproject.com

2 4 6 8 10 9 7 5 3 1

CONTENTS

Authors' notes   1
2014 – Tash   5
Introduction   11

1 'A bit confused, excited . . .'   35
2 'Huddled together in a corner'   71
3 'Today it's looking, tomorrow it'll be thinking' 117
4 'This troublesome body'   155
5 'Please be gentle'   203
6 'Would like to stay'   253
7 'Fatally disruptive'   293
8 'Multiple paradox net files'   331
9 Conclusion   351

2023 – Adam   361
2023 – Tash   371
Bibliography   381
Acknowledgements   383
Image credits   385
Notes   387
Index   395

AUTHORS' NOTES

Anonymity and confidentiality

Calls to Switchboard have always been confidential. Callers themselves can remain anonymous, including to the volunteer who is helping them. The log books contain names and other information about millions of individual callers, although only rarely is there enough information to actually identify someone from that information. The log books are held at Bishopsgate Institute in what is known as a 'closed' collection, meaning that the archivists will only show them to people who have been approved by Switchboard. Switchboard itself has a robust process of understanding why a person is requesting access and how they intend to use the material, and adjudicating whether they have methods of ensuring confidentiality.

In making the podcast and in writing this book, we have worked in partnership with Switchboard. We have changed callers' names and details. (We've kept the dates of the log book entries correct, but have changed the date format to be consistent across the book, as well as the time format where a time is given.)

Our biases

This book is grounded in the stories of people who have, or have had, what are perceived as sexual and gender identities that are given minority status by the rest of society. We have sought to collect stories from as wide a range across this experience as possible. We've tried to fill in the gaps where the log books or Switchboard didn't capture this range, and explain why that may have been the case. This means trying to include stories that also cross age, class, ethnicity and/or racialisation, (dis)abilities, and nationalities. We had to hold all these characteristics in our minds as we collected material, especially where others' identities and experiences are different from our own. We have carried with us the fact that we are both able-bodied, neurotypical, and racialised as white. With the support of the team around this book, we have sought to remain aware of these characteristics and the privileges they bring us, and to make sure they don't stop us from including, and often centring, others. Any mistakes in doing this are our own.

Language

Writing a social history about a group of people is tricky, especially when that group is as diverse and ill-defined as, broadly, people who identify as lesbian, gay, bisexual, transgender, queer, questioning, intersex, asexual or otherwise a person of gender and sexual difference. Many of these terms change meaning and use over time, and in the same time period two different people can disagree on whether to use a word like 'queer' even while it applies to them both.

We have used the term 'LGBTQ+' as a broad categorisation for people who are made to feel that their gender and sexuality are somehow different. We have used 'queer' similarly, albeit especially in stories where the context includes more of a radical and political edge to it. The plus in 'LGBTQ+' is intended to signal that no acronym is sufficient for the varied nature of this broad group. We have used terms that are appropriate for the time we are writing about: for example, the callers helped during early days of Switchboard are described as 'gay and lesbian'. Although now some of those people might use another word for themselves, we believe it's right to use the words from the time and to place this in context, often referring to how words like these have changed.

The log books contain archaic language that offends some people. We have quoted this language, and added context. But readers should be aware that the following pages contain terms that are slurs, or are otherwise old-fashioned ways of describing people. The log books are also slippery when it comes to pronouns, especially for callers who are exploring their gender, sometimes using different pronouns for the same caller. Where relevant, we've referred directly to pronouns to document the ways we change and evolve. Some Switchboard volunteers reveal themselves in the log books as flawed, their notes stained by transphobia, biphobia, racism, ableism, and/or sexism. This is a part of the Switchboard story, and an element of the story of life in Britain's LGBTQ+ family. We have sought to include and contextualise this, too.

We have used 'Section 28' throughout this book, even though that law was variously also named Clause 28 and Section 2A (in Scotland) during its legislative journey.

We have used the name 'Switchboard' to speak of the charity in the general sense, and the name it used at specific times when that is relevant.

2014
TASH

I've heard rumours. People are saying there are boxes – somewhere – full of fun photographs, protest banners, sexy HIV prevention posters, pages and pages of meeting minutes, and call records. It's all the stuff generated in the running of a helpline that started in 1974, where I am now a volunteer.

My role is to listen to anonymous phone calls from people living all over the UK. They ask me a stream of questions about sexuality and gender identity, and in return I listen in confidence, and answer where I can. It's 2014 and Switchboard – LGBT+ Helpline is approaching its fortieth year of operation. I work shifts in the phone room, drinking gallons of tea, wondering what it had been like before. The rumour of those boxes, filled with hidden voices and lost questions, proves too enticing for me to ignore.

Switchboard's building has a storage area, but it's more of a crawlspace above the common room. I squeeze into it one Saturday afternoon. Wedging myself among the water-stained, dust-ridden boxes, folders and files, I find stacks of papers and minutes, photographs of volunteers in chunky sweatshirts answering phones in the 1970s, and posters stamped with the old Gay Switchboard logo in black and white. Tucked behind a folder of pictures, I discover a stash of notepads, each marked with the words 'log book'.

The spine of the first log book collapsed long ago. Tea stains and doodles are sprawled across its cover. Half of the pages fall out onto my lap as I open it, each covered from top to bottom with dates, times, and notes. The entries were made by volunteers over the decades, describing phone calls they had just taken: a teenager whose parents had kicked them out of home for dressing as the wrong gender; a lesbian terrified of having her baby taken away from her; a man arrested for chatting up another man in a public toilet; and a young person wanting to know how to come out. Sometimes the volunteers wrote to each other: in one entry I read, they are having an argument about a double-ended dildo. What secret time capsule have I opened? Whose lives am I peering down at? Who were all these people?

I can barely catch my breath. Every single time-stamped note is a snapshot into the moment when a person reached out for help. I've found a living, breathing diary of queer life, all of its highs and lows, across the country, across time. The oldest log book dates to 1975, and the records continue until 2003. These books that are falling apart in my hands contain a communal, cacophonous voice made up of all the people who have called Switchboard, and all the volunteers like me who have turned up to the phone room to answer their calls.

These boxes of books feel like a secret, a discovery, something censored that shouldn't be seen – because why hadn't they been seen already? As I open up more and more boxes, further volumes keep appearing, with more and more entries, some painfully lost to bad handwriting. The collection numbers sixty-three books in total. The pages are covered in traces of queer life. Volunteers have written in their reviews of gay bars, taped in flyers for political campaigns, and printed warnings of bomb threats sent to the building. They've even documented their rows – accusations from one volunteer to another about dodging the washing-up or leaving questionable stains on the bed sheets used on night shifts. I read over these notes as if they had been left for me, a smile stretching across my face.

2014 – TASH

So the rumours are true. There are countless untold, invaluable stories held in the pages of these log books, spanning forty years of queer life in the UK. I had no idea about what people had gone through. I am a twenty-eight-year-old queer person who knows nothing of LGBTQ+ history, and nothing of the history of this organisation I am a part of. And these boxes had been stuffed into a crawlspace. I feel like I am the only one who can hear these stories, and everyone else should listen up. The log books are a unique archive, and I need to share them. I haul out another box of books and get to work.

16 June 1975
Caller says he has homosexual tendencies – no sexual experience at all – guy was almost in tears about whole situation.

7 January 1982
Guy from Stroud phoned. Wife told him that she had fallen for a woman (they have been married for 21 yrs – kids etc). He was being very supportive, but clearly upset & under considerable stress (he's been publican of a pub with some gay clientele). Chatted for some length. His wife is going to call us sometime today or tomorrow.

13 March 1991
A Black lesbian called today. She's moved from Nottingham and is living with a straight white woman in South London. She's 19 and slowly coming out. She'll definitely ring on Monday night to speak to Femi.

19 January 1992
Caller got cut off during call, he has been thrown out of his accommodation because he is HIV+ and was asking about legal rights. I went to get Legal File and when I came back he was gone . . . Hopefully will ring back.

10 May 1997
Woman caller who dresses as a man, hopes to have sex change but is attracted to gay men. Where can she go out? Men she is attracted to tend to go to men-only bars/clubs. Any ideas?

23 January 2003
A woman from Glasgow rang to find out how to go about becoming artificially inseminated.

28 February 2003
Had a one hour + 10 min call from a bisexual guy today who started off feeling full of shame + shy about expressing himself

INTRODUCTION

If you grow up by the sea, every day you can feel that the world is wide open to you – and that there is nowhere to go.

We both lived at the seaside, Tash in the south, in Plymouth in Devon, and Adam on the east coast, in Cleethorpes and Grimsby. In 1986 we were babies; we had no idea about the world and what it would hold for us.

Even as a little child, Tash was able to express her opinions, said Julia, Tash's mum, when Adam interviewed her in 2023. 'She was fiercely independent,' Julia said, reflecting back more than thirty years, back to a different era in her own life, raising a young family. When she dropped Tash off at nursery, Tash wouldn't allow her to accompany her inside. One day, Julia peered through the window for a thumbs-up from the staff, but Tash caught her. 'She was so cross that I'd gone to check.'

Where Tash was opinionated but friendly, Adam could be a 'little bugger', according to his mum Patsy, because he used to bite other children. 'I think it started at the nursery,' she told Tash. 'He got into trouble there about it.' Later it became clearer that he was resisting physical play. Patsy said, 'It suddenly dawned on me: Adam's more academic than sporty . . .' This is probably why Cleethorpes library became one of his favourite places.

These are the two children who, in 1986, turned one and two respectively, just as a little storybook brought chaos to a library in Haringey, north London. It was a special library, used by teachers to find books that could help them do their job of explaining things to children, opening their eyes to the world around them.

It was the kind of library that good teachers turned to, to give their pupils the sense that even if it felt like they had nowhere to go yet, the world was waiting for them anyway. That is the power of books, and the promise of stories.

That storybook was *Jenny Lives with Eric and Martin*, written by an author named Susanne Bösche. Susanne's book told the story of a girl called Jenny who sometimes lived with her mum and sometimes with her dad and his boyfriend. The words and photographs of the book detailed Jenny's domestic life, enjoying things like lollipops, breakfast in bed, and a garden party. If we had seen this book when we were little, we might have thought it was OK for a child to have three parents, and for two of them to be men who lived together as partners. Although we were babies, our bodies were on a path to becoming the kind of bodies that would feel more at home in families like Jenny's than the ones we found ourselves in. But the year was 1986, and many people hated the idea that a book could open our eyes in this way. Our leaders, our police, and many of our neighbours tried to make sure we did not see Jenny living with Eric and Martin.

The little storybook didn't make it from London to us, out in our coastal hometowns, but it did hit the national headlines. 'Save the children from sad, sordid sex lessons,' wrote the *Daily Mail*.[1] The *Sun* ran with 'Vile book in school: pupils see pictures of gay lovers'. These are the headlines that our parents might have read over their tea and toast in the morning. They also might have heard voices on the radio like that of Baroness Cox, calling for the 'urgent need to investigate the teaching of subjects like the occult, witchcraft and homosexuality'.[2] Cox had heard about poor Jenny and seemed to assume that satanic men fed her sweets before a sacrifice to the gay gods. Cox believed that books like *Jenny* represented a terrible influence on little children like us, forcing us into homosexuality and devil worship. Cox and the right-wing press were ganging up on left-wing councils such as Haringey's that were placing equality and diversity at the heart of their policy agenda. (The Labour Party had won control of Haringey Council in May 1986, on a manifesto declaring 'commitment to fighting heterosexism'. This included prioritising 'the needs and interests of lesbians'.)

Another panicked parliamentarian who hated this sort of thing was Viscount Buckmaster, a member of the Conservative Family Campaign, who said books like *Jenny* condoned if not advocated 'things like incest and homosexuality'.[3] Others still, the Earl of Halsbury and Baroness Knight, got to business drafting a law that would stop the lesbians and the gays like Eric and Martin in their tracks. In 1987 these lawmakers with their silly titles produced a draft law that would attempt to scrub our generation clean of homosexuality.

It is true that Jenny's family looked different from each of our own, but like us, she was treated with an ice lolly on a sunny day; like Jenny, Tash even has a dad named Martin. It is clear in the cute photographs that Jenny is loved and cared for, and yet the description of this portrait that circled around us when we were growing up is that it was a false, immoral family. And that opinion was a vote winner. The Conservatives pushed that line in a general election in 1987 and won a third successive term in government. With that fair wind behind her, in October 1987, Margaret Thatcher addressed her party conference in Blackpool as the newly re-elected prime minister:

> Children who need to be taught to respect traditional moral values are being taught that they have the inalienable right to be gay.[4]

The following year was 1988, when Tash turned three and Adam turned four. We were soon to enter our school careers, under the tutelage of teachers who might have used books like the one about little Jenny. This possibility was stopped because Thatcher's government passed the law they'd been working on since before the election. The legislation banned councils and the public bodies they funded, such as schools and libraries, from 'promoting homosexuality' and 'pretended family relationships'. This provision was entered into the statute as Section 28 of the Local Government Act 1988. (The last piece of anti-gay legislation had been passed a century earlier, in 1885.) With Section 28, the British state had signalled loudly what many people were saying privately: homosexuality was immoral, and must not be accepted into public life.

The pages of the book in your hands hum with stories about what that evil signal meant for LGBTQ+ people. Everyone who is born or comes to live in Britain inherits a history that is insidiously and pervasively hostile towards queer folks. This hostility has taken many forms, from schoolyard slurs to religious practices, from medical pathways to the law of the land. Section 28 was just one concrete form within a landscape of prejudice and an atmosphere of hostility towards queer people across the fifty or so years covered in this book. We refer to Section 28 in this introduction because it is one thing that validated the anti-gay hostility in the air when we were growing up. We were confused about who we were and we couldn't find the words to talk to our parents about our feelings. Paradoxically, Section 28 has also brought us our biggest project as writers and producers to date, starting with Tash climbing into a crawlspace to search for our hidden history.

INTRODUCTION

To understand our urge to look into recent history, we've had to go in search of ourselves, and where we came from. Tash came out to her parents in a burst of anger at fifteen. Both her mum and dad were fine about it but there was no further conversation. Tash was already a turbulent teenager – shouting down the stairs, scratching rage-soaked tears into her diary, and troubling her parents every time she slammed the front door and slouched away from the house. She was already isolating herself from her family, and coming out felt like something that isolated her further.

Adam's life was nowhere near as dramatic as all that, but he still struggled. Dodging daily shouts of 'puff' at school and never feeling comfortable doing the hobbies he enjoyed, he threw himself into his studies as a way to build a new life in a new place.

Even if our parents had spotted that we were a bit different from other kids, even if they had wanted to create a way for us to talk about our sexuality, how could they have done that? Opinion leaders in the media and parliament decided that we were wrong. Men were dying of a disease called HIV/AIDS that news editors, priests, and police blamed on the sin of gay sex. Lesbians were cast as bitter because they weren't pretty and couldn't find a husband. The stories of queer people in our family histories were shushed out of existence. *Jenny* was shoved out of the library.

Children like us, perhaps not knowing about Switchboard or not daring to call it, were refused answers. At school, Tash tried to ask two teachers for help, but they shut her down. Since 'promoting homosexuality' was illegal, those public servants feared for their jobs. Because local authorities funded youth clubs as well as libraries and schools, any recognition of queer life in the institutions where children like us spent our days was forced into the shadows.

For a moment, consider the stories that are handed down to children and teenagers by the adults around them.

We all inherit stories that teach us about who we are. Sometimes these are cultural, as in the case of a family of football fans passing down tales of their team's great triumphs over the decades from one generation to the next. Sometimes they are a mix of culture and ethnicity, such as descendants of migrants learning recipes that their elders brought to the UK. Sometimes the stories we inherit are about the trials of our relatives who were persecuted for the ethnicity that we share with them.

For LGBTQ+ people, this inheritance process is different. We usually grow up around straight and cisgender people who don't know any queer histories, and who don't trace their own line back in this way. We have to look elsewhere for our stories. The internet was slow and shoddy. And Section 28 was doing its pernicious work, bullying people into holding their tongues and gently obscuring the already poor representation in TV and films, making these stories and lineages even harder to find. Our queer elders, whom we didn't know, had found their pubs, swapped books, created in-jokes – they'd built a culture, but it was marginal, and held out of view from us. We were the generation growing up without experience or memories of LGBTQ+ life in the 1980s and before; but our lives were being shaped by legal changes, the AIDS epidemic, and riotous protests, even if we were unaware.

Section 28 was repealed in 2003; by then we were reaching the age of eighteen and finishing our state education. It took us to 2019 before we truly started our own journey to recover the stories that Britain's fear of all things queer had kept from us. Adam had learnt about his grandfather's fishing heritage, and Tash had inherited her grandmother's Catholicism. But as queer people, we grew up in a kind of silence. We may be the children of Section

INTRODUCTION

28; actually we are its survivors. And it is as survivors that we have found our way to our work, to honour voices excluded from history and shape stories that reimagine the future, as a way to understand what happened to us.

The work has not been easy. We've realised that we, and those like us, carry a kind of grief on our shoulders – grief for the halted conversations, grief for the stories left unshared. This is why Tash was overcome with emotion in 2014 when she found the log books. They contained the hidden stories of people with the same problems and questions that she'd had, even when she didn't know it. Our not knowing about Switchboard, or the millions of people like us who had spoken to its volunteers, hit us with a new wave of grief. We'd been carrying this grief without listening to it. This is why we spent years reading Switchboard's log books, tracing ageing volunteers, and making three seasons of a podcast (titled, like this book, *The Log Books*) from 2019 to 2022. A lot of conversations needed to be had. We were making up for lost time. Throughout our childhoods, our troubled teenage years, and our young adulthoods – even for a decade before we were born – Switchboard had been taking care of people like us. This was our queer ancestry and, finally, we could hear it.

―――

Switchboard was a gang of misfits, a stack of folders, and a bakelite telephone with a curly cord. A couple of the misfits wore suits, but most of them were scruffy. They assembled in a small room above a bookshop in King's Cross, London, in 1974. The area was notorious as a den of depravity, inhabited by sex workers, homeless people, drug users, gays and lesbians, and radical leftwing activists. Number 5 Caledonian Road, the birthplace of Switchboard, was, on the ground floor, a 'radical oasis'[5] named

Housmans, a bookshop stocked high with socialist, anarchist, and progressive ideas behind a green and yellow shop sign. In the 1970s, the building opened other rooms for a rotating number of groups to use. Each focused on a different movement: non-violence, peace, anti-militarism, animal rights, environmentalism, and what was then called 'gay liberation'.[6]

This was a hot, frenetic movement. In the UK, from 1970 to 1973, a group of radical activists known as the Gay Liberation Front (GLF) published a manifesto, held weekly meetings of up to 300 people, disrupted Mary Whitehouse's religious conference, the Festival of Light, and co-organised the first Pride march. Their slogans included 'Gay is Good' and the less snappy 'We demand the right to show affection in public'. By 1974 they were burnt out from trying to start a revolution, and some of their members wanted to change the world by doing something quieter than endlessly protesting. Instead of shouting, they wanted to listen.

This is as much as Tash had heard from the volunteers she met while answering calls in the Switchboard phone room in the 2010s, and from those she'd tracked down over the years. We knew the broad strokes, but when we started to work on this book we wanted to see the details. We knew that the idea for Switchboard had come from Denis Lemon, a member of the GLF who'd helped to set up *Gay News* as a fortnightly newspaper in 1972. At Bishopsgate Institute in the City of London, which houses an ever-growing archival collection on LGBTQ+ life in Britain, Tash went in search of the breadcrumbs leading up to Switchboard's beginnings. There, in the basement, she found the *Gay News* archive and started the search. Tash started to pull out the old copies of the newspaper and, to her surprise and delight, it was all there, written out moment by moment.

INTRODUCTION

The idea for Switchboard was found in Issue 31, dated October 1973, in a column headed 'Hello. Can I help you?' The column read, 'Six years after the Sexual Offences Act, six years after gay activism went into business in England, it seems strange to us that we haven't managed yet to get a central clearing house for information about the gay scene. And it's not that there is no demand for one.'

In 1967, the Sexual Offences Act had partially decriminalised homosexual acts between men in England and Wales. This had sent a signal of freedom to gay men, and even to the women whose homosexual acts had never been criminalised. Times were changing. Since 1967 people had been calling gay organisations in ever increasing numbers for information and help. In 1973, *Gay News* reported: 'Every day at the offices, we get phone calls from people who want to know where the gay pubs are in Burnley, or where they can find a gay solicitors who will handle their legal aid case.'[7]

The article announced a forthcoming meeting to try to set something up. At that meeting Denis put forward the idea of a helpline, having heard of something similar in the USA. The GLF collective had space in the basement of Housmans; those behind the phone line idea were now offered the spare room above the shop, and a few people signed up to get things moving. Thanks to Denis being the editor of *Gay News*, the story is documented in print. Three months after putting out his initial call, Denis wrote: 'Actions taken so far have been the formation of a Launching Committee, the appointment of a Treasurer and the opening of a bank account . . . It is planned for the switchboard to become operational by the spring.'[8]

The sound of the phone rang out in the room above Housmans bookshop at 5.05 p.m. on 4 March 1974. This was the first time someone had called Switchboard for help – and the first volunteers were there to pick up the phone. The news was splashed across the cover of Issue 42 of *Gay News* under the headline 'Gay Switchboard Dial 01_8377174'. With a circulation of 18,000 copies at its height, it wasn't a bad way to get your number out.[9]

'I was certainly there that night,' John Lindsay remembered when Tash interviewed him in 2023. John was the only surviving founding member of Switchboard we could trace.

Technically, John found Tash. He had waited for her outside a talk she was giving at the Barbican Centre in London on the history of Switchboard, during the *Out and About* exhibition curated by Bishopsgate Institute in 2023. True to character, John had a bone to pick with Tash on some of the wording used in the exhibition, and Tash was enthralled. She had heard of John, through one person or another, but had never managed to track him down. Many of the people who were active in the seventies and early eighties had left without staying connected to the charity. But there he stood in front of her, not having attended her talk but having waited outside, patiently, to tell her what was wrong. Tash listened attentively and in that moment heard the richness in the history of Switchboard, in the collective memories of those who remembered. She thought to herself, *John is my history*. These queer ancestors held it all in their minds, like precious archaeological finds that need to be recorded and protected. She took his email address and promised to get the discrepancy looked into. For what it's worth, the discrepancy was that the exhibition referred to Switchboard as 'London Gay Switchboard', not 'Gay Switchboard'. John made it very clear that the founding intention of Switchboard was to be a national helpline, for anyone, anywhere.

Having met John, Tash wanted to speak to him for longer. This is how we were doing our history: by talking, and listening. But reconnecting with him after the exhibition wasn't easy. Tash spent weeks trying to contact him. He checked his email only about once a month and, despite being a founding member of a helpline, he'd told Tash that he no longer used a telephone. They eventually arranged to meet and, on a sweltering August afternoon, Tash walked into the library inside the Barbican Centre and began scouring the aisles for the living book that was John Lindsay. She found him hunched over a library computer researching homosexuality in the Renaissance. Aged seventy-six, John wore a long white beard topped with spectacles, an oversized T-shirt softened by a million washes, shorts, and sandals. The pair of them found a spot to sit, Tash clicked on the recorder, and they began.

'There were not very many people,' said John, casting his mind back half a century to the first night at Gay Switchboard, 'only a small group of us.' John and the others were a group of comrades with a mission and a phone. 'Oh, it was just a fairly bare mess. I think there was a table. I think . . . a settee. There were a couple of chairs, it was really only the cardboard boxes . . . it's amazing . . . after fifty years, I remember the phone number.'

Beyond this, John confessed that his memory of the first night was patchy. How could he and the others have known the importance of that moment? How could you know that you were starting something that would continue for more than fifty years?

'The problem is that the people who I can remember are all dead,' said John, carefully placing down the names of those fallen comrades for the record, names like Ali Bucknell, who worked with John on indexing information for the fledgling helpline.

When Tash interviewed John he no longer remembered the nature of the very first call to Switchboard – but he and the others were meticulous record keepers. Where John's memory struggled, the paperwork picked up the story. All that remained of that first night, save from John's memory, was a stack of sheets of yellowed A4 paper with a pencil grid drawn on. The grid allowed for the volunteers to complete the date, time, and type of call, and add any comments. The call categories on the very first log sheet included 'Clubs & Pubs', 'Medical', 'VD' (venereal disease) and 'What's on tonight'. These log sheets continued and later became call sheets and reports, but it's clear from this first night that it's the 'Comments' section that morphed into the log books.

4 March 1974 – PLEASE DO NOT LOSE
5.05 – refer to CHE LIC, unable to give phone no of Surrey office
5.26 – Referred bisexual guy to talk things over
5.35 – Leather. Visitor from abroad.

Within its first thirty minutes Gay Switchboard had taken three calls that demonstrated the breadth of the information needed. They came from one caller looking for leather clubs, a bisexual person who needed to talk, and someone who got a referral to the Campaign for Homosexual Equality, a law reform group that had been running since 1964. That first night, Gay Switchboard took a total of forty-five calls. John and the others had proven their theory: people needed information and support, and a group of volunteers with a phone line could help them. They knew they'd be busy. When Tash asked John if he was nervous on that first night, he answered: 'Oh no, I had a job to do.'

It was thanks to John that in those early days of Switchboard volunteers could rely on index cards full of information when answering callers' questions. John, a proud librarian, pushed his glasses up his nose and told Tash at length about his love of indexing, which began as a child with an encyclopedia. 'The first thing that I started doing [at Switchboard] was building up a catalogue. So that when telephone calls came in, the people working on the

INTRODUCTION

telephone could look at this card index. First of all, it was by going through *Gay News*, and picking up anything that was mentioned.' John didn't know it then but he was mapping out queer life, laying it down on those index cards, recording the movements of those living in their queer bodies, creating the foundation of an incredible archive.

John was immensely proud to have the organisation itself indexed correctly – that is, listed in the telephone directory under G for 'gay'. This listing was a crucial factor in raising awareness for the fledgling service. With a big grin on his face, John remembered that this recognition wasn't easy. 'There were...negotiations with British Telecom,' he told Tash.

The calls kept coming. 'At some point or other, there was a second phone,' John half-remembered. In fact, just over a year after that first call, Switchboard began operating a twenty-four-hour service, seven days a week. More pubs and clubs were opening; more gays and lesbians were finding each other, or trying to. And thanks to things like *Gay News*, more of them were getting organised in the fight for rights. Volunteers at Switchboard were inundated with questions and queries:

> 18 December 1975
>
> For the third successive session I have been on GS [Gay Switchboard] I have been asked genuine questions about gay sex by people who have been worried about it e.g. 'What happens to the semen when it is inside you?' I think this backs up (unintentional pun!) the point made a few volunteers meetings ago – that if we are asked about fucking etc we should not shy away from giving the information . . . It is worth satisfying a few wankers for the sake of those who are afraid of the unknown or have been conditioned by the outside world to think it 'unnatural'.

21 July 1975
A guy who has been married for 16 years and is gay rang to ask for advice as he thinks his wife is also gay, he has 2 kids 1 of 15 & 1 of 10 & needed to talk with someone.

As the seventies ticked over into the eighties, the service expanded. More and more calls came in from men caught by police when having sex in toilets, lesbians locked into custody battles with shitty ex-husbands, countless teenagers found homeless after being kicked out, and transgender people looking for medical contacts. And millions of calls came in, from all over the world, about what was at first a new, mysterious disease. As the decade rolled on, and more people got sick, Switchboard became a clearinghouse for good information about HIV/AIDS and safer sex. The helpline was, of course, also a counsellor to the community during a period of rampant bigotry and state homophobia. And all of this survives as 'history', on paper, incidentally – because the volunteers thought to record it, not for future generations to read, or for an official archival record, but to help with the day-to-day operation of the helpline.

We were not trained historians or affiliated to an institution, but we were possessed with the need to gather all this recent queer history, and to share it. We knew the story would be about volunteers like John, and about Switchboard itself, but also the anonymous callers and the social and political contexts they found themselves in.

Volunteers like John were there to try to clear up the mess of those years and give advice, and they did this in a very simple way, developing what became the Switchboard method: to listen, calmly, without judgement, and to ask non-directive questions. Day after day, hour after hour, they picked up the phone and said, 'Hello Switchboard, how can I help?'

INTRODUCTION

Often callers asked the volunteer a version of the question 'Are you like me?' When the volunteer explained that everyone at Switchboard was gay or lesbian (an identification that later broadened out to LGBTQIA+), sometimes they'd hear a sigh of relief at the other end of the line. Callers relaxed because they felt, *Finally, I'm home.* From 1974 onwards, many calls to Switchboard have represented 'coming out'. A phone call to the helpline is often the first time that the caller has told anyone about their sexuality or gender identity. From day one, the Switchboard volunteer's role in this moment was simply to listen. There is a special type of listening that occurs when the speaker knows the listener, too, has been through something similar.

This type of listening required Switchboard, and its volunteers, to be open. No surprise that it was founded by a group of people who'd spent the early years of the 1970s marching with placards proclaiming 'Glad to be Gay!' They were out and proud, slipping calling cards into lesbian novels in the library, and joining political rallies under big banners carrying the name 'Switchboard', plus the number – *always* the phone number. This is how Switchboard grew: through openness. It was the openness to listen to people who were not heard elsewhere. It was the openness to declare itself to the world, to swing the doors wide and say, 'Let's talk'. And it was the openness to change with the times, to accept new types of volunteers, to adopt new words, to find answers to emerging questions. This openness remained at the heart of Switchboard over the decades, as the position of gays and lesbians, and then the broader LGBTQ+ community, shifted. Our rights gradually became equalised, the internet made it easier for us to find each other, and we saw ourselves on TV shows like *The L Word* and *Queer as Folk*.

Even Section 28 was repealed, in 2003, just as we turned eighteen and started to join the world on our own terms. It would still take some time, however, for us to meet each other and awaken to the lives that had been going on for all those years – the pounding gay clubs recommended by Switchboard, the advice about lesbian sex and how to get it, the volunteers' private dramas, and the unstoppable endurance of helpline volunteers who kept answering questions. We may have felt like we grew up unheard, but in fact Switchboard was listening all along.

———

Before Tash moved to London, she volunteered at Bristol Switchboard, one of the many Switchboards that have existed across the UK but are now long gone due to cuts in government funding and turbulent political climates. Tash was volunteering there while studying at university, having answered an ad in the local *Time Out* magazine stating 'More women volunteers needed – Bristol Switchboard'. Without an interview, without any training, Tash turned up one Tuesday night for her first shift. She was handed a stuffed folder and told to read it, and if she didn't know the answer, to ring London Lesbian and Gay Switchboard. The London volunteers were so much more knowledgeable, like a collective oracle of all Switchboards. When Tash moved to London, she knew she had to apply to volunteer there. Tash was so nervous at the interview that when she was asked to name a sex act between two women, she could only answer 'erm, holding hands?'!

Thrown in at the deep end, Tash received a new education. To start with she learnt endless terms to describe different sex acts, from iceboxing to felching, and was taught the best way to have anal sex for the first time. The next week she was shown how best to handle suicide calls and what the signs of abuse could be. It was a lot, but the trainers knew they had a job to do. Jeremy Adams,

INTRODUCTION

who was one of Tash's trainers back in 2012, had joined Switchboard in the mid-nineties:

> The training at Switchboard was the hardest I've ever had to do. I think there were sixteen of us on the course, and three trainers, so nineteen LGBT people in a room together, which was, firstly: *whoa!* And secondly, I'd spent most of my life hiding behind the job.

Tash found it surreal to hear her trainer Jeremy speak this way about his early days, and how it was so different from his day job. On training, he said:

> You're in a room where nobody gives a shit about what you do . . . and I found that really hard to start with. I remember during the initial training periods, I used to walk around the block a few times, just to get the courage. And of course you're completely filled with doubt, can I do it, oh my god, and the seriousness of what the thing was, you could be talking to somebody who is about to commit suicide. This is real.

Tash really felt that, too, especially when she started to take calls and became one of the many voices of Switchboard. It was this connection that drew Tash so deeply into the log books in 2014.

Separately, at that time Adam was just starting to have sex. He was twenty-nine years old, and until then had kept his body and its desires to himself. He shed his shame and found pleasure – not just from sex with other men, but also through friendship and emotional intimacy. Over the next few years, these experiences began to change the course of his career. He stayed working on staff as a journalist and social media editor for publications but gradually started to make short films, write articles, and produce podcasts about gay life and LGBTQ+ history. In 2019 he jumped

THE LOG BOOKS

into self-employment to dedicate himself to projects like these, to live and create a more integrated life.

By the time Adam went independent, the log books had left the crawlspace in the Switchboard building. Tash had worked with other volunteers to conceive of the log books, the photographs, the meeting minutes, and the posters as an 'archive'. They were all packed carefully into boxes and moved into Bishopsgate Institute as part of the archival collection mentioned earlier. The archivists there catalogued Switchboard's log books over three years. They laid down a way to protect them and preserve their confidentiality while also opening up their stories.

Tash was the first to carry these stories out into the world. She pulled her favourites into a talk which she toured round various institutions during LGBTQ+ History Month in 2019. This is where we met: Tash presenting her discoveries, and Adam shopping for an enticing project. Adam sat in the audience, staring at Tash's photos of scrawled log book entries, with his imagination reproducing the voices of the callers and volunteers down the line. *This needs to be heard*, he thought, approaching Tash after the talk to say, 'Hello, can we make a podcast?'

A door had opened when Tash had found the log books, a door to a community that was waiting to be heard. That night we walked through that door together. We didn't know it at the time, but we were about to become historians.

We found a third producer with radio journalism experience, Shivani Dave, and the three of us got on with it. First, Adam went into the archive as Tash had done, to read the log books. Entries were collected and grouped into themes that would become episodes. Next, Tash and Adam set about interviewing people with memories of the same years covered in the log books. We started talking and listening. We began with the Switchboard volunteers

INTRODUCTION

whom Tash already knew: Julian, Lisa, Diana, Femi, Richard, and Ruth. Tash had spoken to them all in passing and each one enticed her in with a line from a long-forgotten story of Switchboard. We had no idea how much these people would come to mean to us.

Former call handlers let us into their homes, offered us tea, sat patiently while we set up our recording equipment. As they told us their stories, they embellished with their hands – the same hands that had written the notes in the log books all those years ago.

For every answer they gave us, we needed more context. One interviewee might refer to women going to court to keep their kids, and we'd need to ask them to spell out why. Another might joke about a tactic used to avoid a police officer in a train station toilet, and we needed them to give us a history lesson about gay sex. We were finally learning about the context that we were born into, hearing the stories that didn't exist in our own families, and the ones that our government had censored. It was as though we were finding our queer ancestors and hearing the tales of our people for the first time.

The volunteers' memories were captured in our project too, everything from how they felt listening to the callers to their lives rushing from the day job to the phone room, or visiting gay pubs so they knew which to recommend. Given the chance to remember and to talk, they often led us out of the phone room and onto the loud streets of King's Cross in 1977 for a pint. They walked us through the lesbian marches of the eighties, the sexy, semen-stained S&M nights of the nineties, and they shed their tears once more for those whom they had loved and lost. They had never been just faceless voices on one end of a phone call – they were people affected by the same issues as the callers.

Then we went wider, finding more and more people to listen to, lives lived in parallel to the log books. We listened to stories of love, romance, and betrayal. Harrowing tales of the pain wrought by HIV/AIDS, told by men who'd lost countless friends and lovers. They made us laugh, cry, and sometimes grimace at how relatable some of them were to us today. We spoke to people who had called Switchboard decades earlier, sweat returning to their palms all these years later. The memories conjured up the same emotions as we sat there and listened to them – they became nervous, silent callers once more, anxious people with racing hearts. But we were there to hold them, and, unlike the volunteers at Switchboard, we got to hear what happened next. They all gave us their voices, and we recorded their lives, listening and learning. These stories and many more are coming up in this book. But in these pages we intend to do much more than retell stories that were originally recorded for a podcast.

What we realised as we collected stories over three podcast seasons is that we were filling in the gaps in our own history. For the most part our biological family stories didn't contain meet-cutes of women getting together in a lesbian bar. They didn't include tales of men having to evade police just to have sex with each other. Even little Jenny's story of eating breakfast with her dad and his boyfriend was hidden from us. At school we rightly learnt about the movement for women's suffrage, but not the gay liberation protests. We never got any official queer history lessons – it was illegal!

In the log books we finally found the stories we should have inherited: stories of people searching for love, or sex (lots of sex), fighting for rights, finding friends, making homes, building families, and, more than occasionally, trying to bring down the imperialist, white supremacist, capitalist patriarchy. This is why our project was important – it was a reclamation for our entire generation.

INTRODUCTION

The Switchboard callers and volunteers, and every person we've interviewed, are extra parents, grandparents, uncles and aunts, sharing their war stories and their wisdom. This is our queer ancestry. This is who we are. It is an inheritance filled with histories, herstories, theirstories, life lessons, and lived experiences, specifically ones that have not been shared before, or ones that risk being drowned out by other histories that focus on activists and legal rights. The podcast was our education – it opened doors to so many stories, but even more questions.

We were naïve. This was so new to us, and our personal excitement and overwhelm at this 'discovering' made us giddy and gooey-eyed, obsessed with the collecting. Like sugar-addicted kids we wanted more, but didn't notice the impact that it was having on us. Mics in hand we reached out to hear the stories of our elders; and now we have had the space to see how that changed us. This book is the unravelling of our lives as we reframed the stories we heard and saw how they changed who we were – like the log books, we are also living archives.

One feature of this inheritance is its revelation that we share something unique with those who have lived LGBTQ+ lives before us. This is why we have added our own stories and reflections throughout this book. Another feature is that our queer ancestry has huge gaps. The log books are not a comprehensive survey of LGBTQ+ life: for a start, historically Switchboard took far more calls from men than from women. In the podcast and in this book we've used interviews to fill these gaps and add context. The result of all this work – that is, the learning of our history and our discovery of queer ancestry – is our realisation that the lives of our elders, often hidden, have so much to teach us.

In making the podcast we came to see how we were following the tradition of listening to the stories of our elders, one of the only ways that queer histories have been passed down, as opposed to the police records and laws that tell the story of our oppression. We were trying to tell our histories our way, in a queer way. It wasn't about statistics or saucy gay kings; it wasn't about Oscar Wilde or even the radical activists who'd shouted the loudest. Our queer history was quieter, and from people who were largely unknown. This story is grounded in the millions of everyday people who called Switchboard for help and the many who didn't but wished they had, the experiences of the volunteers who listened to them, and, finally, us – the children of Section 28.

The log books are a treasure trove; and the once-living archives like John Lindsay are even more valuable.

During the writing of this book, John died. It was August 2024, and it had been exactly a year since Tash had sat down and interviewed him in the Barbican library. It was hard to hear the news. Tash attended his funeral at Pembroke Lodge in Richmond Park, London. She wore shorts, like John always did. His partner Tim spoke gently, through tears, of meeting John twenty-seven years ago, and of their life together. People shared memories of their times with John in the GLF, living with him in the squats of east London, and how he believed in the power of sharing information. They recounted tales of stubbornness and gruffness throughout his life, but also confusion near the end. In a moment where people were invited to share their memories, Tash stood up and shared hers. She wanted everyone there to know that John had heard Switchboard's phone ring out for the first time, and that by the time of his death fifty years later, the charity had taken over four million calls.

The last founding member of Switchboard that we could find was gone. Tash had managed to record John and capture his

INTRODUCTION

memories of setting up Switchboard, and writing all those index cards, in his own words. And now they are laid out in this book. So many more comrades have been lost. Many didn't survive the HIV/AIDS epidemic. David Seligman, who always wore a suit for his shifts in the phone room and worked so hard to professionalise the helpline, was around when we were making the podcast, but not well enough for an interview. He passed away before we started writing this book. We didn't know enough about the value of David's work until it was too late for us to ask him how he did it. We have evidence of his work in the log books (his notes written loudly in all caps and wide letters), but little else. We don't know what his voice sounded like. This is why recording queer people's memories is important. Memories are often the only 'history' that we have.

Hundreds of hours of audio, pages and pages of notes, voices, and stories – our stories, our history. It is history that everyone should know. We didn't know that when we started this project to collect a few stories, we were at the beginning of something bigger – a journey that would re-educate us, and change us for ever.

1
'A BIT CONFUSED, EXCITED . . .'

Sex, desire, and the freedom of enjoying your body

> 21 January 1989
> There is a young woman who has rung 6 times this evening and gives the tale that she and her girlfriend of the same age want to know what they can do to each other sexually and then wants to know what men do to each other.

Tash's first kiss with a girl was a hot mess. It was a girl from school and it took place one night down a back alley. Although it was grotty behind the bins, nothing could dampen the pleasure Tash felt inside. Every molecule in her body vibrated with desire. The next morning that feeling was cut with terror. She did not want to be gay. She knew what that meant, and how she would be seen: a lesbian. It was 2001, and it was clear what the world thought of people like that. Similarly conflicted feelings can be found in numerous log book entries:

> 9 February 2002
> Female caller under 20, very upset & crying saying 'I don't want to be gay'. Very traumatic. She's starting to explore her feelings, use family/friends as support which I encouraged. Will probably call back.

Tash may have been reluctant and ashamed, but she was also a defiant person. Rather than holding her desire in, she let it out and ran into a world of sex with women. In fact, in her late teenage years and twenties, she hurt some of them by acting recklessly and carelessly in pursuit of her unfettered desire.

Adam didn't want to be gay, either. Adam became sexually active at the age of fifteen, around the year 2000, but only with himself. He had some lads' mags with sexy women in bikinis, and quite a lot of photos of naked guys from the internet, printed line by line with the family inkjet printer. For the next fourteen years he pleased himself. The pictures became videos, his hand his long-term partner. When he first had sex with someone else at twenty-nine, it was gay and it was good, and it changed his life.

When we both read the log books in our thirties, the act felt salacious. We were thirsty for all this sexy gossip we had missed out on. We wanted more. But as we consumed these stories, the related feelings we had held so tightly began to untangle. All the people who had called Switchboard to talk about sex had experienced the same hormones as us. We all desired other people, but somehow the way that we felt about ourselves and who we desired was almost too much to bear.

Who had made us hate ourselves so much?

Our parents hadn't talked to us about sex very much, and if they tried we blocked them. Our teachers were working inside legal and social constraints, bound by the reticence in society to talk to adolescents about sex. We sat through our so-called sex education, present but not included. At an all-girls grammar school Tash was given an overripe banana and a condom. No prizes for guessing which one remained a staple in her life. Adam's teacher showed his class a clip from the film *Trainspotting* because it included an incidental condom use during the terrors of heroin withdrawal. We learnt about men and women having sex to make babies, or how to avoid the babies. All these lessons focused on pregnancy and sexual health, not relationships or pleasure. Where was the sexy

'A BIT CONFUSED, EXCITED...'

detail? The sexual world was revealed to us through the lens of reproductive heterosexuality and disease.

And, worse, some people were working actively against us, from powerful government ministers to campaigners like the ones who dropped this leaflet at a school:

> 9 February 1992
>
> Young woman, 16, phoned to say how angry she was about sex education leaflet given to her at school describing gays as 'seasoned perverts acting to corrupt impressionable minds & bodies etc etc blah blah blah!' She read me out what it said . . . & it's outrageous. The leaflet by a group called:
>
> Youth Concern
>
> % Family + Youth Concern
>
> Who are they? They sound very dangerous and pernicious!

With teachers who were either actively homophobic or censored by the state or by groups like 'Youth Concern', if we'd had questions, the only place we could have turned to was Switchboard.

What Switchboard did from 1974, and through our adolescence, was revolutionary. Volunteers were committed to answering callers' questions about sex and sexual health without judgement. The log books show that for many people the moment they called Switchboard was the first time they had spoken about their desires with anyone. Many callers lived at home under a policy of 'don't ask, don't tell'. The silence these callers faced at home, at school, in society, was deafening. As we read the entries, we were reminded of our own sexual histories . . . and just how difficult they had been for us.

We were born into a time when the dominant social attitude was against us. In the British Social Attitudes survey of 1983, respondents were asked their views on sexual relations between two adults of the same sex. Half said these were 'always wrong'. In 1984 and 1985, our years of birth, the figure went up to 54 per cent and then 59 per cent. By 1987 it was 64 per cent. A further 11 per cent said it was 'sometimes wrong', meaning that when we were little, three-quarters of British people were against homosexuality.[1]

We both grew up amid shame, confusion, and fear. Much later, through the log books, we noticed that the careful listening of Switchboard volunteers could show us a better, alternative way, even if we didn't benefit from it when we needed it. There is an entry in Switchboard's first log book that says:

> 12 June 1975
>
> Transexual call: fuck society for twisting people.

During one of Tash's early journeys into the log books, this line made her stop dead. She took a picture immediately and sent it to friends, asking: *What's changed?* It made Tash think about a time in her twenties, when she asked her dad when he first thought she might be gay. He replied saying that he had always known from the way she liked to play. When Tash was four she asked everyone to call her 'Jase', after Jason Donovan; her family had been supportive and thought she had a little crush on the *Neighbours* actor. But it wasn't that. Jason was her role model. She wanted to play at being a 'he', but she was a kid and lots of kids do this when they are little. When she read that log book line about society twisting people, she saw that something else had grown on top of all of her innocent play in wanting to be Jase. Maybe her shame wasn't just about her sexual desires.

Since sex was one of Switchboard's primary calling cards from the moment the phone lines opened, when we began to collect stories

'A BIT CONFUSED, EXCITED . . .'

from the log books, we started with the sexy ones. Before the internet, people had been calling Switchboard with the most fundamental questions:

21 September 1995
Caller rang to thank us for advice given a week or so ago about having sex for the first time – it all went brilliantly!

This person had called Switchboard because he'd wanted to take a first step to discovering his desires. Volunteer Julian Hows never forgot those kinds of questions. 'Is it painful to be fucked? Is it painful to fuck?' he remembered. When Adam recorded his stories in 2019, he fired off classic queries fast, like a stand-up comedian telling an old one. 'The thing of lubricant, of relaxation, of taking things gently. There was more to sex than fucking, anyway.'

Adam sat across from Julian, recorder in hand, lapping up every word. He had not spent much time in the company of outrageous queens like Julian. As he told his stories, Julian twinkled his eyes and flung his arms about, relishing the sex gossip, even, possibly, flirting with Adam.

Julian explained how he and the other volunteers built a diverse and filthy knowledge base of sex acts, dirty places, tools, terms, and toys. These people had archived our sexy histories without even knowing it. What a treasure trove to reach us all those years later, as we sat in a formal, silent archive reading the log books. Perhaps they are the filthiest books in existence.

'We had the complete list,' grinned Julian. 'There became the famous thing of wearing a teddy bear in one's left-hand back jeans pocket. [It] meant I was a cuddler, and wearing it in the right-hand meant I wanted to be cuddled.' Julian laughed a ragged smoker's laugh and summed up Switchboard's role in talking about sex:

'The community asked a question and then amongst the volunteers we'd sort it out.'

There was no stupid question about sex, remembered Femi Otitoju, who was an integral Switchboard volunteer for many years. 'One of the ones I remember most of all was, "I've managed to persuade this woman over to my house, she's coming and she's staying tonight, and I've never had sex with a woman before and I don't really know what to do."' Femi explained how she used to handle those kinds of calls. 'You'd start with very practical things like, "Do you masturbate, how does that feel for you?"'

Women would ask if penetration was acceptable to lesbians; men would ask if anal sex was compulsory, and how to not cum too soon.

Through listening and asking questions, volunteers like Femi came to understand what a caller liked to do with their body already, and what they wanted to try. The volunteer would sometimes give options, suggesting techniques and moves – but always making sure the caller knew they should be in control of their body. This is how the threads of feminism and gay liberation, as political movements, made it into the practical support offered by Switchboard volunteers. The volunteers were doing this work in the seventies and eighties, long before Tash and Adam needed sex education, but even by the time we got ours in the nineties, it was nowhere near the quality of that offered by people like Femi to those who managed to call Switchboard. When we read the log books and interviewed the volunteers, it dawned on us what we had missed. We'd been longing for something unnamed, until we heard our elders like Femi name it.

As a teenager Tash felt like a freak, not daring to look at girls she fancied in case they noticed. She didn't dare to snog other girls during games of spin the bottle. She was ashamed of the feelings in her body. She didn't want to stand out. The idea of someone sitting down with Tash to listen and to talk like Femi had done to all those callers seems like something from another world – and yet it was so close to us.

As Adam was growing up in Cleethorpes and Grimsby, without knowing it he probably passed places where men met for sex. That is the queer life: it is both ubiquitous and invisible at the same time. Switchboard volunteers have told us all about the many symbols that different LGBTQ+ peoples have used to connect, sometimes secretly, with others. Queer people love a symbol, especially when it's about sex – badges, pendants, karabiners, earrings. For men seeking men, one symbol was so important in the seventies and eighties, and so complicated, that it led to calls like these ones:

> 22 September 1976
> [Newspaper clipping] South Humberside. Slim 38, own home etc. wants to meet bloke with black handkerchief in left hand pocket or right.
> [Written by volunteer] Okay you infomaniacs – I just had a guy on the phone asking what this is about. Left for dominant, right for submissive. Yellow means golden showers, but black? Or red? Maybe we should have more readily available info on leather/denim/s&m things??

> 4 October 1976
> A guy phoned asking if we knew 'The Handkerchief Code' We didn't know. Does anyone else?

The 'hanky code' is a way to signal a sexual desire and your role within it. You choose a handkerchief in a colour that symbolises the specific sex act, and you stuff it into your jeans pocket so the colour hangs out on display. Whether you wear it in the left or the right pocket says exactly what you'd like your relative role to be in the sex act. So when one caller asked what a red hanky meant, the volunteers realised they had to pool their knowledge and make sure they were all up to date. That's why one of them carefully drew a table of the code across a full page in the log book on 16 October 1976. When Tash came across it during her research, she devoured it, line by sexy-fun-hilarious line. We suspected that the volunteer had had a laugh with some of the entries . . .

LEFT HIP POCKET (butch and sadistic)	COLOUR	RIGHT HIP POCKET (passive and masochistic)
Fist fucker	Red	Fist fuckee
A. Fucker	Blue	Put your heels on his shoulders
A Whipper	Black	What else? A Whippee
Came straight from the office, didn't have time to change	White	Had time but is signalling non-conforming to the code
His hang-up (or down) is size – the bigger the better	Mustard	Has eight inches or more
69s are what I have in mind tonight	Robin's egg blue	Anything but 69 tonight

'A BIT CONFUSED, EXCITED...'

Unlimited, but wants to discuss pre-Columbian art first	Puce	Looking for a discussion on pre-Columbian art
Hustler – selling	Green	Hustler – buying
Golden shower – pisser	Yellow	Golden shower – receiver
Drag in disguise	Lavender	His sister Kate
The insouciant habit of anything, anytime	Orange	Nothing. Never. His legs are glued together with Bostick
Shitter	Khaki brown	Shitee

Julian could even have been the joker who made this entry. He told us he had a multicoloured hanky. 'When you pull[ed] it out, like a magician's hanky, it became all the colours!'

As the hanky code reveals, sex practices can be varied. LGBTQ+ people are often particularly adventurous, and also happy to talk about what they get up to. If you can imagine a kink, Switchboard has heard about it:

> 13 August 2001
> Caller rang wanting to know about 'adult babies' groups – people dressing up in nappies. Couldn't find anything on database (Checked fetish/other). Anyone know of anything?

27 August 2002
Anyone else take a call from a guy in his 30s near Lancaster who says that he doesn't fancy men or women, just people dressed up in Rubber Fishing Gear? He sounded very genuine!

25 February 1994 – 6 a.m.
First call for an hour. I've just found out what a toilet slave is. Yuk.

2 January 1976
Guy called would like to form a group for gays who are podophiles (ie lovers of feet). If an extensive and exhaustive list of people who have the same penchant could be prepared he will ring in a month or so to see who is interested.
I had an amazing ½ hour talk about my feet (he almost chatted them up!), his feet, dancers' feet, his lover's foot (one lost in war). The great thing about S/B is that I managed not to have hysterics not having had experience of this before. In fact I got quite fascinated.

Another volunteer replied to the last entry to recommend that the caller advertise in *Gay News* to find others who were interested in feet. We loved coming across entries like that, showing how much the volunteers took callers' interests seriously, but also revealing that Switchboard was staffed by humans. Two of the volunteers above were, at least in the privacy of the log book, a little dismissive of their callers' kinks. The service was non-judgemental, but when it comes to sex and fetishes, we all have our biases.

Calls like these often stuck in volunteers' minds years after they'd been taken. When Adam interviewed former volunteer Jeremy Adams in 2019, he could still recall one of the first calls he took soon after joining twenty-five years earlier, in 1994. 'It was a morning shift, and the person said, "Hello I just want to talk to you before my master hangs me, is that alright?"'

Even though he'd been trained, Jeremy didn't initially know how to address someone who was in a master–slave sexual dynamic within a BDSM context. During his interview with Adam, Jeremy sat in a black roll neck jumper in his office in the theatre where he was working, and he explained in his calm and inquisitive tone: 'Of course this was a relationship this person had with this master, and every Tuesday at eleven o'clock they went through this ritual hanging. Perfectly normal.'

Learning about the BDSM world is a particularly deep education for many volunteers. 'It's so easy to start putting our interpretation [on them],' said Jeremy, '"Are you happy being a slave? Are you happy being hanged every morning?" But actually that's what they wanted to do and that's what they liked doing. You're perfectly safe, you're happy . . . all the different people in their different lives, and the different things they do.'

It is through calls like these that Switchboard developed its unique training in how to be non-judgemental. As Jeremy says, whatever your initial thoughts were, you had to put them aside. This was the power of Switchboard: callers knew they would not be judged. Sometimes, though, it's impossible not to have a laugh about this stuff.

> 10 January 1993
> Caller (w): 'Can you tell me about Clone Zone?'
> Me : 'yes it's a shop selling everything from lycra shorts + underwear to leather harnesses + nipple clamps. Predominantly gay boys but some women use it. Why, what do you want?'
> (thinks she's looking to buy a dildo)
> Caller: 'Well I've just found an access receipt in my husband's pocket!'
> !!

4 March 1995

I had a call . . . #1 this guy phones and says:

'Hello, can you tell me about S&M please'

I thought he said M&S – i.e. Marks & Sparks. So I said 'what are you looking for',

'something new and different' he replied.

'Well' said I, 'you ought to try the big store at Marble Arch, they put new lines in there all the time.'

'New lines? Oh no I'm not into piercing.'

The penny dropped.

―――

Although Switchboard pooled an orgy of information about sexual practices and subcultures, it was not set up to link people directly together. That's why volunteers suggested callers advertise in gay newspapers or go to certain places to find like-minded people. It's why teenaged Tash went to a place called Zeros in Plymouth, seeking a sexual match in a queer club. We are both of the generation that straddles two sexual epochs: the era of the dating app, and the era before. Grindr launched in 2009 and changed almost everything in the interactions between men who have sex with men. By the time Adam started to have sex in 2014, Grindr was ubiquitous, and it definitely helped him to make up for lost time in exploring his sexual body with others. Other apps launched, catering to different bodies, sexualities, and preferences. But before all of that, websites helped people to connect. Gaydar Girls opened up an online world for Tash while she was still at school. After connecting via scratchy dial-up modem, she was presented mainly with offers of threesomes from 'straight' couples – not what she wanted, but still a world filled with potential. Others included Man Hunt and Gaydar, and the forums on Gingerbeer, which was a community website for lesbian and bisexual women in London.

A lesbian called Fisch said she got some of the weirdest responses when she chatted to women on Gingerbeer. 'I think they were more your woolly jumper . . . lentil-eating lesbians,' she remembered, when Adam spoke to her in 2021. 'I just said, "Does anybody fancy some casual sex?"' Although she got a digital cold shoulder, she did meet up with some people that way. But as someone who was active in the dyke sex clubs of the eighties and nineties, Fisch said that meeting online wasn't right for her. 'I'm old-school,' she said. 'I'd rather see what someone smells like.' As a dedicated sniffer, Adam knew exactly what she meant.

Fisch's story connected with those of callers to Switchboard who were looking to share physical space with someone else. If the log books make it clear that people want to discover their desires, the stories we've collected of people doing this reveal just how much sex and desire are bodily experiences – visceral, sweaty, smelly.

This is what people like Fisch wanted, and what all those callers who asked for help in exploring their fetishes wanted. It is also what the men who had sex in public wanted. For centuries before apps like Grindr, websites like Gingerbeer, and helplines like Switchboard, men had been meeting in public toilets and the dark corners of parks to get off with each other. The log books are a chronicle of this unique part of the queer experience. They contain countless entries about 'cruising', the practice of looking for sex in a public place, and about 'cottages', places such as public toilets that were known as spaces where men met for sex. These are histories we know about, but these entries are unique because they are told through the voices of those who lived in these moments. These are the people behind the police records, the mugshots, and even the lucky escapes. We were looking at our history, being told by those who lived it, not by those who tried to suppress it.

> 15 May 1975
> Does a gay beach count as outside cruising? Well, where do we draw the line with what information we give? Are we simply keeping on the right side of the law or are we moralising in the way the creators of law want us to? Aren't we supposed to disagree with what the law/tradition/other people . . . say we should do? Whose game are we playing – ours or theirs? I know it's debatable but what does the team think?

> 28 October 1975
> A caller asked specifically for all-night cruising places. I told him. Is this now ok?
> I don't intend to offer such info unless asked for it specifically, and will give warnings and respectable alternatives.

Specific acts in cruising and cottaging were criminalised even after the partial decriminalisation of homosexuality in 1967. There was a common assumption that men having sex in a public toilet were particularly turned on by the location and the risk of being discovered. This was true for some. But for many men, sex in this way was their only option. They may not have been out, as 'gay' or 'bisexual'. They may not have felt comfortable going to a gay pub or a gay social group. They may not have been able to have men come home with them, if their desires were secret from the people they lived with – housemates, landlords, or family members. As we did our research on this in 2019–24, Adam experienced the exact same issues in sex spaces and his own sex life.

Most of the calls regarding this public sex were about police actions against the men who were doing it, and we knew that would be a big piece of work to investigate. Initially we stuck to researching the fact that it was happening and, most interestingly, how it was sparking debates among the volunteers in the phone room.

> 12 October 1975
> On the subject of cruising: The trouble with the cruising scene is that the whole concept has become abused and distorted.
> Surely the idea of cruising is that a guy goes, say, to Holland Walk (of which I used to be very fond) in the hope of meeting someone with whom to trick, or if he is fortunate enough, with whom he can form a more lasting relationship. (I was lucky and met someone there whom I loved and lived with for 3 years, until he had to go back to the US). On returning to that place it seems that the whole scene has shifted to the dark stretch of pathway at the top where groups of gays stand around with their hands in one anothers' parts.
> Can you imagine how this must strike people who are using the walk simply to get home at night? Is it unreasonable that the fuzz [police] get complaints from the public and act on them (which they are obliged to do) or even do so on their own initiative? Shit! I know what these people are doing and yet each time I see the whole zombie-like scene it gives me the creeps. Faceless forms groping at each other.
> I have actually seen two cops go up to a het couple who were snogging on a bench in Holland Walk and ask them to leave – without hassling the gay guys at all! So why should gays expect to be allowed to indulge in masturbation in a public place without trouble? That includes cottages.
> But apart from anything else – it's much nicer to do things in a bed.

This entry drew a few responses from other volunteers, agreeing or disagreeing, and another who added a ditty:

> WHY BEAT SOMEONE'S MEAT IN A STREET
> OR SHOOT YOUR LOAD ON THE ROAD
> WHEN YOU CAN WANK IT
> BENEATH A BLANKET
> AND PERHAPS EVEN DISCOVER
> A LOVER

That poet then added, 'It's been rather quiet tonight.' Broadly, Switchboard seemed to be in favour of public sex, knowing that being against it would put the volunteers on the side of homophobic public policy and the state. As Julian remembered, it was easy to argue in favour of cruising in public places because it involved only those who actually wanted sex:

> This whole idea of it offending public decency or something like that? Well, no, because most people who were using [a cottage] for normal purposes of a toilet came in, went to the nearest cubicle, went straight out again . . . it's not as if people were accosting people who were not using it for that, because there'd have been no point anyway. What was the point when there was so much delectable flesh on offer anyway?!

Volunteers like Julian were nothing if not sex-positive, and they were often sex radicals. We felt liberated meeting these queer elders who had such progressive thoughts. It pushed us to explore our own, and Adam found his way into sex clubs more and more when he wasn't in the archive. Some volunteers, however, had let their personal prejudices make it on to the pages of the log books, as in this exchange about the use of poppers, a drug common among gay men:

'A BIT CONFUSED, EXCITED . . .'

29 August 1975
[Volunteer David:] People who sniff poppers need an extra physical kick from sex as they get no emotional satisfaction.
[Volunteer Anon.:] You sanctimonious tie-wearer

We both loved reading these debates in the pages of the log books. They often carved out the same ethical positions as the ones that we experienced much later; no doubt the question of what is morally acceptable and what is not will continue far into the future, too. But Adam's particular response to all the chatter about public sex on the phone lines, as revealed in the log books, was one of amazement. He'd previously suppressed his desires and been one of the people Julian was describing: blind to what was going on in train station toilets and the corners of parks. Opening up sexually had opened his eyes, too. Then, through reading the log books, Adam was able to see his place in a glorious history – a history of bodies discovering themselves and each other, enjoying pleasure, and living their freedoms while evading the forces that would stop them. (Also, it's just hot to look around and tune into the web of sexual energy that governs our public interactions.)

Tash had a different response altogether: where were the women wanting to have public sex with women? And all the other people in between the binary genders? Where were their illicit, sexy stories? Tash had had sex in public, from parks to graveyards, beaches to secret rooms in the backs of bars, as well as in beds under duvets at night while the cat slept downstairs. There was something different here that Tash was drawn to, much like the writer Amelia Abraham. In an interview for *Granta* in 2024, Abraham explained why few people except masculine-presenting cis-men would feel safe to head out into the dark of night for a walk, let alone in search of sex. 'Cruising is not as accessible for many people, such as some disabled queer people,' said Abraham. 'It is perhaps riskier for Black and brown people in terms of policing, and it is less physically safe for trans people and women. Yet it is often talked about as a radical practice . . . "as gay as it gets", as it were – and I have felt frustrated by that sentiment for these reasons.'[2]

Tash found herself longing to be part of that disruption in the log books, which itself was a complex reaction to an act that has grown out of oppression. Even though there were no stories of women cruising in the log books, that didn't mean that it didn't happen. What unified both of our experiences in reading about public sex in the log books was the experience of an absence. Tash found that something was missing, and Adam hadn't even seen something that was there. We realised as we heard about all the queer sex in our histories that we felt this absence – for ourselves, sometimes, and also for all the people who wanted to discover their desires but couldn't.

This was a theme explored in a stage show produced by Breach Theatre and first staged in 2023, *After the Act*. The title referred to Section 28 and the show was created and performed by people who, like us, grew up in the wake of that homophobic law. Our interviewee Ed Lees saw *After the Act* in 2023 and found himself weeping at the end. 'It's really hard to capture an absence and how it impacts on you,' he said. He'd grown up without queer role models or a queer person to speak to. And it's why when he did come out and started to expand his discovery, he went to a different continent to do it. 'I was so scared in those two years of exploring and coming out,' he remembered, realising that he'd travelled to spend time in Buenos Aires partly because he needed to be away from friends and family if he was going to practise being the real Ed.

The absence that people like Ed and us have wanted to fill pre-dates Section 28. It is there throughout history, produced by other homophobic laws, the violent enforcement of patriarchy and the gender binary, and much more. We were brought into a society that had been excluding queer people for centuries, and that would still have continued even if Thatcher's lot had failed to pass Section 28. Switchboard started to address this all in 1974. It could only directly help the people who managed to call, but for those people it was a lifesaver. The unique thing about being LGBTQ+ is the need to find a time, space and language to discover your body and its desires. How did Switchboard volunteers set about this enormous task? How did they gather knowledge of sex and how to talk about it?

From day one of Switchboard it was important that all listening volunteers had the same level of knowledge. This was not an easy task, staffed as it was with gays and lesbians whose lives might not otherwise have crossed. 'I remember sitting next to a gay man hearing him talking to what I perceived to be a lesbian, about lesbian sexual practice,' said Femi, 'and I must say, more than once I was more than slightly surprised at some of the things . . .'

We had both seen Femi's name in pink pen dotted across the log books, and pictures of her at various Prides in amazing dresses and leather capes. We knew we wanted to speak to her, and she was one of the first people we contacted when we sought elders to interview. Adam was the one to do it, nearly giving himself a heart attack as he cycled uphill towards her house and arriving, out of breath, just on time. He was pleased he'd pushed himself, as Femi had the air of someone who would remember if he'd arrived late. She welcomed him in and they sat down on a soft sofa. Her large, tidy house was intimidating enough, but then Femi herself – the former volunteer with the pink pen – sat across from Adam waiting, and he had to ask her about lesbian sex in the seventies.

Often the male volunteers' knowledge of lesbian sex fell behind, Femi told Adam. She said that the helpline worked on the principle that everybody had to be prepared to talk to anybody about anything. One day, she said, it became clear that certain colleagues needed a refresher course on lesbians' body parts and what was possible with them. She smiled at the memory; it was remembering stories like these that softened Femi. (And in fact, over multiple interviews with us both over the years, her seriousness turned playful.)

'Some of us lesbians got together and decided that we would do an in-service training session on lesbian sex and sexual practice,' she said to Adam. It is no surprise that Femi took on this role during her time, as she is a natural trainer. She founded a business in 1985 to advise public and private organisations on diversity, and pioneered training around unconscious bias in the workplace.

Talking about vulvas, even to men, came naturally too. 'I thought, *I'll teach them biology* . . . So I bought a great roll of lining wallpaper and drew a massive great diagram as big as my dining-room table.' The point of Femi's workshop was to centre this anatomy in a conversation about pleasure. When Tash first heard this interview she was transported back to herself as a teenager; how much better, how much more authentic and expansive, would sex education have been if it was done like this?

'I drew this great big vulva, clitoris, hood, rolled it all up and took it on the bus to the West London Day Centre, where we tended to hold our in-service training sessions,' said Femi. 'I don't know what happened to the elastic band . . . but as I came down the stairs on the bus, this wretched thing fell out of my hand and rolled down the stairs and opened up.' Femi tilted back with laughter at the memory. 'There were some very shocked people at the bottom of the stairs. We had a lot of fun in those days!'

Presumably Femi's training session went well, and the men of Switchboard were more equipped to talk about lesbian sex (and ditto the bus passengers). 'Getting gay men to at least know what women did in pairs together was always a revelation,' Julian said, 'but I'm sure it was just as much a revelation to some lesbian women of the strange practices that boys got up to as well.'

Lisa Power is another volunteer who is open about how much she learnt at Switchboard, describing it as her 'university' as a lesbian. Speaking to Tash in 2019, Lisa recalled sometime in the late 1970s when she heard a male volunteer refer to a sex toy she couldn't imagine. 'I'd never seen a dildo at this point,' Lisa said, her fringed bob framing her face. 'I talked a good talk about sex but I wasn't that experienced,' she said, 'and one of the men said something about double-ended dildos, and I said, "I don't believe you, you're making that up!"'

Her incredulity is even recorded in the log book of the time, much to her embarrassment. That record is a significant piece of queer history, because Lisa went on to run the first mail-order lesbian sex-toy business in the UK. This led her to learn more about the products being manufactured. 'Actually double-ended dildos were shit at that point, 'cause they were rigid,' she told Tash. 'They were hard plastic. Put two people on a double-ended dildo and you kind of waved at each other from the far ends.' Both Lisa and Tash fell apart laughing at this image.

Lisa, like Femi, told these stories in such an open and frank way. Listening to our queer elders educate us on how sex should be discussed, even though we were well into our thirties already, we felt our muscles lose some of their tension.

From anatomy to toys, the volunteers had to learn it all if they wanted to answer questions about sex. They also needed to keep up to date with the evolution of language:

> 17 March 2000
> Call from young (17) woman asking if I knew what a 'PILLOW PRINCESS' was – apparently it's a lesbian term . . .
> May call back to see if anyone else knows.

This is why we talk about discovery. Our journeys into understanding our sexual bodies are mapped out in the log book entries from callers and the volunteers who scribbled down their notes, comments and questions. Through the log books, we saw that sexual feelings led to more questions, more chances, more potential.

Sometimes callers didn't have a question. They just wanted to let someone in on the good news:

> 12 January 1976
> AMAZING! SUPER! MARVELLOUS!
> A girl phoned, she's had her first sexual experience with another woman over the weekend, and it was super. And she was so happy and so pleased that she wanted to tell someone about it. She was bubbling over.

Adam too remembers 'bubbling over' in one of his early sexual experiences with another person. His body began to shake, flushed as it was with hormones, and he and his partner had to stop and breathe and calm down. He was experiencing something that his body had not been through before, the electricity of pleasure with a second body. Most of us are filled with the desire for this, and one thing that is clear through the work of Switchboard is that it is as much about our understanding of ourselves as it is about lust for another. With Tash, that understanding came in quiet moments – the first time a lover called her handsome, or when finally, at thirty-five, she had her hair cut short for the very first time. As Joshua the hairdresser snipped shorter and shorter, Tash watched her hair fall to the floor and felt the same mix of desire and terror from her first kiss. Spinning her round in his chair, Joshua declared Tash a 'Disney prince!' Tash felt like she was going to cry. Prince Jason, perhaps.

Very early on in Switchboard's operations, volunteers had seemed to realise the power of self-exploration, too. They settled into a pattern of constant learning, listening, sharing, and learning again. It helped that Switchboard was cradled by the gay liberation movement of the 1970s, standing on the shoulders of second-wave feminists, a growing sexual openness, and innovations like the Pill and poppers. And often calls were simply from someone desiring someone of the same sex or gender. But still, as Diana James put it when Tash interviewed her in 2019, volunteers had their work cut out if they were to try to support a caller who was experiencing an attraction while unsure about whether they themselves were a man or a woman.

'[We'd have] some young person phoning up from a rural [place] saying "I don't feel comfortable with my body, every time I look at my body it feels wrong to me, I hate my body",' Diana remembered, explaining that it was often difficult to unpick how such a caller felt about themselves, their gender, their body, other parts of their identity, as well as everything else about their desire for another person – and what the combination of all this could mean for them. 'It was a minefield for people.'

Tash had never met anyone like Diana before. The first time was at Switchboard. It had been decades since Diana had set foot in the building (at the time of the interview she was living in

Cornwall) and they thought it would be a nice place to come together. As Tash was getting ready in the office, she looked out of the window. She instantly recognised Diana waiting across the street, dressed in a leather jacket and tight blue jeans, with long red hair and glasses. Diana was leaning against a wall, looking down the road. It was a scene right out of the 1980s. It was as if she was ready to transport Tash back there. Tash waited and watched her for a moment, thinking about the last time Diana had stood on that street. It could have been thirty-odd years ago, maybe just as we were taking our first steps into school.

Society's collective understanding of LGBTQ+ experiences evolved over Switchboard's first five decades, none so much as that about gender. 'The terminology was so damning, even within our own community,' Diana explained. 'You'd get a trans man phone up and they could get really negative information [from a volunteer who might say], "No you are just a butch dyke, loads of butch dykes have these feelings."'

In the 1990s and early 2000s, through growing understanding of transgender experience, the troubles of callers like the one in Diana's example became clearer, and volunteers understood more and more that a person has both a gender identity and a sexual orientation (the label of which is relative to their gender identity, and only ever for the convenience of describing yourself to another person). This is not easy to understand, and it is one of the reasons why so many of us struggle to discover our desires in the body that feels right. We started to come to think of this as 'gendersex' – how it feels to be desired and to express your desire, in the gender that feels right to you. A month after Tash kissed the girl behind the bins, she clashed with a friend in a way that revealed as much about the 'gay' kiss as it did about the person Tash perceived herself to be. The girl she had kissed had asked the friend if Tash was bisexual. Shocked, the friend had said, 'No! She fancies boys!' When the friend relayed this to Tash, laughing about how ridiculous it was, Tash felt a fire in her chest. 'Why did you say that?!' Tash said, full of fear that she may never get to kiss that girl again. As Tash started to explain how she felt, she quickly assured her friend that she still fancied boys (which wasn't true) and that she only fancied the girl she'd kissed because she *looked like a girl*. Perhaps this made her less likely to be perceived as a lesbian? It didn't make sense, but Tash, who was yet to open up her more masculine side, couldn't allow herself to be perceived as anything other than femme and, with that, the girls she fancied too. Tash carried the shame of that moment for decades. It was while reading the log books, and after years of therapy, that she was able to forgive herself and understand what had really been going on in that moment. Teenage terror and adolescent angst, but make it queer.

Diana had had these experiences and made these discoveries herself, in the early eighties, just before she started to volunteer at Switchboard. She remembered thinking: 'Could I be a lesbian?' She had dismissed that idea initially because she 'only saw images of butch women, you didn't see images of femme women or femme-ish women at all. So I thought, well that's not me, so perhaps I'm bisexual. I thought maybe there's that. I didn't really know.'

Tash sat and listened to Diana in awe, growing more fascinated by the moment. They had spoken on the phone a couple of times by then, but being in that space, in the roots of the building where both Tash and Diana had taken calls, felt so important. It was early on in our history-collecting journey and Tash was all eagerness and nerves, whereas Diana was calm. She was straightforward and unfazed. As Tash would come to learn, this was because of the life she'd had. Tash felt connected to Diana. She wanted to find what

Diana had found inside herself: certainty, or perhaps a deep understanding of who she was.

The idea of someone being brought up as a boy or girl feels so strange to us both now, but of course it's happening all around, and it happened to us both. It's not so much about our bodies, which are all so different and varied; some of us have vaginas and some have penises, and some have signs of both (there are as many intersex people in the world as there are redheads). But whatever our body parts, the categorisation of gender that is placed on top of us can be confusing, and painful. Tash was called a 'tomboy'. As a child, she was raised as a girl but would scream when put in dresses. She hated having long hair. Shopping trips for clothes just made her feel awful. Tash wanted jeans, long shorts, T-shirts and jumpers. She didn't understand what she was struggling with and didn't have any way to express it. As a person who is short with a smaller stature, Tash was never perceived as anything other than female, but this started to change when she cut her hair. Men called her 'mate' when they saw only the back of her head, and not her round, more feminine face. Suddenly the short hair and all the 'mates' started to make life feel a bit more fun for Tash.

When we think about gender, it's important to understand how much of it is our 'perceived' gender – a response to whom we are interacting with or responding to. A person will have a sense of their own gender identity, but there is also the identity that others perceive them to be. These can sometimes be different, which can be hard to experience. So many of us have grown up trying to grapple with that, feeling a resistance to what was being put onto us, tattooed into our blood, etched deep into our bones. That takes a lot to unshackle. People who were raised as boys but with similar confusions to that experienced by Tash often had a harder time of it.

Ed Lees didn't know who he was, either. Ed is the same age as us, and so was likewise educated under Section 28 and raised during a time of hostility and invisibility. He spoke gently, thoughtfully, and generously when Adam interviewed him in 2023, reflecting with hindsight on how as a child he must have seemed 'a little bit odd' to the other children, especially the other boys.

'I used to get taken the mick out of [for] how I walked, which I think was probably a bit of a mince,' said Ed, which was a fear that Adam had also had at a young age. They'd both tried to walk like the other guys – in a 'manly' way – didn't cross their legs, and even stopped listening to the pop band Steps. For Ed, this self-censorship all came before he was sexual, before and during puberty, before he started to sleep with women and men. His experience helped us to see how gender and sexuality are mixed together in our bodies, something that bisexual people often experience in a particular way. When Ed started to have sex with women, and enjoyed it, the question of who he really was made him afraid to explore sex with men. 'I would love people to grow up without that fear,' he said.

When he was figuring out how he could be in a relationship with a woman while also thinking about men, he realised something one day and said it to himself: 'I don't want to be in a situation where I have this niggle that I haven't tried something or I haven't explored or haven't understood something about myself.'

Ed did a lot of exploration, thinking, experiencing, reading and counselling – because this stuff is hard to figure out, especially when you are raised in silence. This is why people call Switchboard. The sensation of feeling something about your body and knowing that you must explore it is compelling. You might be able to shut it down, as Adam did, but it is always there.

THE LOG BOOKS

As society's understanding of LGBTQ+ experiences changed over Switchboard's first fifty years, there also came a significant change in the language used to describe gender identities, an evolution that will continue into the future. It is through the use of the words etched into the pages of the log books that we can track the profound evolution of our shared understanding of gender identity, often in relation to sex and sexuality. It is clear from the log books that gender and sexuality are distinct experiences in our bodies, but also inextricably linked:

> 27 November 1995
> Woman phoned who thinks she's a gay man. Fancies gay men but wants to penetrate them. Therefore wants to change her sex so she can sleep with men.
>
> 6 January 1992
> V. long call. In 40s – had first sex with a man last month – a TV – he didn't know until 'too late'. Has no problem about sex or sexuality but needed confirmation he wasn't 'abnormal'. May phone again & likely to ask for me.
>
> 17 April 1998
> Male caller. Asian transsexual undertaking gender realignment programme in London. Selling sex and in relationship with his/her pimp who is totally controlling his life. Suffering physical abuse from boyfriend when he gets drunk.
> Caller feeling very violated and unaware of what to do. Totally losing his confidence and out of control of his life.
> Gender realignment is also most important.
> Caller referred by Samaritans who he considered unsympathetic. Asked if he could call again for support. I assured him he could call and talk at anytime.

'A BIT CONFUSED, EXCITED . . .'

The log books often include the terms 'TV', for 'transvestite', and 'transexual', or 'TS'. These terms were used commonly in the seventies through to the nineties and early 2000s, and at the time of writing this book they were being used more commonly once more. 'Transsexual' in the log books was used to describe people whose gender identity was different to what they were assigned at birth, and 'transvestite' was used to describe people who dressed in clothing usually associated with their opposite gender (almost exclusively this was men dressing as women). Volunteers did not always handle calls from 'TV' or 'TS' people with the compassion they deserved, not least because many people in the 'gay and lesbian' community did not accept them. But by and large enough people at Switchboard had the right impulse: these callers were part of the family, and they needed their help and understanding. More and more transgender people were going to call Switchboard, especially when they saw Hayley Cropper appear in 1997 as the first trans character on *Coronation Street*, a television soap loved by millions. That year, volunteers got together for this training, advertised internally via the log book:

1. TV/TS – Why they're just not the same . . .
This workshop will allow volunteers to discuss how they feel about the increasing amount of TV/TS calls we receive at LLGS. Why do we get these calls? How do the callers feel about calling us? What is the difference between TV and TS? What referrals should we make? And what are the places for TV or TS callers like? Three trainers' experience in this field will facilitate this interactive and frank discussion on an increasingly relevant phone topic.

When Tash needed to reflect on log book entries like this, revealing Switchboard's internal self-improvement mechanisms, she turned to Lisa Power. We had learnt that Lisa's brain was full to the brim with information, and we would come to her time and again during our research, just as you might look something up on Wikipedia. Lisa put her encyclopedic knowledge down to being 'a dyke who's been around for donkey's years'.

The fluidity of language, though, meant that even Lisa struggled to understand what was going on for some callers. 'We used different languages and we had different explanations,' she recalled. 'I think a lot of people that we talked to were transgender but didn't have the vocabulary or the imagination to describe where they were heading.'

On top of the language was the actual matter at hand of knowing how best to help the caller. This challenge was also felt when taking calls from people with disabilities.

10 May 1997
Does anyone know the name of a group for amputees? Man called wanting to get together with people who wouldn't be freaked out by the fact that he has only one arm.

28 November 1998
Looong call from 35-year-old disabled man, who has been cottaging for 5 years, but wants to have sex with a woman.
Very confused about his sexuality and kept going round in circles. Is probably likely to call again.

2 December 2000
Malcolm called, handicapped in a residential home. He is not sure if he is gay and started to ask for information on wanking (brochures and leaflets). He sounded very sincere. Lots of things came up in the conversation.

Every disabled person experiences something different, but each of them is held back by the challenges that society places in front of them – from physical obstacles such as stairs to social barriers like ignorance about neurodiversity and the prejudice that disabled people are not sexual beings. It is clear in the log books that Switchboard volunteers, who were mostly able-bodied, were not always fully equipped to support disabled callers, but for the most part they tried. Technology like 'touch talk' and Minicom, which were in effect early versions of instant messaging, offered support to more people who needed it:

> 5 August 1996
> Should we be logging disabled calls? We don't always know if the caller is disabled, but it would be good to see how often disabled people call us. Also shouldn't we be training volunteers to use Minicom? I know there's info in the folder, but Minicom calls are panic-inducing and often abortive.

> 18 January 1997 – 3.30 a.m.
> Took a call on the touch talk service – you dictate replies through an operator – from a terminally ill house-bound guy from Liverpool who wanted an escort.

The descriptions in the log books of some calls from disabled people show just how much some people have to face:

> 28 August 1998
> Call from married guy in east London who has MS, though fairly mobile. Various physical problems including impotence. He has had a few sexual encounters as passive partner due to impotence. Talked for an hour about isolation and trying to get friends/support – visiting London cafés/clubs. He wanted to go to Heaven but only to talk as couldn't dance and alcohol wouldn't be good with his tablets!!? He has lost all his friends – feels Asian community and his family against him. Has been married for 18

years, but wife has had several affairs and currently seeing another man who is physically threatening to him, so he is afraid of leaving the house at times.

. . . Will probably call again as feeling depressed at times due to degenerative illness – isolation, feeling threatened in marriage/wife's lover.

. . . What physical disability groups exist for him?

It's clear from this log book entry that being disabled can be an incredibly isolating experience, and especially so if your desires are harder to discover or experience. There is a dual prejudice at play, one that is also experienced by queer people of colour, or anyone who has more than one identity that is the subject of oppression. 'Disabled people aren't wanted around,' said Kath Gillespie Sells, in an interview at home with Adam in 2021.[3] Kath was one of the UK's most significant disability and LGBTQ+ rights campaigners – knowing that these two aspects of human experience both face intersecting ignorance. Kath volunteered for Switchboard, and in 1990 she founded Regard, the national network for disabled LGBTQ+ people. 'I've got a loud mouth, nothing else,' she said. 'And I can smell injustice miles away.'

One volunteer who read the log book entry about the caller with MS suggested Regard as an organisation that might be able to support him, writing the idea in the margins of the log book. But beyond that, it is clear from these last few entries, and the many more that mention disability, that the sexual bodies of disabled people were ostracised. 'Disabled people aren't [seen as] sexy,' said Kath. 'And in general terms, certainly the LGBT community has not been that interested.'

Tash had seen Kath in the building at Switchboard, on shift, but it wasn't until Adam interviewed her that Tash began to understand the breadth of the work that she had done. Our project had started to collect stories like Kath's, and we were committed to sharing them as widely as we could. The world needed to know that Kath's campaigning reformed the Pride in London organisation to make sure that Pride marches included disabled people. And in building a network through Regard, she made an army of campaigners whose work led to the passage of the Disability Discrimination Act in 1995. This law made it illegal to discriminate against people due to their disabilities in relation to employment, the provision of goods and services, education, and transport. The law was rolled into the broader Equality Act in 2010, which Kath regretted. 'Once you marry disability legislation into others it loses a lot of its strength,' she said. When Kath died in 2023 she left behind a world that was kinder to disabled people, but one that still had a long way to go before it could claim to treat them as first-class citizens with valid sexual desires.

When we decided to delve into the log books, one of the first things we looked for was sex. That's because we thought it would be fun – and it was! We had a riot. We'd managed to look back through time, and we saw just how much Switchboard volunteers had prioritised the pleasure of their callers. They never gave up, not even in those moments of indignity:

20 March 1992 – 9.15 p.m.
Sweet, distressed, underage* gay man whose boyfriend has a vibrator stuck up his bum – irretrievably . . . they had no condoms & were trying to stay safe! I think I persuaded them to brave

* In 1992, for a male having sex with a male, 'underage' meant any age under twenty-one. From the tone of the volunteer, who didn't raise any safeguarding questions, it's most likely that the caller was aged eighteen to twenty-one.

casualty sooner rather than later, but they may well ring back.
Desperately embarrassed & needs lots of support.

There was so much sexual exploration going on for callers and volunteers but, looking back through our modern lens, we noticed a gap. Few people during Switchboard's first few decades had the language for asexuality – and it just didn't show up in the log books or our interviews. This absence made us realise how isolating it can feel for asexual people to emerge into a (queer) world that is so full of sex and desire, as the log books are. It is yet another human experience that leads to shame being placed on us.

Otherwise, what we discovered in the log books was just how sexually open volunteers like Lisa, Femi, Julian, and Diana had been. They'd had to be, since they were often the first or only people some callers could speak to about sex. The message down the line was always: explore yourself. This idea hit both of us hard, in our mid-thirties. It confronted us with the fact that in our different ways we had both not always had the strength to explore ourselves – even though our elders had been counselling callers to do just that since a decade before we were born.

In the end, discovering our desires is the thing that has made us who we are. Our interviewee Ed had a similar experience, after a long-term relationship with a girlfriend and then exploring sex with men: 'One of my best mates said to me, "Look, you and Rachel were a wonderful couple. I love you both. You were great then. But now you're more 'Ed'." And that was really great to hear.' The stories of our peers like Ed connected with our own experiences, as did the countless earlier calls to Switchboard:

18 November 1994
[Caller] has also had sex for the first time + decided it is one of the best things that has ever happened to him – he is so happy as

a result. He thanks Richard [a volunteer] for his excellent advice (take the plunge + see how you feel about it!) and asks us to keep up the good work.

Indeed, the way these histories connect with our own pasts, and even our presents, has been fascinating to us. Even though we were in our thirties by the time we began delving into them, it seemed that we were still discovering our own bodies. This is why that line in the first log book struck Tash so deeply: 'fuck society for twisting people'. Maybe this was why we were 'doing history'. When we read and heard about all the ways that Switchboard volunteers had helped callers to un-twist themselves, we realised that we were in that process for ourselves. The log books not only taught us the breadth and depth of desires and queries that people have, but also revealed to us our own endless need to listen to their stories.

Tash had remembered her desire to be seen as 'Jase'; Adam had begun to reflect on why he held off from sex until age twenty-nine, when queer people had apparently been happily shagging around since forever. Our bodies were yearning to be themselves, to connect with other bodies. But all of these desires had been clashing with the clutter in our minds.

Since we both loved to dance, we wondered what we could possibly find when we read log book entries about nightlife. We had to ask our elders to take us by the hand and lead us back in time, into the darkness and the lights of their favourite gay bars.

2
'HUDDLED TOGETHER IN A CORNER'

The timeless euphoria of finding others like you

10 July 1993
Donald from Skye phoned for a chat. Apparently he spoke to a nightshift volunteer last Saturday and says 'Hello & Thanks' to whoever that was. He is thinking of leaving the island and moving to a town or city on the mainland to explore his gay self so he has lots of questions to ask. He is 22 and fairly cheers up a nightshift with his wry sense of humour. He will probably be a regular (& drunk) & makes extensive use of swear words.

We don't know if Donald made it to the mainland, let alone a gay club. But we do know that he wanted *something* more. Maybe to meet *someone* new. 'I didn't know any other queer people,' said Clare Truscott, one of our interviewees. Clare was animated, her hair a riot of shaved scalp and scarlet-coloured curls. She came out in 1982 in Preston, in the northwest of England. 'I'd not read about any other lesbians, I'd not seen one, or seen photographs of one, or read about them in the papers.'

Clare's stories were seasoned with reflection, but the main dish was always the things that happened, retold with her no-nonsense northern attitude. 'I had accidentally got myself a lesbian flatmate,' she said, of how the whole queer thing started. One night the two of them squeezed into a phone box. They called the Preston Gay Switchboard, one of many local 'Gay Switchboards' that popped up in the seventies and eighties, responding to the burgeoning gay nightlife scene and the number of people testing positive for HIV.

'We rang this number and they said, "We're having a lesbian social here tonight and you've just missed that, but we're about to go to the pub."'

Clare the femme punk was commanding Tash's full attention. 'It was on the street we were living on!' she grinned. Clare and her flatmate bustled out of the phone box and marched along the pavement in search of the tiny brass plaque that marked the discreet doorway. 'And that was my coming out,' Clare said. 'I had my first lesbian shag that night and it was lovely!'

Clare helped us fill the gaps left by the log books. With callers like Donald, we could only imagine how he found his 'gay self'; but the frequency with which folks like Clare found theirs in pubs and clubs pointed to one of the likelier answers.

Stories like Clare's made us each reflect on our own times in LGBTQ+ spaces: Adam trying to serve Britney Spears' moves at the Royal Vauxhall Tavern, Tash bouncing up and down at a night called Fanny Pack. Both of us chatting and flirting with other queer people, meeting our friends, shaking off the busy week.

As we worked, we began to collect nightlife log book entries like ticket stubs. We also asked everyone we interviewed about their nights out. We wanted to bathe in their stories. We wanted the drama, the pleasure of the dance, the locked eyes, the bright lights and the dark rooms, the bodies clubbing together to find the same beat, the same beat we have found together at queer techno raves in Belgium and drag bars in Newcastle, sweat dripping down our faces, eyes closed and moving to the thumping bass of the music. This is how music reaches us; we both seek out the night and the dancefloor, sometimes in unison, sometimes separately. There is a connection in the movement of our bodies that we feel. It is our expression, it is our freedom, and it is all ours to thrash around in. We may have met each other in the archives, but we connected on the dancefloor. This is why we were hooked on our queer elders' stories; they were ours too.

After Clare told Tash her story about the lesbian pub down the road, Tash heard herself spilling to Clare about spending her teens driving to gay clubs across the South West to a soundtrack of 'Fast Car' by Tracy Chapman. From Eclipse in Truro to The Vaults in Exeter, Tash hit the dancefloor in search of Alex Parks, a Cornish singer who won a TV talent show and the hearts of tiny queers like Tash. Usually Tash just ended up in a car park, asleep on the back seat of her Nissan Micra, only to be woken at dawn by a parking attendant knocking on the window. Surely there was somewhere better than this, she thought, somewhere bigger, somewhere gayer. That is the pull that drew Donald away from the beauties of Skye, Clare from Preston to London, and Tash from Plymouth to Bristol.

Adam, by contrast, did not realise that, subconsciously, one of the things that drew him to live first in Nottingham and then London was the chance of a gay scene. He stared at Nottingham's gay club NG1 every time he walked past. He looked down on clubs as arenas of chaos, far from anything he wanted to be or do. He avoided alcohol, and was always ready to go home before anyone else. It would take Adam another decade to discover what a queer space with beats and boys could offer him – but as soon as he did, it was all systems go. If the architects of Section 28 didn't want us looking at a storybook, they would have fainted if they had seen what we saw at the disco.

The club was our playground and we revelled in it. We were pulled towards the log book entries about nightlife – they all still sparkled after four decades.

We wanted to hear every speck of detail from our elders. We asked them to pretend we were with them, to describe the smell of the club. We wanted to be with them in those past moments, to see and feel how their club nights compared to ours, to inhabit some space together, outside of time. But we had to wonder whether elders like Clare remembered their glory days through rose-tinted lenses. This would have to be a question in our work on this project: we'd have to reflect on why we wanted to hear fun and positive stories, and why our elders still needed to tell them, too. When it came to nightlife, more than any other realm of queer life, were we all just drinking a full pint of nostalgia?

———

As we thumbed through the log books, we found entries from all across the country. The most common type of call we encountered was people asking Switchboard to recommend somewhere to go. We were even surprised to find callers had asked Switchboard about gay pubs in our hometowns of Grimsby and Plymouth. And in fact, before we could really reflect on the history of queer nightlife, we first had to understand how on earth, before the internet, Switchboard volunteers knew what was going on, and where. Index cards, databases, files and folders – they all came tumbling down on us when we began to explore this essential duty of the helpline. Without realising it, volunteers were mapping out a record of queer lives and movements across the UK, and, decades later, they also helped us to connect with our queer ancestors.

19 May 1975
PLYMOUTH – CHE reports
Lockyer still gay (Oak Bar) all ages, 9–11pm. Best weekends. Gay men + women.

'HUDDLED TOGETHER IN A CORNER'

Mr Harry's Club. 2230–0020 (except Sundays 2400). Bar + disco. Gay + straight. Gay men + women (all ages). Entrance 60p or membership £2 (30p entrance). Extra charge for cabaret, sometimes. £1. Drinks expensive. Snacks available.
Millbrook 454. Gays **not** welcome.
Antelope pub. Definitely not gay. Never been gay.
Cascade club – was gay in small bar, now straight disco, possible for rent (sailors).

3 March 1997
Caller reported the 'Cheers' in Grimsby was burnt down a couple of months ago. It's still on the database – has it risen from the ashes? Caller had moved away, so might be out of date himself. Any vols. available to volunteer to research/investigate/update any of: Lincolnshire, North Lincolnshire, North East Lincolnshire (both new 1996 counties that used to be Humberside), South Yorkshire, East Riding and Nottinghamshire?
These counties are vacant at the moment & Info Group needs vols to adopt them!

Sometimes a place being 'gay' wasn't enough. Callers often wanted somewhere to go where they would feel more at home, and included:

5 February 1989
Caller rang asking about disabled access – and wheelchair access particularly – in London pubs . . . I had to guess from memory (I did tell the caller that this was what I was doing). There was no way that I could guess about the width of doors or their suitability for wheelchairs. I know that it would be a lot of work to collect this information but, in the short term, it would be a help if there's even a few places that we could recommend as being wheelchair-friendly.

17 December 1975

Womens Clubs

A woman called asked if there was anywhere for women to go after 11pm. As far as I can see there isn't – is this really so? Any suggestions?

15 May 1976

Umpteen calls tonight for other info about an all Black Gay Club in Brixton

. . .

See above, one guy phoned saying its called The Underground, behind the Odeon, High St, Brixton – NOTE: BLACK PEOPLE ONLY UNLESS WITH A BLACK MEMBER.

10 May 1997

TV/TS

Female caller who dresses as man, hopes to have sex change but is attracted to gay men. Where can she go out? Men she is attracted to tend to go to male only bars/clubs. Any ideas? Also where would women in her position meet women cross dressers? TV/TS files don't appear to cater for female cross dressers.

As these entries show, volunteers were diligent in collecting information on all the queer nightlife spaces. They amassed huge files stuffed with intel. They hung a map in the phone room, plotting it with colour-coded pins to mark different types of pubs and clubs. Without realising it at the time, they were playing a crucial role in formalising the 'gay scene'. This included the volunteers themselves, of course, who often updated the files with their own personal experiences. People wanting a night out could always consult the listings in *Gay News*, the *Pink Paper* and *Capital Gay*, during their respective periods – or they could phone Switchboard where volunteers tried to be hot on where was hot:

10 May 1975
Would it be possible to keep a guide as to what drag artists are appearing where. It's amazing the number of calls I personally have received asking where so and so was that night. Even a short guide would help. E.g. regular venues around the pubs.

26 April 1978
There is a new file (black) which has fairly comprehensive details relation to Transvestites & Transsexuals. This includes info as to which bars, clubs etc they can go to. This file should be compulsory reading for all volunteers.

The volunteer who wrote that last entry made the nightlife file a set text because they knew that nightlife was central to the mission of Switchboard; they knew the power of being in a space where they felt safer, being queer, than in the outside world. Many of the queer spaces in London gave free admission to volunteers carrying a Switchboard identity card, so those volunteers could more easily keep tabs on nightlife and make accurate recommendations to callers – and connect them with each other.

The need to connect with others was especially great for youngsters. Marc Thompson went to his first Black gay party as a teenager on 13 July 1985. He remembers the date because everyone else seemed to be watching Live Aid. 'It was filled with Black gay men,' he said of the party he attended instead. His handsome face beamed as he added, 'Mind was blown, and I was set for life.'

When Marc told Adam this story, it was like he'd been telling it for years. In fact, a lot of the parties from that time merged together in the memory. 'They were usually in somebody's house, not a club. There would be a DJ playing songs I knew, my parents knew, my older cousins, very Black British, some food being cooked, a bunch of people in the kitchen, jokes, very gay, very male. Very Black British Caribbean.'

Adam could imagine younger Marc, as stylish as ever, elegantly cool, floating around parties like that, with lovers rock music on the decks. 'You'd get somebody, or invariably they'd get you. Slow dance, up against the wall, very little movement, a lot of action taking place . . .' Marc crubbed with guys who were a few years older than him, and it felt like he'd found somewhere to be. 'This is the first generation of Black gay men born here or coming here, creating their space,' he said. 'It had never happened before.'

The men at these parties created somewhere to be Black, gay, and British all at the same time. For other people the combination they were seeking might have been different, but in one way or another each was looking for their queer space to hold them. This is what callers wanted when they asked a Switchboard volunteer to recommend somewhere to go.

'I remember as if it was yesterday,' said Lyn in a podcast interview in 2019. Aged seventy, Lyn spoke softly, carefully, and with great tenderness towards her younger self. She told Adam how she'd been on a date with a man and felt nothing. 'I was driving back in the car,' Lyn said, 'and I thought "I can't do this, I'm not being true to myself."' As soon as she got home, she found the number for Gay Switchboard and dialled it. 'I spoke to a volunteer called Val,' she said, 'I was crying, and she really helped me a lot.'

On the phone, Val comforted Lyn, digging into Switchboard's files to offer the name of somewhere to go. Driven by the need to be true to herself, Lyn hopped on a train the next day, arriving in a bar in Green Lanes in London around 9 p.m.: 'I got a drink, and I sat down and just took in the atmosphere.' That moment of being in a queer space for the first time, inhaling, taking it all in, still lived inside Lyn decades later. 'I looked at the side of the bar and there were two women, and they were stood together drinking.' Every molecule of her body savoured the sight. 'And they were looking at each other, face to face, and it was as if they were the only women in that room. And I thought, "I want that!"'

Sometimes our interviewees adopted the tone that no scene was as good as the one they experienced, and that nightlife had definitely gone downhill by the time we interviewed them (often long after they had stopped going out). It's easy to see why any one of us can look at our best nights out like this:

> 22 December 1985 – 8.18 a.m.
> Caller: 'Just calling to thank you for a wonderful evening last night at a club recommended . . . must dash before the guy who picked me up wakes up!'

As we heard countless stories like these, we wondered whether we were destined to be nostalgic too. Would our nostalgia just indicate how time shifted, scenes morphed, and hormones changed proportions? Or would it mean something else? Perhaps that survival meant remembering the past as better than it was?

> 19 April 1975
> Chaguaramas – reported not gay at all. Straights have been making comments when gays dance together. Gays have been huddled together in a corner so they will feel ill at ease – so what is going on?

In 2003, Tash and her first girlfriend also found themselves in a bar surrounded by straight people. They held hands under the table. They flirted with their eyes. And then they went to the toilet to snog – away from any internalised shame, it was the only place in the bar they felt safe doing so. Aged seventeen, Tash had already grown used to unwanted attention. It seemed that she could barely go anywhere without the fear of being glared and gawped at like an animal in the zoo. The best part of three decades had passed since someone went to Chaguaramas bar in the West End of London and felt the same. Fortunately, they'd called Switchboard so that volunteers could warn other callers about that place. Sharing such reviews, especially the clientele ratio of straight to queer, has long been a tradition in our queer family.

In the same year as Tash's toilet session, Adam started university. He fell into a group of other students who went on a weekly night out to a club called Ocean, and didn't once wish that it was gay. The possibility of sex was not alive for Adam: the idea of being attractive, of wanting to be desired, of wanting someone else – all of it was there, somewhere deep, but not turned on, like an electric circuit with no voltage running through it. This is how he kept a distance from the pleasures that others allowed themselves in the club. He danced, and he liked it, but he might as well have been dancing alone. Even on a family trip to London and on a walk through the historically gay area Soho, he kept himself secret. The only times he went to a gay space for the next decade was as a tourist: joining queer friends, but staying at the edge of the dancefloor.

Tash, of course, thought, *Fuck it*. She'd dropped her religion, grown tired of Wetherspoons, and wanted to be where the queer people were. Nothing could stop her: she headed to the rough edge of Plymouth, lied about her age, and crossed the threshold into The Swallow. On one side of the pub a bunch of butch women played pool; on the other, a group of gay men painted the air with their gossip. It felt amazing and terrifying all at once. The same emotions assaulted Adam too, when he finally joined in. Although it wasn't his first gay party, one specific night out at the Sink the Pink party in Bethnal Green Working Men's Club became etched into his memory. He joined new gay friends, wearing trashy drag and dancing free. It was a silly night, with silly pop and silly people – and, *Yes*, Adam thought, *this is how I could be*.

He had not yet met Tash, but he finally caught the same bug she'd had for years. 'I've got a gay bar illness,' she had written in her diary after one night in Zeroes, the gay club in Plymouth. 'I just can't stop!'

It's funny to read back this entry and muse at Tash's use of words, but what is clear is the sense of euphoria burning through her veins. The connection was made. She, and later Adam, slipped into the same beat that Marc, Lyn, Clare, and those in the log books had all danced to. The spaces were different, but the purpose remained the same, no matter the decade. Callers from all over the country were desperate to be out on the town, with others like them, knowing they were sexy, hoping for a snog, necking a shot, feeling that Heaven was a place on Earth.

Their reasons were all the same as ours. The more we looked back at nightlife in the log books the more we understood how important it had been to find the right place.

> 13 April 1976
> Phoned in to say that someone had been thrown out of a pub in Forest Hill for wearing a gay badge. That's the Bricklayers Arms. The landlord said 'It is in the best interest of customers that Paul should be permanently banned'. So there is going to be a demonstration at Thursday at 8pm in the lounge bar with everyone wearing gay badges.

The volunteers we interviewed always spoke of the night shift being the hardest time to take calls, especially in the seventies, eighties, and nineties. They would hear from callers who had been attacked, verbally abused, kicked out of clubs, and even arrested. Their queer nightlife, their refuge, came with risks. Nightlife seemed to be a strange thing to be nostalgic about. Even if it felt like a safer world inside the club, the moment you stepped out, *they* were waiting. Something as small as a badge could mark someone as different from the dominant expectation to be straight and cisgender. Even the women who wore trousers didn't have a chance:

> 23 August 1975
> Leeds CHE + GLF are asking gays to boycott the New Penny (formerly Hope & Anchor) as management are refusing admittance to women wearing trousers.
> York lesbian group looking for new meeting place as landlord has become 'oppressive'. He is also refusing to serve people wearing gay badges.

The badges again. Pages and pages of entries about badges, in fact – and in Bishopsgate Institute where the log books are kept, we also looked at hundreds of badges that our elders used to wear. 'Glad To Be Gay', they said. 'Lesbian Liberation', 'Practising Homosexual', 'Lesbians Unite In Armed Snuggle', 'Dyke', 'Gay Liberation', 'I Am What I Am'. Each badge had its own simple message, and collectively they made a choir singing a song of resistance to the kind of treatment the callers above had to face. Badges were political, and so, we discovered, was nightlife. The pub or club was often the place where the unstoppable force of queer freedom met the immovable object of heterosexual patriarchy.

'HUDDLED TOGETHER IN A CORNER'

21 September 1992
A young woman rang up distressed about the fact that she had been 'man handled' out of the Ace of Clubs for asking for ice in her drink (!) which was repeatedly refused by male manager & female server also. Shocked by treatment on first visit & wanted to warn people about this – she also will be getting in touch with newspapers etc to publicise her experience & warn other women.

Femi told us that this sort of behaviour was 'indicative of the difficulties we faced at the time'. Even when you got into the pub things weren't straightforward: 'If you ordered a pint of beer you'd get two halves. They wouldn't give you a tankard, in some pubs. And, of course, [for] the lesbians it was our badge of honour that we'd drink pints.'

Tash, an avid pint drinker who would have worn that same badge, couldn't quite believe this from Femi. Standing at a pint-sized five feet and three inches herself, Tash has long resisted sexist behaviour and perceptions by trying to take up as much space as possible. Suzanne Ciechomski did the same in the 1970s:

> It was very difficult to be gay, to be out and gay. You'd get a lot of hostility on the street. We used to wear lesbian badges and that felt like a risky thing to do cos you could be identified as a lesbian and several times one or other of us did get beaten up, and it was quite frightening going into a pub as a group of lesbians . . . and having cropped hair and dressed as a lesbian, wearing a huge fluorescent badge that says LESBIANS IGNITE.

Tash listened back to our audio of Suzanne and smiled at this image of someone standing up for who they were, despite the fear. Suzanne took up karate to be able to defend herself. 'You wouldn't expect that kind of thing to happen today,' she said; but in fact, at the same time she was giving Adam her interview in 2019, two queer people were recovering after being attacked in central London when they were kissing. Melania Geymonat, a gay woman, and her partner Chris, a bisexual woman, were taunted and then punched by male teenagers on a night bus. Suzanne described it as a scene she thought she had left behind. 'I found that really shocking in this day and age,' she said, 'and it saddened me.'

We were challenged to think what our 'history' project could teach us about our own times, and how we and our elders could have felt so warm and fuzzy for the risky business of going out.

But the facts from the log books were clear: you can't keep the queers down. Despite the hostility, the scene flourished in the eighties and nineties. Gay bars, lesbian parties, women's club nights, and trans spaces: all grew out of a need to escape 'normal' life and find safety and community among peers. People were looking for their tribe, and an escape from the world that made their very existence political. They were looking to prioritise their pleasure. In the case of lesbians, as Fisch, an artist and drag king, reflected, 'It's important to be able to create those spaces because that's where we grow up, that's where we find ourselves. That's where we can relax, you know, you can snog a girlfriend, you can flirt. You haven't got the threat of some straight bloke wandering in and just thinking, "Oh, this is a good laugh".'

One feature of the women's scene that came up again and again in our research was the dominance of the idea that a woman had to be either butch or femme, which is to say presenting themselves in a more conventionally masculine or feminine way.

23 October 1975
A girl rang up saying that she'd just moved into London – into a large flat. (Kennington?) She & her friend go to Louie's, Rod's [bars]

etc which they enjoy – but with the net effect that they know more gay men than women. They're thinking of holding parties for girls of their age (around 20) who want to avoid the butch/fem scene.

As Clare remembered of her time on the scene in the eighties and nineties, there was 'loads of aggro' between women about this. It's something Tash definitely experienced growing up as well. She wore skirts and dresses to play with being femme, but it didn't feel good. She felt like she was in drag, and not just for the night. But she was stuck not knowing how to be another version of herself that wasn't 'butch' as she saw it. The two options she saw the world presenting her with as a teen felt too strapped into the binary of being a woman.

Gay men created their own binaries, too, from the sexual preferences of tops and bottoms to the gendered fulcrum of whether a man, like the lesbians, should be more masculine or more feminine. Plenty of other categories formed through the seventies and eighties for gay men too: clones, disco queens, bears, leathermen, theatre gays . . . all could be incredibly freeing while also sometimes feeling like straitjackets.

For punks like Clare the labels were especially political when it came to sex. All sorts of queer people created different binaries between kinky sex such as sadomasochism (SM) and more regular, or vanilla, sex. This could just make the way others saw your gender even more confusing; as Clare said:

> I always thought the SM dykes were more fun. The vanilla dykes were very poker faced, no sense of humour, no sense of style, no conversation . . . Although I was a very feminist-focused woman, because I liked wearing some feminist-focused things, many would write me off as a femme and I remember saying I am not femme, this is not a lifestyle/sexual role; this is a dress!

Tash eventually dropped the dresses she hated wearing and grew to feel more herself when she went out in a shirt and tie. And yet the first time Adam wore a dress on a night out he felt gorgeous and queer, and on that night he couldn't stop looking at a sexy boy in a wedding gown. We continued going out to clubs and doing our research at the same time. We endured eighteen months when we couldn't go out at all due to Covid, and were forced to think about it at home instead. The histories we were collecting – whether dark or light, from the archive or from all the stories we'd heard, about clothes or music or spaces – all connected us to our own feelings. All along, we had just wanted to be seen.

There is an idea that some people go on a night out in order to be 'seen' doing the acceptable thing or the cool thing. This is not what we mean here. We mean that, as we heard our elders tell their stories about enjoying the music and the people, we could tell they were talking about being accepted for who they were. Clare was a kinky punk in a dress, and why the fuck not? Marc was a Black queer man eating the food of his childhood, but this time at a party with others like him, in the absence of heterosexuality. If life was a pick-and-mix, the world of the night meant gorging only on the sweets that gave you the sugar rush of being you. We'd both been going out for years by the time we read the log books and heard from our elders, but now we understood why we found it so much fun.

If having the sex we liked was a private pleasure, going out was a much more communal one. When we went out, we were creating the stories of important nights, the nights that helped us to be seen as we wanted to be seen. Tash began to look back differently at the chaos of her career as a club monster in her twenties. Adam felt the colour blooming into nights out that had previously been grayscale. We were in the process of archiving our own powerful, self-actualising memories. As with our elders, this memorialising was tinged with nostalgia, but it was more than nostalgia. The memories each contained a voltage, and it was this that sparked when we spoke to our elders. Their memories, it seemed, were a whole new kind of archive. We'd been focused on the log books, the extraordinary written record of questions for Switchboard, but the more we used them as prompts for our interviewees, the more their memories came to life, and the more we realised that a central drive for our project was to collect these memories, just as Switchboard had collected the call logs. If Bishopsgate Institute preserved the log books, our project would do the same for the memories of our elders.

Recognising the importance of the archive of memories we were creating was a huge turning point in our work, and it led us to the King's Road in Chelsea in 1982.

After going to that lesbian night in Green Lanes after phoning Switchboard, Lyn stayed on the scene. She heard about Gateways, a place for women in Chelsea, west London. The basement club with the green door was already a legend by 1982, and Lyn knew that she had to try it out. Around the same time, a woman called Elaine Fitzgerald had phoned Switchboard too. She was newly out of a marriage to a man, coming out as a lesbian, and looking to meet women. She called Switchboard, and she too spoke to a volunteer named Val. Switchboard was not a matchmaking service, but somehow via the helpline Elaine and Lyn were put in touch. Their combined memories were among the most radiant we collected, as clear and beautiful as crystal. As Lyn told Adam about getting dolled up for the night, pulling on her fur coat and carrying her large handbag, Elaine chuckled beside her. 'Obviously she didn't realise that gay women didn't carry great big handbags,' said Elaine.

They hopped in a taxi and directed the driver to the King's Road, too cautious to request Gateways by name. When they stepped into the basement club they absorbed the scene. 'We looked around,' Elaine remembered, 'and we just had this magical feeling. It felt like a homecoming. I know it sounds a bit corny, but it really did, didn't it?' In the retelling, she looked at Lyn, who smiled and nodded, and they held each other's gaze for a moment, thirty-eight years after that night.

'They were playing Joan Armatrading,' said Elaine, naming the song, 'Willow'. 'So we had a dance to that.' Like old partners do, Lyn contradicted her. 'That was later,' she said. 'Remember?' Elaine waited, as Lyn explained: 'There were fast dances and then the music changed . . . I looked around and you looked at me, and . . . we danced to "Willow".'

It is not hard to imagine that Elaine, from Leytonstone in London, and Lyn, from a small village in Derbyshire, might never have found each other. Even without the connection from Switchboard, would they have connected in the world outside of Gateways?

Having met partners and lovers in the nightlife scene, we could both relate to Elaine and Lyn's romantic and sexy story. The possibility of a space where you can find people like you, to love and be loved, is what kept drawing us out into the night. For Tash, it was the queer community in the dark corners of Twat Boutique at Dalston Superstore, the tiny dancefloor of Ghetto, parties with names like Booby Hatch and Crap Fag, lazy afternoons at First Out café, sweaty nights fuelled by mephedrone at the Joiners Arms, and first dates at the George & Dragon. In the 2010s, when it felt like there were more lesbian nights than gay male ones, those spaces became her home, those people became her people. Meanwhile, for all the glare and glam of the commercial gay scene, it was the queer basements and dark genderless techno boxes where Adam discovered that he felt most sexy, where he found his club kids, his family for the night.

Finding the right people to connect with was also essential for the trans people who phoned Switchboard for nightlife recommendations:

> 2 November 1994
>
> Call from TV who sounded extremely isolated. Wanted to talk forever. Seemed to be putting up a lot of barriers and was quite pessimistic about the prospect of going to the Phoenix again (which was 6 months ago). Various referrals (orgs/clubs/bars/adverts) made but was quite keen on maintaining contact with other TVs on a 'safer' basis. He suggested that maybe other vols would know TVs that might be willing to meet him/go out with him.

We sat down with our queer elders for the podcast and this book between 2019 and 2024, when transgender and gender non-conforming people were under severe attack as a social group. Looking back through the log books and talking to our queer elders, we learnt that many of the clubs and pubs, including women-focused spaces, were inclusive. They welcomed trans people. But there was also hostility and discomfort, not dissimilar to what we have seen in the 2020s. The log book entry above from 1994 was echoed in some calls that Tash took as a volunteer at Switchboard. The need for 'safety' is a very relatable one, and something that Stephanie Fuller, a Switchboard caller, was looking for in 1993. She told Tash about a specific night, her first night out as herself – as a trans woman, as Steph – which she found to be 'terrifying, absolutely terrifying'.

Steph told the story while cradling a cup of warm tea. She explained she had wanted to go out that night in 1993 as herself but wouldn't have felt safe on public transport. She decided she would have to drive into London instead. Before leaving home, she even stood in the hallway to check if she could hear her neighbours before forcing herself out of the door. 'You'd [have] thought I was smuggling someone out the country or something!' she said. 'But yeah, just even leaving the house was difficult.'

> 14 March 1994
> Please could we have a list in London Ents of places recommended for TV/TS men. I can't think of anywhere else to get this information (at Switchboard) and I do think it's important for us to be able to tell callers ourselves rather than having to refer them to another helpline.
> Secondly I wish people would make a point of signing entries in the log book – legibly. It used to be a rule.

Underneath this entry another volunteer recommended 'The WayOut Bar behind Selfridges every Saturday night.' (Trans people also used the *TV/TS Newsletter* for similar listings.) The WayOut is exactly where Steph was heading on her first night out as herself. After all, one of the taglines for the night was 'Where Gender has no boundaries . . . and neither does love!' Steph climbed into her car late at night and hit the road. Telling the story to Tash, she laughed as she remembered driving past the club twenty times before parking up. She even checked her rear-view mirror to pick a moment when no one else was walking on the street outside. It was a 'heart-in-mouth moment', her breath quickening at the memory.

Finally she took a deep breath, pulled on the door handle and placed her heels on the cold pavement. She stepped out in a big coat with a black fur collar. At the memory of that night, Steph's hands pulled up an imaginary collar, and she smiled. 'It's very Spice Girls,' she chuckled. 'And then I think I saw them wearing it subsequently. So I think I was ahead.'

As Tash listened to Steph, she got goosebumps, she could feel the power of this moment in Steph's past. The strongest part of Steph's memory of that night in 1993 was the build-up, the preparation, the travel, the arrival. For trans people like Steph, the WayOut Club was a destination. It was a place where trans people could prioritise *their* pleasure – being their true selves. The existence of that space was enough to inspire many of them to want to be themselves, and to find a way to make that happen. Steph hadn't even thought about what would happen on the inside. She hadn't even thought about what she would *drink*.

'I was obviously nervous, like a nervous kitten,' she remembered. Another nervous trans woman sat down beside her, and they began to speak. The woman had taken a ferry from the Isle of Wight and driven nearly four hours to get to the WayOut Club. She would have to leave the club at 1 a.m. so she could get to the first ferry and be home before anyone realised she'd been out. 'I totally understood why they felt that was the only way they could do this,' said Steph. When she left the club that night, she was exhausted and buzzing at the same time. Girl power! 'I remember getting home,' she said, 'shutting the door behind me [and] just breathing . . . the most enormous sigh of relief.' It was the first moment of the rest of her life.

The log books also showed us that the need for spaces wasn't just limited to the letters of the LGBTQ+ acronym, but other aspects of an individual's identity too – their race, their culture, their heritage, as Marc had alluded to. All too often, as the log books reveal, the need for inclusive spaces came from the racist exclusion and segregation experienced on the wider, predominantly white gay scene.

> 30 April 2001
> Does anyone know of any Black/Asian friendly saunas? I had an Asian guy on the phone saying he felt uneasy in a sauna he visited. I subsequently rang a number of saunas to ask if any Black or Asian guys used them – my responses were not impressive.
> Caller might ring back in a week.

White people on the scene, or those running the spaces, often made non-white people feel unwelcome. People of colour were also assumed to be into stereotypical things, which is exactly what Femi experienced on a night out once. 'I remember turning up with one other Black woman, the two of us going to this gay club, and the guy on the door said, "It's not a soul night."' Like Femi, many people were forced to look further, to create spaces and establish new club nights. This led to parties like Sistermatic, Precious Brown, SHAKTI, and Club Kali in London; Saathi night in Birmingham; and, in Leicester, Bar Bindi, all for queer people with South Asian heritage.

> 11 March 1993
> SHAKTI having a disco on 12 Friday March at club RECESSION from 10–2pm

DJ Ritu played at SHAKTI, having already cut her teeth on many dancefloors in London in the 1980s, including a five-year residency at the London Lesbian and Gay Centre starting in 1986. It was around that time that Rita Hirana moved to London. 'I felt really alone and isolated,' she said. 'I didn't have any connections.' She was looking for the kinds of parties that Ritu was creating.

Tash watched Rita's eyes bring her memories alive with excitement and vibrant emotion, but also with an undertone of vulnerability. She told Tash how one night she made it out to SHAKTI and even met the DJ, Ritu. It was 1991, and, as Rita puts it, 'I kind of felt I found another home.'

Rita was experiencing what DJ Ritu was trying to do with nights like that. In an interview with Adam, Ritu said, 'I have grown up to be a person who doesn't like to see other people feeling alone, so I've always tried to bring everyone together.'

Ritu had grown up in Ilford in east London in the sixties and seventies, in an atmosphere of exclusion and prejudice. 'The National Front were marching through Ilford High Road all the time. I got called the "paki" word every day as a child: on the street, in my school, you name it. We were frightened of skinheads and there were skinheads around us all the time. So I didn't feel I belonged, and then there was the sexuality side, and I didn't feel I belonged. I felt alone, very alone.'

Both Ritu and Rita found a home in those clubs and on those dancefloors. Rita saw other South Asian lesbians around her living and dressing in the ways she wanted to, which was a huge relief. She said that she thought to herself, 'You know what, the world will not come crashing down if I go out with my hair out. And it felt so strange to go out and have my hair out in wild abandon and wear the make-up I wanted.' With her long black hair cascading down her back and her red lipstick as her power weapon, Rita emerged into the night. 'I felt like I was just learning to be who I am.'

When Tash interviewed Rita, it was clear that she'd spent a lot of time thinking about her life, and the journey she had been on. She took time with her answers, was incredibly self-reflective, and didn't try to hide any vulnerability. Rita had worked hard to be who she was, and she wasn't afraid to show it.

But it wasn't all acceptance and liberation. She said she experienced and witnessed 'intercommunity segmentation' that saddened her. 'I started getting aggression from other lesbians . . . But I thought, well, hell, I've been alone all my life. So I'll create my own space, and whoever wants to join it can join it.' Rita wanted to lean into her self-discovery, make every single day count, and found herself and Ritu dreaming up a new space. It would be named after the Hindu goddess Kali who, to Rita, represented the fierce feminine energy the scene needed. 'She battled demons and chopped off their heads and made a necklace out of them,' said Rita. 'And I thought, yeah, you know what, if there's going to be something that's going to oppress you, get rid! She was my role model.' Club Kali was born in 1995.

Both Ritu and Rita spoke of Club Kali as a celebratory space, a home away from home, and it thrived. Shortly after Club Kali opened its doors as a regular night, they were hosting parties at The Dome in Tufnell Park, which held 500 people. Coachloads of people came down from Birmingham, Manchester, Leicester, in fact from all over the UK. It was a space where queer South Asian people like Rita and Ritu could celebrate themselves, feel less alone and, crucially, not be disrespected due to their heritage. Rita and DJ Ritu talked of those years of Club Kali with nostalgia, yes, but also something deeper than that. We listened to their stories and we heard their yearning for connection; we learnt about the power they harnessed in order to build connections, not just for them but for thousands of others. Yet again we were hit by how much these nights meant to these women.

They wanted a place where they could feel welcome and included, a place where all aspects of their identities were held, equally. The disabled people who called Switchboard wanted the same. But whereas volunteers could send South Asian callers to

'HUDDLED TOGETHER IN A CORNER'

SHAKTI and Club Kali, they struggled to know what to recommend for disabled callers. As we read the log books we saw plenty of evidence of volunteers listening to disabled callers and supporting them, but sometimes there was the hint that creating disabled access to spaces was one job too many. In one entry, quoted above, a volunteer recommended collecting info on wheelchair-friendly venues even though 'it would be a lot of work'. In another entry, the volunteer noted that spaces and groups seemed to not think about accessibility at all:

> 17 March 1974
> I've just taken a call from a disabled gay guy in Hants who was asking about how gay groups etc would react to his being disabled, and pointed out that it's very frustrating to be sent somewhere and find when you arrive that you can't get in because of all the steps or the narrow exit, etc. etc. (and what about access to the toilets, will there be anywhere)

The log books show us that people go in search of spaces and places because they are driven by feelings of isolation and loneliness from within the LGBTQ+ community, especially from some people in it. When you think you've found your space, there are still so many barriers to break down, and often those are physical too.

What kind of message were these pubs, clubs, spaces, and even Switchboard sending when this question hadn't even been considered? It was loud and clear: *We haven't thought about you.* This meant some callers were excluded from exactly what they were longing for – a place to be free, with people who saw you for who you were.

The same was true of older callers who left their traces in the log books. Across thousands of pages we didn't find one mention of spaces where elderly people specifically felt welcomed, from club nights to social groups to care homes. Calls, and Switchboard's service, tended to be more geared towards younger people who were either 'on the scene' or wanted to be. Older people did call, and Switchboard listened, but judging by the log books, the idea that their isolation could be salved by dancing together, or even just getting together for a chinwag, didn't seem to occur to anyone. And yet the request that comes out time and again from the log books is that callers were looking for it – community. Just as the disabled callers were held back from going to clubs by some physical obstacle in the building design, *all* queer people were held back by society's obstructions: prejudice, discrimination, exclusion, fear, shame. Only the solidarity of a community can erode those.

That is what Rita and DJ Ritu were creating in Club Kali, and it is what, one night, Ritu invited her parents to experience. She wanted her mum and dad to see what she actually did for a living as a DJ. Many people she knew didn't have their parents' approval, but Ritu thought she could get it, and send a message. 'So my mum and dad came along, they sat right in front of the DJ booth,' she said to Adam, beaming. 'Two elderly people, Mum in her sari, Dad in a suit. Probably they're sweltering away. It was very hot, and they were just calmly watching everything going on around them and I saw people, punters just coming over to them and kneeling beside them and asking for their blessing.'

This 'blessing' was just an informal thing, requested by queer South Asian people who were not respected or loved by their own parents. No one had expected that DJ Ritu's mum and dad would find themselves being asked to substitute for all those others, but it is just what happened. When we heard stories like these, we thought about the language of Section 28 and we wondered:

which is the 'pretended family relationship' in this scene? The supporters of bigoted laws like Section 28 refused to see the beauty, the *connection*, of the people whom DJ Ritu brought together that night.

Ritu's mum later told her about one trip to the toilet, when about six people called her the respectful term of 'aunty' and thanked her for being there. One of them said to her, 'I wish my parents were like this with me, and I beg you for your blessings.' Ritu breathed slowly through the memory, then said, 'Makes me cry even thinking about it now.'

---

27 October 1982
Our 1,000,000th call came through today at 12.58pm. It was from an american tourist but he wouldn't give us his name . . . Bob Workman was here to take photos and the champagne flowed!!!

'I remember that call very well,' said Julian, thirty-seven years later, perhaps still under the influence of the champagne. 'It was from an American tourist who had just landed from Chicago [and] was looking to find where the Coleherne was.'

The Coleherne pub in Earls Court, London, was clearly very famous before it was the subject of Switchboard's millionth call. Also, perhaps, infamous. The pub appears frequently in the log books as the place where many men were entrapped by police into breaking homophobic laws, and often arrested. Richard Desmond told Tash about the Coleherne when they were looking over old log book entries together as fellow volunteers in 2019. Richard looked at the entry with resignation and commented, 'Just ordinary handwriting, writing what was all too likely to be a normal thing: "the coleherne has been raided".' The fact that so many men went to the Coleherne despite its reputation as a police trap meant that it was somewhere worth taking a risk for. It was such a special pub because it drew all types: poor and posh, young and old, leather daddies and opera queens (and in fact those two were often the same).

We loved hearing about these legendary gay spaces: the Coleherne, The New Penny, Bolts disco, Gateways, Heaven, Two Brewers, the Royal Vauxhall Tavern. We loved hearing how men like Richard found their tribe. For Richard, the tribe was leather, which was a significant part of the nightlife, as the log books showed us:

> 16 October 1984
>
> Anyone into leather? Next Saturday 20 October MSC [Motor Sports Club] is holding leather auction for our benefit. If you would like to be there its being held at Ship & Shovel, Crown Passage.

> 4 July 1992
>
> Please note that the BACKSTREET is a STRICT DRESS CODE LEATHER + RUBBER CLUB ONLY. Please do **not** send beginners there as the owner has complained about having to turn people away sent from S/B [Switchboard] because they are not suitably dressed.

In fact, when The Backstreet opened in 1985 it just so happened to be on the same road as the previous home of Switchboard's resident leather queen. The first day Tash met Richard he was on shift, supporting a caller, brow furrowed, eyes focused, leather jacket on. He was everywhere at Switchboard, an essential cog in the machine, always with something to say in his often quick and abrupt manner. But if you listened to what he was saying, it was always incredibly valid. It wasn't until Tash asked if she could interview Richard that she got an invitation to his home. You can learn so much about someone from their home, the decor, the placement of items, what food they have in their fridge, and what they offer you. Richard would always prepare something for Tash in his council flat by Victoria Park in east London: lunch or cake, tea or coffee, all ready to go – Tash always accepted. His place was busy, with lots of art and musical instruments strewn everywhere (his partner being a musician), and it was warm and welcoming. Richard would sit on the sofa and Tash on the beanbag (both leather, of course). Richard told Tash proudly, 'I have been a gay leatherman since I bought my first leather jacket when I was sixteen.' When she teased him about being known as Switchboard's resident leather queen, he laughed: 'I'm not the only one, there are more of us, honestly. Some of them have even got motorbikes!'

Through the log books and our interviews, we learnt about the blossoming of an SM scene in the eighties and nineties. As elders told us their stories of running SM and fetish nights, or just attending them, the themes of queer nightlife became clearer. For some people, music and dancing is the thing that brings us together and makes us feel included and part of a community; for others, it's desiring very specific kinky things with each other. Even this was about community – and it's why Derek Cohen and others set up a fetish club at the London Lesbian and Gay Centre in 1991.

The regular night was called Sadie Masie, and Derek loved telling people, especially those from the USA, that it was 'an S&M and disco club for lesbians and gay men and it's funded by the local council'. He still seemed surprised by the progressive politics of London in that era himself. 'And if their heads hadn't exploded at the idea of SM lesbians and gay men dancing, the last bit just finished them off.'

In fact, Adam's head exploded when he heard about it from Derek. During the course of our research some local councils were threatening, not supporting, several sex-positive queer parties. After complaints from residents, in 2022 Tower Hamlets Council tried to cut the already tiny number of licences it gave to venues so they could host sex on their premises. For Derek's generation and Adam's, these kinds of parties had become essential, sex in shared homes not always being the easiest thing, the venues boosting the chances of finding a sexual match.

During the making of the podcast and this book, listening to elders like Derek, Adam became more sexually adventurous, sniffing out different spaces and flavours. It was energising to compare the stories of elders' sexy nights out, including to spaces that had closed down, with the equivalent stories in our time. From gay saunas to fetish parties, Adam experienced something similar to what Derek and the others had: sexual community.

In fact, SM culture is so often misunderstood as being all about sex. It *is* about sex, but it is also about relationships, friendships, self-expression, tenderness, and even love. People who go to clubs that feature sex are looking for the same as anyone else going to any other type of club: to feel less alone; to find people. Part of Adam's sexuality is being able to enjoy sexual contact with lots of different people (not always at the same time), to be in clubs with nudity and where lots of sex happens, and to do specific things with those who share the same fetishes. But this sexuality can feel isolating, because most people do not want to have sex like that. Adam has found himself explaining himself to people a lot, just like in the old days when gays had to beg for acceptance. So to enter a space and know that everyone there on a basic level accepts that they are creating something outside of traditional relationships or usual social conventions becomes very significant.

Maybe community was the thing that we were all always looking for. Maybe even in that moment of Derek telling Adam his memories, a new community, just the two of them, was made. These interviews often felt to us like a shared space, with a sense of home.

Sadie Masie's didn't last forever, not least because it was one of the more controversial nights given a home at the London Lesbian and Gay Centre. Some women objected to lesbians being part of SM culture, arguing that it was oppressive to women. The centre also struggled with staff turnover, financial issues, and a theft of a lot of cash. It was the changing political priorities that wounded it fatally, however, starting with the abolition of the Greater London Council in 1986, and subsequent public bodies not seeing the value in a centre for gays and lesbians. The night closed in 1992.

But you can't keep the kinky queers still. Venues fold, parties struggle, and the SMers get organised:

> 24 August 1994
>
> <u>Clit Club</u> – for anyone who is interested – its future is uncertain. It did move back to the Elephant at Vauxhall in July but another had not been planned.
> Simply because FIST a mixed event makes more money !!!

In the log books we also track the movements of those nights from space to place, some popping up all over and others, like the Clit Club, having to rethink their future. The short-lived Clit Club was women only, but it faced competition from a night called FIST. Like Sadie Masie's, FIST was 'mixed' (meaning catering to all genders) and designed around people into BDSM (Bondage and discipline [B&D], domination and submission [D/S], and sadomasochism [SM]). As Clare remembered, you needed solid eardrums too: 'As you'd walk in, the sound just hit you,' she told Tash. 'It was absolutely physically loud. Some pounding music.

Very hard house music. And the smell of poppers. Smell of smoke and poppers. Because of course, you could still smoke in pubs and clubs back then. Every club was very smoky back then. But at least it was easy to wash the smell off your rubber!'

The people whom we spoke to about the varying BDSM nights always described them in such detail with all their sensual markers, poppers especially being a staple of any queer night scene. Tash used to sell poppers in the cloakroom of the Queenshilling, the gay bar she worked at in Bristol, often inhaling for her own pleasure to the beat of a particularly good song. Such a distinctive scent, and such a rush. Adam loved poppers so much, especially how they help queer friends on the dancefloor to kiss each other for fun, that he ended up writing a book about them.

Fisch was involved in promoting kinky queer nights in the 1990s. And the feeling she loved the most, the feeling that Adam related to as she talked, was freedom. 'There was never a feeling that "oh, we are going to get into trouble",' said Fisch. 'Never.'

For people who were, by definition, trouble – people who lived their lives on the edges (and the edge) – sex clubs and nights out offered validation. *We are trouble and we're going to revel in it*, they said. If the leaders called our relationships 'pretended' and people spat at us on the bus, in the club we could just be among our kind. 'Everybody loved everybody,' said Fisch. 'Everybody wanted to dance and that's what I wanted to do – I just wanted to chat and dance.'

When we heard statements like this from contributors like Fisch, we thought they sounded simplistic. This was the nostalgia that we'd worried we'd get into. And yet Fisch's memories about living so freely rang true with us. We felt something that wasn't just a dream of how wonderful things were in the past or how much fun you can have in the club. The badges, the clothes, the sex tribes, the gender poses we all struck – they were all about being free. It actually *was* simple. When we asked our elders to talk about their nights out, we realised, it was because we wanted to be with them in the past moments when they'd felt the most free. This is how we could feel together with them, down the decades and through the gendersex chaos: the shared memories were stories of freedom. This is how we connected, this is how we found the beat they'd been dancing to already, and how we joined in.

You can't archive dancing, but we knew we'd have to try. We loved asking our elders about their moves. The thing about dancing in gay clubs is that 'you could really just let go of all your worries and woes,' said Rita. 'And then you know, you crossed the threshold and went out into the real world at three o'clock in the morning. And you had a different life, but you were energised, you were stronger.'

Rita's memory is common among those we interviewed. Many of them talked about how the club helped them to forget what was waiting for them outside, at work or at home. We understood this feeling. Dancing especially is such a full-body activity, a sort of public sex, that you can barely do or think about anything else. This is exactly what Rita felt as soon as she stepped on to the dancefloor too: 'I thought, "Oh, my god", it's like, I cannot explain how my heart burst open. With life . . . suddenly, I was emerging.'

And this is how Rita reached Tash through the years: *Emerging, yes*, thought Tash, *that's how it feels, to be in the right place with the right people, the people who saw me, and to dance.*

When we dance, we feel free. On the dancefloor, LGBTQ+ people can perform to their chosen songs, explore their gender and their sexuality, create a future full of queerness on their very own stage. *This* was it. *This* was what all those callers to Switchboard had wanted. *This* was what the volunteers had sought for themselves on their nights off from the phones. In 2024 a friend saw us reacting to a set by the performer Hey, Baby doing an act fusing techno and punk. Our friend commented that we both danced the same: as lawless teenage boys. When we moshed with Hey, Baby, who has a song called 'PSYCHOPARTY', it felt like we were portraying the preferred versions of ourselves for each other, shedding a sense of shame, becoming who we wanted to be.

It's an act of care to give yourself this freedom, and it's an act of care to help your friends to experience it too. On nights out good friends all have one eye on each other, a gentle web of safety, vibrating with trademark dance moves and others who are trying to 'make a move'. Hands held to help with heartbreak, and arms wrapped around each other swapping gossip in the smoking corner. The club cradles our love for each other and our dance is how we celebrate it.

No matter the dance! Even the Switchboard volunteer who left the following message in the log book was looking for the same as us:

> 3 August 1982
> HAVE SOME FUN THIS AUTUMN
> Is anybody interested in forming a gay Morris dancing group to tour the pubs and clubs? Bung a note in my pidgeonhole/envelope. Tony Konrath. PS. I especially need to hear from someone who knows how to Morris dance!

We don't know whether Tony managed to get that troupe together, but if anyone could help, it would be Switchboard. Mostly, however, the musical references in the log books are about pop:

'HUDDLED TOGETHER IN A CORNER'

> 3 November 1990
> Caller rang to say how could he become gay! 16 year old absolutely besotted by the lead singer in Erasure. Dresses like his idol, has his hair styled the same, copies his mannerisms too. Lead singer is gay so our 16 year old also wants to be gay too. How? What is the secret. Any answers.

This caller wanted to be just like Andy Bell, the singer in Erasure. It can feel so freeing to become someone else, as any performer will tell you. But really these personas, whether your own or somebody else's, are just an imagined, better version of ourselves anyway. This is why music has long been a core feature of queer community. Artists have often been the first examples of queer representation that a young queer person sees. Performing their stories through music, like dance, they give us the belief, individually and collectively, that a more positive future lies ahead for us:

> 18 May 1983
> NME has a very positive article on gays this week – about Bronski Beat which are also featured on the front cover. It would be stupid not to advertise in the publication as a follow up to this sort of article . . .

If Switchboard's Development Group did follow through on that suggestion and advertise in the *NME*, it would have led to some calls. The power of the lads from Bronski Beat putting themselves out there as visibly gay no doubt led to more connections between queer people. And then there is their music itself, of course: most famously their song from 1984, 'Smalltown Boy'. It's about a young gay man who is bullied at school and unloved at home, and leaves to find a better life. Sung in Jimmy Somerville's plaintive falsetto, mixing darkness into the dance beats, it became a queer anthem, never leaving the dancefloor.

In 2024, as we worked on this book, the song turned forty and it was ready to be celebrated again. The tune was remixed and updated by the artist and producer Planningtorock, who added their own voice to it:

> I was twelve years old when I first heard this song, and it had a massive impact on me, as a young, gay, queer, trans person. And it's still just as relevant today. Young, gay, queer, trans, and non-binary kids are still having to run away.

In October 2024 'Smalltown Boy' became the centrepiece at a concert marking the anniversary of Bronski Beat's album *Age of Consent*, which had been named to draw attention to the inequality in law for gay and bi sex in 1984. The concert took place at Queen Elizabeth Hall in the Southbank Centre, London, and featured performances from not just Planningtorock but also non-binary pop star Tom Rasmussen, and the Pink Singers, an LGBTQ+ choir who'd sung on the 1984 album. The night was put together not by people of Bronski Beat's generation but by the younger generation, our generation, in much the same way that we were trying to mark and celebrate our queer elders through our work. In fact, one of the night's producers, composer and sound artist Lulu Manning, even weaved recordings from our podcast into an audio soundscape which played out between the songs. The voices we had captured were brought back to life, giving them another space, taking us all out for the night once again.

The memories, the songs, the togetherness – they were decades old, and yet now they were celebrated by people from younger generations, because the feelings were the same. When we interviewed our elders and spoke about the songs they danced to in the

1980s and the songs we danced to in the 2010s and 2020s, we got a dizzying sense of timelessness. In those conversations, when were we exactly? Their time or ours? It didn't matter. Simply, in those moments, we were together. Our elders taught us that dancing *is* something, and it is the ambiguity of that something that we encountered when we went looking for memories of nightlife from our elders. When we tuned in to the beats of their bodies, we connected to our own. Outside of time, we were all stomping and sashaying to the same rhythm.

Of course, plenty of people who called Switchboard looking for people like them did not want to dance. They wanted a gay chess group, a lesbian hockey team, or a night out at the theatre. Nightlife can exclude some people, and they can feel very isolated when so much of queer culture is geared towards the night. Switchboard helped, recommending social groups, sober spaces, newsletters, bookshops, and more. We saw the value in these kinds of spaces in the pages of the log books and heard about the power of groups such as Imaan, founded for queer Muslims in 1999. And, in fact, when Tash began researching her hometown of Plymouth, she found out about a radical bookshop run by two lesbians that sat just a stone's throw from her school. The shop was called In Other Words, and somehow it had managed to stay out of sight even for a person who needed it. Tash found archival photos of the bookshop's window displays set up to oppose Section 28, and even snaps from a book launch for *Jenny Lives with Eric and Martin*. She also learnt of a newsletter called *The Outback* which was circulated across the South West by two lesbians. It had lists of LGBTQ+ clubs, pubs, nights, and groups, and so many of them were in Plymouth. Running from 1996 to 2007, it covered the years when Tash was searching for those spaces. Tash didn't find that newsletter or the bookshop, but the people behind them were there, creating community just as much as a nightclub owner or DJ could.

———

The log books contain plenty of stories of the darkness of night-life, as with the troublesome trousers and badges mentioned above. If we wanted to understand our elders' experiences, we had to grapple with the dangers of being queer on a night out. And, as it happened, we knew exactly how this aspect of nightlife was not at all history. As regular clubbers we were both used to the hostility of the sexist, heterosexual patriarchy. Covid brought somewhat of a break from this, but only because all the clubs were closed. In August 2021, we were making season two of the podcast, but the time came when we could finally shake it off again. The clubs had been closed for well over a year, but one of our faves, Riposte, was back with a day rave. When Adam stepped off the bus to meet Tash, he looked emotionally bruised. During Adam's journey a man had looked at his short sexy shorts and muttered a homophobic slur. The story made Tash so angry: Adam's beautiful display of queerness had been used as a weapon against him. (And the man was wrong because Adam has really sexy legs, actually.)

As we found in the log books, going out had never been safe:

20 August 1983
Caller reported that a man smashed the windows of The Alternative with a large car-jack last night. None of the women were hurt inspite of the flying glass.
The man apparently said that he wanted to 'get' his wife whom he thought was drinking there at the time. The police came but did not hurry so the caller said.

She is worried, probably with very good cause, that the trouble will be blamed on the women & the pub, rather than on a violent straight male. It's possible that it could adversely affect the pubs renewal license.

This call is emblematic. As Switchboard was recommending pubs and clubs to callers, it also had to track how safe they were, logging violent attacks like the one above and tensions between clientele, all the better to give full advice to callers. Our interviewees, like Switchboard volunteer Jeremy Adams, had plenty to say about this. 'I remember days when you'd be sitting in a bar somewhere and somebody would just open the door and throw a live firework in,' Jeremy told Adam in 2019. These memories came as thick and fast as the ones about the fun times. As the log book entry above shows, homophobia is not usually the only form of hatred on display in violence, but also sexism. Places where women could feel safe, and not dominated by men, featured a lot in the stories we collected:

4 November 1986

When speaking to women re: ents calls, please ask them to go to The Bell, Kings X on Saturday. It was full of men tonight and it's usually 50/50. We don't want to lose another place that is only half ours.

In the 1980s, The Bell pub sat in what was then the dodgy area around King's Cross train station – very close to the Switchboard phone room. The Bell was an alternative to the mainstream pop-tastic gay scene. It played punk and new wave, and hosted radical leftist activists and a LGBTQ+ crowd for boozy nights and even fundraisers. This also made it one of the pubs that was easily targeted:

8 October 1983

Problems at The Bell this evening – about 6 skinhead fascists invaded. Management evicted them. Some verbal hassling and so on eventually police called to clear them from the area. A **few** people got very excited & had a go at the management – but this was really unjustified. **No one** was hurt or physically attacked. The management got fed up with being abused, and closed early. Nightworkers explicitly support managers' actions.

Numerous other pubs experienced similar troubles:

23 Monday 1985 – 22.18

Guy rang to report an attack outside the two brewers [pub in Clapham]. Wasn't +tive that it was QB [queerbashing], but suspected it might be, apparently something similar happened to his mate a fortnight ago. Funny how they come around full circle, it was me a month ago.

As we read through the log books we felt the same fear as our elders. It wasn't easy to know of the joy and the connection that nightlife could bring us queer people, and then to see how easily it could be shattered.

30 April 1999 – 9.30 p.m.

A bomb exploded in the Admiral Duncan pub in Old Compton Street 3 hours ago. So far we do not really know exactly what has happened – we have heard varying reports that 2, 3 or 7 people have been killed and about 40 injured. There were two people down on the rota for this evening, but Ceri and Boo have been very quick to phone round and other volunteers have rallied round and we now have about 8 people taking calls – we are getting lots of calls related to the incident – many people including some of those here present are worried about friends of theirs who may well have been in the area this evening . . .

We both knew of this attack, were old enough to remember it happening, as teenagers, but now we were confronted with it as queer clubbers it hit differently. Now it was in the log books, and had found its way into our project.

At 6.30 p.m. on 30 April 1999, a nail bomb explosion in the pub killed Nik Moore, John Light, and Andrea Dykes, who was pregnant. Seventy-nine people were injured in the attack, which was committed by David Copeland, a domestic terrorist who had the express political aim of starting a war. The bombing of the pub in Soho was Copeland's third attack in three weeks. Before attacking the gay community, he'd targeted the Black community in Brixton and the Bangladeshi community in Brick Lane. Copeland's war cry was clear: he was a homophobic neo-Nazi militant and white supremacist. He knew that a queer venue like the Admiral Duncan would strike at the heart of the LGBTQ+ community, just as his other targets had hit at theirs.

As a South Asian woman, Rita was already dealing with aspects of racism, gender sexism, and misogyny. She had just been sacked from her job for coming out as a lesbian, and then Copeland's bombs hit London. 'When that happened . . . I just felt like, Kali, are you messing with me?' Rita told Tash how the bombs put her in a state of shock. Before the sacking she had felt like she was just starting to get her life together in London. She had thought, 'I'm starting to flourish here. This is my real home.'

Our home was violated: the city, the streets, the markets, the pub. It started with a loud noise that Jeremy Adams heard from inside the nearby Queens Theatre. Jeremy worked in the theatre, alongside his duties as a volunteer and co-chair of Switchboard.

'We just heard this noise,' he told Adam when asked to remember the day of the Admiral Duncan bombing:

> Nobody was quite sure what it was but knew that something . . . there was the kind of sense when you hear something like that that something is not right . . . I came out of the theatre into Old Compton Street and walked into something that was like, devastation, people bleeding, people on the floor, police everywhere, it was sort of horrific. It was sort of terrible. People did all they could to help.

In one sad way, no one was surprised. Jeremy and the other volunteers at Switchboard were used to living with the prospect of violence. 'I remember Switchboard was regularly getting all kinds of threats,' said Rebecca Swenson, a volunteer at the time of Copeland's bombings, 'people ringing up saying "I'm going to put a bomb through the door". Just general nastiness down the phone lines.'

When the Admiral Duncan attack happened, Rebecca got the news while at another volunteer's house. Without hesitation they both went straight to Switchboard, knowing that there would be an influx of calls. Rebecca told Tash how people rang in worried about family members. More often than not the callers knew the person was gay but they had never talked about it, and now they couldn't get hold of them. Volunteers set up extra phone lines in the basement. As Richard remembered, 'We listened to our community grieve . . . This was a very specific, very nasty attack on us.'[1]

We were too young and too far away from London queer life to be affected by the bombing, but as we collected memories about it, our own memories returned to June 2016. The mass shooting in Pulse, a queer nightclub in Orlando, Florida, shocked the world – but especially LGBTQ+ people. It happened on a Saturday night and was all over the news on the Sunday and

Monday, with horrible stories of clubbers cowering in the toilets. Forty-nine people died, plus the killer himself. Tash, at that time the volunteer in charge of Switchboard's social media, posted messages of support to those impacted by the attacks, and encouraged anyone affected to reach out to Switchboard. Volunteers headed to the phone room in London to pick up those calls just like they had done in 1999. Gradually, a plan emerged among LGBTQ+ people in London, and by Monday evening they had started to amass in Soho. The Admiral Duncan pub, which had been a similar victim seventeen years previously, was the altar of what became a vigil. Adam stood on the street, held by a friend, and wept. It was a mixture of horror, grief, and fear that this could happen to any one of the thousands on the street that day. The London Gay Men's Chorus wrapped everyone together by singing 'Bridge Over Troubled Water'.

This vigil made it clear how queer people connect to each other over continents and decades. We may sometimes be divided, but we have more solidarity. Our pubs and clubs are sacred to us. Our haters know that too, but they can't stop the party. For Switchboard volunteers and callers, the phone room was equally special. The bombing showed how the phone room was its own community. Rebecca took solace in that. 'How grateful we were for that space,' she said, 'and how quickly it could have been taken away.'

This concern was stronger in the weeks after the Admiral Duncan bombing, as Copeland inspired others to his cause, some of whom even threatened Switchboard:

> 7 May 1999
> An awful man called and ranted at me down the phone for a good minute telling me how sick I was and how much we as a 'community' (my word) deserved this. Not wanting to reciprocate

with hate – what do you say? Never have I been so insulted by such sickness and hate.

Underneath this entry another volunteer wrote, 'Isn't this a sure sign the bombs may be triggering off further homophobia? Should we not prepare for it?' Sure enough:

9 May 1999
Caller from Stockwell reports constant homophobic abuse from a gang of youths ever since the bombing. Police apparently not taking case seriously + caller is in constant state of fear and spoke to me in a highly paniced state. Gang is constantly attacking his flat + he is currently in a state of siege.

That gang of youths took permission from Copeland's example to engulf this person in a 'constant state of fear'. But such fear cannot last. The log books show us that no one has to be at home alone, isolated, fearful. Reading between the lines on the scruffy pages, it is clear that the volunteers know what freedom feels like. Callers can tell this, too. It's why they asked where to go out, where they could be with the community, where they could feel free. That is what we've looked for, and it is why Rita went out in Soho not long after Copeland's bomb. 'I thought, no, that's just another aspect where the world is trying to take something away from me,' she said, 'and I'm not going to let it.' As Jeremy put it: 'So when you're in a place and someone opens the door and throws a firework in, my response to that is, "Fuck you, that is not going to stop us, how dare you."'

Jeremy's and Rita's resilience was grounded in their knowledge that being LGBTQ+ is a human right, that it is beautiful and powerful. But they also knew that specifically queer spaces are essential to this. When they are attacked, we are all attacked. That is the paradoxical thing about an act of violence by a Nazi like Copeland: it makes our spaces stronger, and it reveals the connections between us all.

After her shift in the phone room, Rebecca returned home and found a series of answerphone messages left by her grandma. 'I had never talked to her about my sexuality,' said Rebecca, 'and I rang her and she said, "Thank goodness, I've been so worried about you. Are you and your friends OK?"'

We wanted to tell Rebecca's grandma that we were OK. We were OK because we'd found people like her granddaughter, who'd been out to the club before us, who could take us there safely. It seemed that even the darkest stories about pubs and clubs could be lit with love.

We have grown up to love being queer and to love our queer nightlife. It is as much a part of who we are as the blood that pumps around our bodies. The beat drew us to the dancefloor, into the log books, and into our elders' memories. We found ourselves relating directly to their stories of nightlife, because those stories were so similar to ours. Nights of silliness, of freedom and friendship, of love. Nights of fucking and of dancing, and isn't that the same thing anyway? Nights of bodies, of connection, of community.

Whatever the year, whatever our part in the LGBTQ+ family, we all wanted to dance because it helps to shake free from what the writer Matthew Todd called the 'straight jacket' of being queer. 'It is the damage done to us by growing up strapped inside a cultural straitjacket,' he wrote, 'a tight-fitting, one-size restraint imposed on us at birth that leaves no room to grow outside its narrow confines.'[2]

The log books taught us how much more queer clubs meant than just having a good time. And our elders' stories came to mean much more than nostalgia. We'd each taken very different journeys to get to the club, but we both had the same experience when we were there: queer spaces allowed us to be our free selves. And if the club allowed us to be ourselves as queer people, talking to our elders about their nights out allowed us to grow into ourselves as historians. We saw so much value in their memories. The collective memory was as priceless an archive as the log books were.

Nightlife gave us all room to grow. The beats of our bodies hit the same rhythm as those of the elders who created spaces for us. Even when we don't realise it, queer people dance with our elders inside us. That is euphoria. In the club, we are living memorials to our queer elders.

3
'TODAY IT'S LOOKING, TOMORROW IT'LL BE THINKING'

How the police stamped on our freedom

6 May 1988
BROWNIES SAUNA
A caller who works for Brownies rang to say that it was raided yesterday. About 50 police entered premises at 8pm ish and carted off most of the customers. Brownies will reopen tomorrow (7/5/88).

The note in the log book was just three sentences, but the volunteer who wrote it told others exactly what they needed to know: if callers asked for information about Brownies, a gay sauna in south London, be sure to warn them. Police had recently smashed into Brownies and arrested the men inside. Reading that entry thirty-five years later, seated behind a desk in the hush of Bishopsgate Institute, Adam leant forwards. The volunteer's note raised more questions than it answered. This often happened when we read the log books – their writers lured us back through time, only to leave us stranded. Fortunately, when it came to the Brownies raid, Adam could find out more because Bishopsgate Institute has a full archive of *Capital Gay* newspaper. Adam asked the archivists to bring out some back issues from the weeks after the raid.

While he waited in the hard wooden chair, he thought about what it must have been like in Brownies that night. He pictured the interiors of the gay sex clubs and saunas he had been inside. He conjured the unique cocktail of nerves and horniness, the musty smell of sweat, cum, bleach, and poppers, the dimly lit corners, the men looking, circling, looking, touching, tender at first, and then, fucking. He wondered: how would this all feel if fifty shouting police officers barged in?

'This stinks of Nazism, it's like Germany in 1935,' said a man who had been in Brownies on the night of the raid. The story had made it to the front page of *Capital Gay*, where that punter was quoted. Adam was completely hooked by the report, reading it with urgency as though it were today's newspaper. For the three weeks prior to the raid, it had emerged, police officers had pretended to be customers in Brownies, wearing only towels and observing the men they were preparing to terrorise.

A man named John Ellis regularly went to Brownies at the time, to hang out with other gay men, be naked, relax, chat, and flirt. He told Adam that it was a dive of a place, rough and dingy, but he spent plenty of time there. The men in Brownies knew that the police could barge in at any moment. For fear of the law, the people running Brownies often toured the place with a bright torch to make sure no one was having sex. 'I got ejected a number of times for having sex,' laughed John. 'They'd say, "Get your clothes on and leave."'

Fortunately, John wasn't there on the night the police bashed their way in using a sledgehammer. They broke down the door and charged in, wearing rubber gloves due to their ignorance of how HIV was transmitted. Six customers were arrested and charged with gross indecency. Adam went through the later issues of *Capital Gay*, following the case through the legal process that culminated in the sauna's owner Ken Levy and his staff member Alan Malin being found guilty of running a 'disorderly house'. This charge sounded to Adam like a name for a queer club night, but in fact it was the crime that Brownies' staff lived in fear of committing, and why they policed the space themselves. Adam found it hard to fathom: a sex space where sex was banned, and terminology that seemed archaic, even laughable, but also deadly serious. Sir David Hughes-Morgan, the judge in the Brownies case, sentenced Levy to six months in jail and Malin to three, saying that he had to make an example of businesses that facilitated homosexuality. Hughes-Morgan said that any man could have walked into Brownies off the street to take a sauna, witnessed homosexual activity, and been invited to participate. 'The possibilities are quite devastating and the sentence must demonstrate society's shock and horror,' he concluded.

Adam read this judgment with a different kind of horror: the suggestion that gay men lure men into sex against their will was a classic homophobic trope. The real crime was that a judge – someone supposedly fair-minded – had said something so prejudiced. The reality is that there was no problem with confused men wandering in off the street; the actual threat was from the police who barged in. 'I was afraid of being arrested,' said John, 'because I would have been sacked from work. I would have lost my job.'

John's fear was not misplaced. It sunk in with Adam just how constrained these men were, how unjust the legal process, how strong the social censure. The log books told us so. They showed us people who lost their jobs, their careers, their partners, their homes, their children – all for engaging in consensual sex acts or, sometimes, even just flirting.

John spoke openly with Adam in a soft Northern Irish accent, intrigued that he was being asked about his sauna escapades in the eighties all these years later. He remembered that atmosphere of fear and intimidation. It was the peak of the HIV panic, a homophobic fever was about to be passed into law as Section 28, and the police were rounding up gay men. John told Adam, 'I didn't want to be in Britain at all.'

Every signal John and those other men received from mainstream society was that being gay was wrong. He wanted to enjoy his body, explore pleasure, but the full force of the state was saying no.

When Tash heard about these police actions she thought: *that checks out.* Tash had never trusted the police. They were almost all men and Tash had learnt to be wary of blindly trusting straight men. Her interactions with the police came when she started driving. She was periodically stopped for not having her car lights on or for driving too fast. Or they would search her car for drugs when they thought Tash was stoned. On each of these occasions, the officer was male, patronising, and would project his state-given authority into the air around him. Tash hated them, and how they treated her. At first when she read the log books she enjoyed the sarcasm of the Switchboard volunteers who wrote these stories of police versus the gays. They often read like the plot of a film from the *Carry On* series, with the image of a blustering cop chasing a swishing queen.

The more Tash read, though, the more solemn she became. *I've been arrested*, the callers said. *I don't know what to do. I wasn't doing anything wrong. The police trapped me. My life is destroyed. Please don't tell anyone.*

As we gathered all the stories, we could see the full scale of what had happened. It became clear that a huge part of the life of a queer man was about evading persecution by an organised gang of violent thugs: the police. Queer men called Switchboard late at night in desperation. Adam had to pause frequently and breathe, thinking: *What would I have done?*

The weight of the log book entries alone was enough to show us that as historians we had to look into this matter of the police. But the theme also seemed to connect in various ways to the world we came from. As small children in 1988 we were not about to go anywhere that got raided by the police; but in the same month as the Brownies raid, the government passed Section 28. This law, we now felt, turned our teachers into police. It empowered some, and frightened others, into trying to stop us from being queer in whatever way our bodies tried.

As we listened through the deafening silence we'd inherited, we started to hear the stories of our queer ancestors trying to have sex while evading the police. They were always men, or at least that's how the stories were told. For reasons we'll explain, sex between women has not been criminalised in the UK. Queer women have had to fight to assert their rights and freedoms against the state, just not in a fight against police in the same way queer men have.

These stories are also based on the state records of arrests, and limited by the language of the years we are exploring. The police targeted those who were legally considered to be men, for having sex with other men. Not captured in these official statistics, but definitely present, are many trans women's stories. They are often folded into the histories of gay men, as that was how they were frequently categorised by the state.

This was going to be a complicated story to unpick. We wanted to understand this terrible dynamic, between the police and our community. We were ready to see how the power of the state had framed queer lives, and curtailed our own.

―――

Even as Adam came close in age to being sexual, the police were still chasing down gay men. One case in particular brought the whole culture into the glare of the public. In April 1998, the pop star George Michael stepped into a public toilet in Los Angeles and did something that was later classed by a court as a 'lewd act'.

His pattern of public sex, including his cruising on Hampstead Heath in London, became public knowledge.

Adam was thirteen years old at the time of all this tabloid drama, noticing that the famous man had done something wrong involving gay sex.

By October that year, George Michael had completed his community service *and* recorded the song 'Outside', with lyrics hailing public sex, and a music video featuring sexy cops and disco balls. Guilty, yes, but shamed? No. This was a cultural moment in which the singer courageously declared his sexuality and satirised the laws against it, and Tash and her mum danced to the song in the kitchen. George Michael became almost as famous for cruising in the bushes as he was for his gorgeous singing. But for Adam, the idea that gay sex was policed settled into his mind.

A pop star had drawn the public's attention to the way that the state was regularly pursuing victimless 'crimes' – and the tabloids and the public were shocked. Very few people would have had a sense of the scale of police persecution, other than Switchboard's volunteers. Their log books are packed with stories like George Michael's and this one from one of our interviewees, who asked to remain anonymous:

> I was in a park at night. With no one in sight, apart from the chap who was with me. I like to call it 'admiring the beauties of nature in the park'. Everybody knew how dangerous it was – whatever happened it wasn't going to happen to you. So when it did, it wasn't very nice. It was five minutes before the magistrate but boy did I get the lash of his tongue before a hefty fine.[1]

For us, listening to this man's wavering voice brought the log books to life. His was not one of the countless cases reported to Switchboard, but it is similar to them. Another contributor told us

'TODAY IT'S LOOKING . . .'

how police officers would appear behind men in a darkened park and threaten them with a hefty torch across the back of the neck. It scared us to think of how the police could use violence against these men, and how the courts would convict them. Parks, saunas, toilets, even private parties: the police were everywhere . . .

> 7 July 1993
> Call from a punter in Poole, Dorset. To let us know there has been a lot of police activity there at the Gay beach at Sandbanks.

> 5 February 1977
> Just received a phone call from St Austell in Cornwall. The caller informed me that 28 men have been arrested for 'gross indecency' there. There was a police raid at a party and all the men were taken to the police station, stripped, searched, and some kept overnight. All the men have now gone underground after being released on bail.

Jeremy Adams remembered taking calls like these, hearing the fear in the men's voices. 'There was a huge risk in being gay,' he told Adam, adding that often reports of arrests actually came from men who lived straight lives but also enjoyed sex with other men. 'There was always this risk that your life would be destroyed,' he said. 'For a lot of people it was like, "Oh god, if somebody found out, if I was arrested, my life would be over, I'd be sent to court, my name would be in the papers".'

Traumatic calls like these often came at night, much like the calls about violence in nightclubs and pubs. 'In those days we had a night shift which ran from eleven at night till eight in the morning,' Lisa Power recalled. 'You might not be inundated with calls, but you might need one person to be taking the call and another person in the other room on the coin box phoning the police or a lawyer. Or trying to sort something out for someone. It was quite helpful to be two-handed at that time.'

Some men, like Julian Hows, enjoyed the chase of cruising dangerously. By the time Adam interviewed Julian in 2019, Adam had had quite a few of his own sexual adventures, some even in public, but Julian's memories of cruising in the seventies were still a revelation. He got caught once, and his retelling made Adam's heart race. 'I was about eighteen,' said Julian of the incident, in the toilet, or 'cottage', at Oxford Circus in London. 'Someone was waving their willy at the urinal and I walked over and they went to put their hand out and then suddenly the person next to me said, "You're nicked!"' Although the plain-clothes officers escorted Julian up to the street to book him, they were too incompetent to detain him. 'I just belted it, dear!' he said, howling.

As usual with reading the log books and collecting queer memories, there are lots of paradoxes in stories like Julian's – or, at least, in how we've reacted to them. The more we read, the more we heard laughter and anger, often on the same page. People like Julian brought this colourful complexity to life, even though it was bizarre to hear a man the same age as our dads talk about reaching out to grab other men's willies in a public loo. Julian could laugh about it even while it destroyed other men's lives. Of course, he knew it was serious, and as a volunteer no doubt he handled such calls with care. Clearly it was a significant part of our queer history, and of the experience of our queer ancestors. We needed to find out more about how Britain came to be the kind of country that, during our lifetimes, wanted to stop men from fucking.

We read back through legal histories, as though we'd been assigned an essay topic. The first part of our lesson was how none of this was about what happens between women. This is a common occurrence in queer history. The gap is usually the result of women's experiences being ignored by (male) historians and archivists; in the case of the criminalisation of sex, it is men's sexist lack of imagination that means that sex between women has never been banned in the UK.

Henry VIII outlawed buggery in 1533. A further law designed by Henry Labouchere in 1885 criminalised more homosexual activity between men under the term 'gross indecency'. In 1921, Baron Brabazon got in on the lawmaking, claiming that lesbians were a group who needed stamping out. Some fellow lawmakers added a controversial clause to the Criminal Law Amendment Bill to criminalise gross indecency between women in England and Wales (it has been argued that this clause was added by the bill's opponents as something controversial enough to scupper the bill entirely).[2] The idea was quashed when other lords argued that, surely, female homosexuality was not enough of a problem to warrant the ink that an act of parliament would be written in. 'The overwhelming majority of the women of this country have never heard of this thing at all,' said one earl, F. E. Smith, in parliament, adding that there was not 'one scintilla of evidence that there is any widespread practice of this kind of vice'.[3]

Were the lesbians of the past good at covering their tracks? Or was it simply inconceivable that a woman would be able to peel her lustful eyes away from the draw of the male form? Either way, the lords didn't see the lesbians. They were made to be invisible, and Baron Brabazon's amendment failed.

It seems weird that there can be this invisibility while some men are all too preoccupied with *seeing* queer women. By the time we were into our history project, Tash had hundreds of personal stories about this, from the man who threw a five-pound note at her face as she kissed her date and asked her to 'Do it again, love', to the constant stabbing of words like 'slut', 'dyke', 'lezza', and 'whore' thrown at her in public. Once a man pushed his crotch into her when she was kissing someone, and many men have asked her what really goes on between two women. Sometimes these insults come from women and children. Even when Tash shouted back, something inside her went quiet. These interactions all scarred Tash; they shaped her, changed her muscle memory. As with the opinions of lawmakers in the past, these actions against queer women are always rooted in sexism, objectification, and disgust at homosexuality. Perhaps the police and the state have never needed laws in order to keep queer women in line because society taught us all so well that women should be controlled.

The more we looked into the history of 'gross indecency', as it applied to people earlier than the men from Brownies, the more it appeared to us as a system of control. It had been used to bring Oscar Wilde and other pansies into line, and to claim that Alan Turing was not a patriot because he didn't have sex with the right gender. The law went further afield, too: Britain was a country devoted to expanding its imperial power. This meant that as the country exported white supremacy and colonialism around the world, the extremely British concept of 'gross indecency' tagged along. British supremacists transposed their legal system across the seven seas, leading to homophobic legislation in many other countries. This even extended to women, too, in Trinidad and Tobago, the Solomon Islands, Barbados, Sri Lanka, Botswana, Malaysia, The Gambia, Zambia, and Malawi.[4]

Another paradox hinted at in stories like Julian's is that even though men were being chased down by police, the Sexual Offences Act 1967 was supposed to have decriminalised sex between men. (The reform was pretty narrow in scope, though. It only decriminalised sex between a maximum of two men, who were both over twenty-one, as long as they were not in the armed forces, and only doing it in private behind a locked door, and only in England and Wales.) Julian, a Londoner, came of age after this reform, and yet still found himself hunted by police. The reason is that although the law gave some sexual freedom to men, it also clarified which acts were still forbidden: gross indecency, plus 'importuning' and 'soliciting', which are just legal words for coming on to someone sexually. These were crimes committed publicly, and they didn't even have to involve touch. The message from the state towards men was clear: you can fool around with each other, but no one wants to see it. This legal clarity was seen by many police officers as a mandate to catch men who were snogging in parks, winking across a bar, and, of course, shagging in toilets. The police were so emboldened by their powers that they often boasted of high arrest rates and invited television crews to document what they were doing:

30 March 1990

VICTORIA STATION ARRESTS

Police have made multiple arrests at Victoria Station toilets today – more than 50 men, they told one arrestee. They also told him LWT [London Weekend Television] were filming the arrests for a documentary; which should be interesting, as all he'd done was wash his hands twice because he was nosy as to why people were standing round looking suspicious!

As we found log book entries about the police, and legal history articles that helped us to understand the context, we kept thinking about how all these arrests would have been recorded officially. Often the only place where we queers appear in official archives is in police records, of men being arrested for having sex with other men, and state documents discussing the laws on how to control us. We knew we had to look at the other side of this story, and this took us to The National Archives.

The National Archives occupies a site in Kew, southwest London, predominantly a big concrete brutalist building with a lake out front. Documents end up there from central government departments and some other public bodies; it is a legal requirement that they identify records of historical value and transfer them to Kew for permanent preservation. After reading so many stories in Switchboard's log books about police chasing down men for having sex, we wanted to see what documents The National Archives might have stored about this. Had government ministers ordered this persecution? Had anyone lobbied government for or against it?

One of the first things we found in Kew was research by a civil servant, started in 1976, the year Adam's parents got married, and just two years into Switchboard's operations. The official's name was Roy Walmsley, and his intention was to try to understand the impact of the 1967 act that had partially decriminalised sex between men. What Walmsley found seemed to have surprised him: 'Since the Sexual Offences Act 1967 was passed,' he wrote in his final article, dated 1978, 'the recorded incidence of the offence of indecency between males has approximately doubled, and the number of persons prosecuted for the offence has trebled.'[5]

In Walmsley's article, entitled 'Indecency Between Males and the Sexual Offences Act 1967', he posed several theories to explain the numbers. He mentioned changes in the attitudes of homosexuals, the public, and police, and then proposed a perhaps unexpected consequence of the legal reform. 'A third hypothesis is that the Act itself is the source of the increases in recorded incidence and prosecution rate: it provided the police with a basis on which action could more confidently be taken against those involved in homosexual acts in public, and it introduced summary trial for the offence of indecency between males thus making it easier to bring prosecutions.' (A summary trial is a trial by magistrates without a jury.)

When you sit in the reading room at The National Archives, you're expected to work quietly. Other visitors on the day Adam did his research into this file might have heard him sighing and grumbling, however. He huffed his way through the various drafts of Walmsley's article that lay inside a bundle of paper from the Home Office Research Unit, among correspondence between others in the Home Office, from civil servants to ministers, and to external reviewers, including a psychiatrist and a probation officer. As Adam thumbed the various papers, it became clear that Walmsley's colleagues and ministers of state did not consider it unfair that prosecutions against gay men had risen since 1967. They did nothing about it. The fact is, even after 1967, it remained a position of public policy that homosexuality was immoral. The police were doing their rightful duty to enforce laws against it.

One person who reviewed Walmsley's figures was Superintendent Moss of the Metropolitan Police. She reported to the Home Office that she did not find Walmsley's figures particularly high, and stated that the public wished the laws to be enforced. See it, say it, sorted.

Walmsley's findings would not have surprised Switchboard volunteers or their callers – the gay community knew exactly what was going on. The whole ongoing operation felt like a stitch-up, run by cocky cops given cover by the establishment. As we began to build a wider picture in our understanding, we were led to gather more and more interviews. 'I was found guilty of importuning, and I was fined twenty pounds,' recalled Terry Stewart, a man we found through our research as someone whose life had been blighted by his run-in with the law in the early 1980s.

It's one thing for a senior police officer to say that the law was hers to enforce, and another for an individual person like Terry to have his life affected by what came to be seen as clearly unfair laws to begin with. 'The only evidence that was presented to the judge was the statement of both the police officers, which was exactly the same,' Terry said. 'I thought, "Well they are just lying through their teeth." My barrister did ask them how many times had they arrested people in that toilet over the last twelve months and they said 500. So clearly it was a little honey pot.'

Terry spoke to Adam in 2019, some time after the police had largely stopped persecuting men like him. Terry, though, was still stained by his conviction. Over thirty-eight years he'd had to declare it when applying for work or to join an organisation. 'I won't get past the front door,' he said. As he spoke, he could barely control the anger which had lasted as long as his criminal record. In 2012 the government launched a scheme to disregard some historical homosexual offences, namely gross indecency and buggery, but that scheme didn't cover Terry's offence, nor the vast majority of cases (including soliciting and certain acts in a public toilet, which remained illegal). A route to get a pardon for those offences launched in 2017, but only if the applicant's offence had been disregarded. The nation's morals had shifted somewhat, but even the new laws didn't match them, leaving thousands of men like Terry still tarnished as sex criminals.[6] What's more, the government knew that this would be the case. When the Home Office began to plan the disregard scheme in 2010, officials found 50,000 convictions on the police database. Of these, only 16,000 would be eligible for a disregard.[7] By October 2022, a decade after the scheme launched, only 208 disregards had been granted.[8]

'TODAY IT'S LOOKING . . .'

Make no mistake that this is a miscarriage of justice. As Terry suggested, the police played fast and loose with evidence. Most men pleaded guilty just to make their case go away, so the evidence was never tested in court. In the rare cases when it was, it was important for the news to be shared. In early 1984, *Capital Gay* reported three such cases, and a Switchboard volunteer suggested a new way of supporting callers:

17 January 1984
In the last couple of weeks, at least 3 men have been acquitted of charges of importuning in and around Earls Court in the summer '83. These are important acquittals for a variety of reasons.
The police are unlikely to stop entrapping and arresting gay men – their tactics are likely to change, eg moving from Earls Court to Notting Hill to make arrests.
But if we tell callers that people are pleading not guilty and are being acquitted, it can only encourage our callers not to plead guilty but fight.
If we tell callers that in all 3 cases the police evidence was discredited, in all 3 cases the judge pointed out to the jury that the police evidence was dubious to say the least (that's judge-ese for saying the police are lying), it again, can only encourage our callers to fight and win.
Since the news that 3 men were acquitted appeared in Capital Gay, 5 men have contacted GALOP asking if they can re-open their cases and change their plea from guilty to not guilty. Unfortunately I had to tell them they can't re-open the case, but it only shows that people need encouragement and examples to fight cases.

In 1991 the gay rights campaigner Peter Tatchell got hold of a set of convictions figures, conducting his own analysis to show that consenting gay and bisexual offenders were 350 per cent more likely to be convicted of sex crimes than heterosexual and violent sex offenders. *Capital Gay* published the analysis under the headline 'Scales of injustice'. Tatchell sent the report and his numbers to the Home Office, demanding an independent study. The department replied to say his analysis was unfair because gay and bi men were more likely to know each other and be willing to admit guilt, which led to their higher conviction rate.[9] It must have been maddening for Tatchell to receive this pat response, just as it was for Adam to read it three decades later. The British establishment, in upholding state homophobia, refused to consider the bind in which these men were held.

It's true that in hunting down men seeking men, the police were enforcing the law, but the law was homophobic in letter and in practice. Although policing decisions were left to local constables, the central state was clearly giving officers cover. They were obsessed with using this and their powers to intimidate and persecute people. They often took steps to solicit sex from men – simply so they could arrest those men and charge *them* with soliciting. Officers blessed with good looks and bodies that filled tight jeans were especially valuable in this enterprise. They became known as 'pretty police' – and the log books are stashed with them.

> 11 March 1991
> Caller reports Pretty Police activity at Green Park Cottage – policeman was in ripped jeans, blond, around 20+, very very cute – beware.

The thing about Switchboard's volunteers is that even in these serious matters they had a sense of humour: they even held fundraiser balls with the theme of 'pretty police'. The dreadful tactic was so brazen that they had to mock it.

'TODAY IT'S LOOKING . . .'

The testimonies continued to mount:

24 June 1993
Received call from a man in Milton Keynes – police seem to be entrapping people in the park. Guy's lover arrested. Met others in police station in similar circumstances.

Although enforcing gross indecency laws was technically a police duty, entrapment was illegal. So, under pressure from the likes of Chris Smith, the first openly gay MP, the government did look into entrapment, and in fact produced hundreds of pages across two hefty folders that eventually landed in The National Archives. Dating from 1983 to 1990, they contained correspondence between ministers, police officials, and civil servants as they sought to research homosexual importuning, soliciting, kerb crawlers, sex workers, car thieves, entrapment, and agents provocateurs. The party line, held time and time again in these official documents, was that entrapment should not happen. 'No member of a police force should counsel, incite, or procure the commission of a crime,' said one note that was sent to HM Inspectorate of Constabularies. 'There is plainly a continuing need for care to avoid plain clothes officers placing themselves in situations [*sic*] where accusations can be made that they have acted as agents provocateurs.'[10]

When Adam first read these files in Kew in 2023, he bristled. He had to read them again and again to understand the message, because he was effectively being gaslighted by a government from decades ago. No one was answering the charge, supported by piles of evidence, that entrapment very plainly *was* happening. The government was clearly not interested in holding the police to account for it. Adam furiously took photos of the files, the typewritten pages, the scrawled notes, the Whitehall lines of nonsense.

THE LOG BOOKS

Maybe it is words like 'national' and 'archives', or maybe it is the brutalist architecture: the collections at Kew are imbued with something that ought to feel like 'the truth'. But here in the official government records we had found an evasion of the truth. We only knew that because we'd already spent so long reading through the log books. Those scruffy pages that had been shoved into a crawl-space were clearly the more credible source of what had happened to men at the hands of the police. Thousands of callers had given their testimonies of entrapment to Switchboard over the years, and we had corroborated them by taking the time to find and speak to men like Terry Stewart. It was discoveries like these that made us see the value in our work. We had no boss, no institution, and never enough financial support, but we were determined to set the record straight. It felt like we were serving our elders like Terry – speaking for our ancestors who'd been silenced by the state. If that's what 'doing history' meant, we resolved, then that's what we were doing.

This is how we came to see Switchboard's archive as just as important as any other, and often more so. One particularly valuable testimony came from a police officer who called Switchboard one morning in the wee hours.

> 17 April 1986 – 3.30 a.m.
>
> Long call from gay policeman. 23 years old, 6 years service, who was very upset when his sadistic colleague insisted on arresting 17 year old in toilet after giving him the come on. The guy pleaded not to be charged and inform parents but no avail. Father attacked him (the 17-year-old) on arrival and after charging he was sent to a hostel. Apparently they are given 3 weeks plain clothes toilet duty and expected to make arrests. The pressure has turned from harassing the black population to the gay community meanwhile burglary etc soars. Our bobby says most of the others are OK but

about 10% are bastards. He gets very depressed, as he enjoys a lot of the work and all his friends are in the force but thinks he may have to opt out which will probably mean moving to another town and losing a £9,500 salary.

It's hard not to feel sorry for the caller in this log book entry. He seemed to be in the process of realising that police officers can be bad people who abuse their power and that the force as a whole – his employer – may be institutionally homophobic. What mattered to this caller was that the police were not able to recognise the human dignity of gay men like him.

We wanted to speak to a police officer about this. During production on the podcast, when we put out a call on social media, we were surprised that one came forward. Her name was Lorraine Moir, and she retired from Herefordshire Police in 2012. In our interview Moir spoke firmly and authoritatively, as you might expect from a former officer. However, it also felt like she had something to get off her chest. She explained that policing in the 1970s and 1980s was fuelled by heterosexual male testosterone. 'Policing was about enforcing the law, but with policing the gay community it carried a stronger message. It wasn't just about a message of "this is illegal", it was a message of "I don't like what you're doing" as well.'

She was downplaying it, but she was right. It was surreal to hear that from a former police officer, while we were reading all those log book entries about men who'd been entrapped by people like her. Moir, herself a lesbian, was contrite. And even the British state, in its paltry pardon scheme, had admitted wrongdoing. We had to record all this, of course, and traverse how our research had raised questions about the morality of past actions. Moir herself was clear: the police during her time had been homophobic and sexist. She recalled being on duty one night with a male officer, patrolling a lay-by that was well-known as a spot where men met to have sex with each other. 'I remember this one officer asked this chap to get out the car and was really in his face,' she said. 'Nose to nose. [He was] very intimidating, threatening, to say, "I want your details, we're gonna write and tell your family this is what you're doing". It was bullying, no doubt about it, it was never professional.' In the bar after a shift like that, officers laughed it all off. 'It was seen as a game,' said Moir.

If it was a game, the dice were loaded in favour of the police, and the consequences of losing were grave. Men targeted in actions like the ones described above lost their jobs, homes, families, and sometimes even their lives. 'There are people that I know had mental breakdowns,' said Terry. 'They've lost their mental wellbeing. Others have committed suicide.'[11]

Even the police struggled with it: Moir kept her lesbian identity secret at work. Other officers had an even harder time. One of our interviewees, a man named Paul Marquess, told Adam about a time when he took a man home from a gay Saturday-night disco. 'On the Sunday morning, we had a long talk,' said Paul. 'It turned out that he was a police officer . . . he had been very much in love with another boy who was also a police officer, then both in their twenties. His boyfriend had killed himself, because he could not reconcile being a police officer with being gay.'

People in the armed forces had a uniquely hard time, because it was explicitly illegal to be openly gay while serving until 2000:

> 7 April 1992
> A caller 'Mike' rang to tell me a lot of men have been arrested for cottaging in Plymouth (by a group of TEN policemen) including his

friend Jonas, who is in the Navy – Jonas is 40, in the closet and frightened to lose his job, also his solicitor has refused to help him, telling him it is an 'open and shut case' and in any case not worth as it could cost £1000s – thanks a lot!!! So I've recommended a gay solicitor – also I've asked Jonas to call us regularly to let us know what is happening.

This sort of persecution was all too familiar to a tall, gentle man named Phil Collins, whom Tash came to interview. He joined the Navy at the age of nineteen as a trainee engineer officer. He hoped to find exciting work, with good pay, and education. 'Subconsciously I must have thought there would be lots of opportunity to be around other men,' he remembered in an email sent after the interview. (Sometimes our contributors told us their stories on mic, and sometimes they found themselves returning to us after a few days of reflection, realising they had more to say.)

Although Phil had been bottom of his class at school, he said he performed well in officer training at Dartmouth Naval College and settled into the rigid military life. 'It was made very clear in the first few days at Dartmouth that being gay or doing drugs was not acceptable. Not that I was doing drugs, but I certainly thought I might be gay.' Phil was posted to the Navy's engineering college at Manadon in Plymouth in 1985 and began to see guys in his free time. His personal life came into conflict with his professional one: he was breaking the law. This was a 'nerve-wracking' condition.

His partner David, who was also an officer, decided to resign and pay back the cost of his training. He was subjected to a long interrogation with the Special Investigation Branch (SIB) of the Royal Navy Police. They wanted to know what he did in bed, and with whom. 'The SIB had a certain reputation of being overly interested in people's sex lives and in the way they sought to uncover homosexual "rings",' wrote Phil. 'Not unlike the Gestapo, but without the physical torture (I think).' Again, the log books provide further documentation of SIB's bullying methods.

> 7 November 1982 – 4.15 p.m.
> Guy phoned to warn that the Royal Naval Air Station at Culdrose in Cornwall are having a purge on gays by the Special Investigation Branch. They will clap anybody in the service suspected of being gay in a cell overnight to sweat it out and then interrogate you in the morning whilst going through your personal possessions.

Tash was particularly drawn to Phil's story because it happened in parallel to aspects of her own life. Phil was stationed in Plymouth in the same year she was born there; Tash's dad Martin was in the Navy and studied at Dartmouth too. Phil had a very different experience to Martin, who didn't remember ever having been aware of what queer colleagues might have gone through. Tash couldn't help but feel a mix of complex emotions rise up in her – why wasn't her dad aware? Her dad, who told her he'd always known she was gay from the age of three – why didn't he push for change? Probably the same reason most people didn't: they didn't think it impacted them; they didn't make the connection. A few years later, when Tash was six years old, a woman felt the full force of suspicion and interrogation – and she phoned Switchboard because she had nowhere else to go:

> 10 January 1992
> A woman in the armed services rang having been charged/accused of being a lesbian. She is not a lesbian. She was interrogated for 2 days by her commanding officer (she is a

commissioned officer) and told not to have any contact with anyone in the armed services. She is presently at home, v. upset and shaken. Her rooms at barracks were searched among items taken were a couple of D. H. Lawrence books and photos of her and a female friend in Switzerland.

She was accused by a junior colleague, with whom she was working, of using her seniority to psychically and sexually take advantage of her. I calmed her and referred her to Tanner + Taylor solicitors. She may well ring back. She loves us because we are her only friends at the moment. Please treat her lovingly.

We don't know what happened to this caller, but her experience probably stands for so many other servicepeople who didn't reach out to Switchboard for help. Phil didn't phone for support, instead just living through the agony of knowing what could happen to him and his career if his partner David was forced to reveal the nature of their relationship. In the end, David didn't betray Phil, but the truth came out anyway. Phil's experience was easier than David's, but he was still quickly ushered out of the Navy with 'self-confessed homosexual' marked on his medical record. 'It could have been a lot worse,' he said.

Years later, Phil joined Switchboard as a volunteer. His experience of living on the margins, and finding a way to survive despite social and legal pressures, is the reason why callers have always contacted Switchboard.

The charity has long had a difficult line to tread when it comes to working within or against prejudiced laws. Some volunteers have found it impossible to handle calls about persecution and not issue a call to arms:

21 July 1975

Caller rang to inform us that there is definite purge on Holland Walk. Eight people arrested Friday night. Fined £40 each on Saturday morning. All pleaded guilty. But all other reports I've had indicate that there is nothing unusual in that – they do it every now and again. What are we going to do about it? Us, gay people?

Over and above their calm words on the calls, volunteers were clearly angry – and many wanted to take action against the police persecution. The tradition of queer people assembling against the police is just as much a part of our history as fighting the police for trying to stop us. It is not only the riots outside the Stonewall Inn in New York between police and LGBTQ+ people that fuelled a movement; similar conflicts sparked in the UK, too. In London on 27 November 1970, 150 members of the Gay Liberation Front set off flares and fireworks at Highbury Fields to protest the recent case of a man named Louis Eaks who had been found guilty of an act of gross indecency there. Police actions against gay people also led to the creation of the radical activist group OutRage!, after the homophobic murder of Michael Boothe in April 1990. In grief and anger, fifty people turned up to a meeting and decided to form a group to 'assert the dignity and human rights of queers'. OutRage! would fight back against the violence and discrimination they were experiencing, including at the hands of the police – and they did, with high-profile protests and actions through the nineties.

LGBTQ+ people, and Switchboard, were always vigilant towards the police. It can often feel like we're just one step away from a huge crackdown on our bodies and our freedoms. It is always worth considering police tactics and overall strategy. Underneath the log book entry quoted earlier in the chapter about a raid at a gay party in St Austell, a second volunteer wrote: 'This is frightening – perhaps they're trying to see if it works in a small town first – think about it.'

This was not paranoia, as we know police officers even regularly checked in at the Switchboard office. The sense from volunteers is that these reminders were not always friendly. Switchboard was not a protest group, but even its role of listening to and informing LGBTQ+ people attracted police attention. Volunteers worried about this constantly. In October 1975, they had a furious debate about whether it was right for them to recommend cruising spots. There was an ethical imperative to help the callers live their best gay lives, of course, but also a legal concern that this would put callers and Switchboard in police crosshairs. In a very long log book entry, the volunteer John Payne asked: 'Is it the right issue for Switchboard to get busted on?':

> Once it becomes widely known that cottaging etc is condoned by Switchboard, people who are arrested outside Jack Straw's Castle [pub and cruising spot] when asked by the police might give the response 'Well, Gay Switchboard sent me here.'
> This could motivate the vice squad to increase the % of fake calls and collect a horde of tape recordings for use against us in court

John's proposal was that Switchboard's primary role with callers asking for places to cruise was to suggest organisations 'where they stand a decent chance of making friendships'. Four volunteers wrote notes of support for John's mini essay. No one recorded support in the log book in favour of recommending cruising spots to callers, but we could imagine volunteers arguing about it between calls. However, another volunteer had a practical reason against making recommendations:

11 October 1975

The Great Cruising + Cottaging Saga, Part MCLXMVIIII

Apart from ethical/legal considerations, in order to recommend cruising areas we should have to put them on the files. The Information Group can't cope with things now. For *!?s sake don't invent any more work!

As with many voluntary organisations, Switchboard had to strike a balance between the moral thrust of their operations with the reality of a never-ending workload. In any case, Switchboard had to be prepared for John Payne's worry, about the organisation being 'busted' for its connection to gay sex, to come true. The volunteers had to read up on the law and, most of all, protect themselves. On 14 September 1976, a volunteer typed up a note and taped it into the log book for all other volunteers to see. The note makes it clear that Switchboard knew that it wasn't just the men cruising in toilets who were under threat:

<u>Don't ask a policeman.</u>

In the event of the police (uniform or plain clothes) calling at these premises in pursuit of any enquiries, the following courses of action should be adopted by the volunteer on duty.

1. Don't let them in unless they have a warrant.
2. If they don't have a warrant, tell them you have no authority to let them in and they must make an enquiry appointment with either the chairperson or the secretary whom you should immediately inform.
3. If they have a warrant, examine it, and if it's valid, let them in but phone David Offenbach immediately. Also inform Chairperson and secretary.
4. You must not make any statement without David Offenbach or substitute being present.

5. Always be polite but firm.
6. Take down the number, rank and name of the police involved and the station from which they've been sent.

As a child of the fiery gang who ran the Gay Liberation Front in the early seventies, Switchboard knew its political rights. Sharing advice like the list above was a common practice of other radical groups and organisations of the time, from the Black power movement to women's liberation groups. Switchboard sat firmly in this tradition, while also under pressure internally to be as politically neutral, and therefore safe, as possible.

Although volunteers needed their own way to respond to police, they were focused as always on supporting callers. Switchboard volunteers could not give legal advice, but they knew a man who could. Not only did David Offenbach advise Switchboard, as per point #4 above, he was also on hand to advise callers. 'When people telephoned they wanted to come and see us as soon as possible,' Offenbach remembered, recalling those countless referrals from Switchboard in the seventies and eighties, early in his career. 'People were very anxious about their careers, their reputation, often about their family circumstances and what the consequences of a conviction for gross indecency would be.'

Adam interviewed Offenbach in his home in north London. His voice wobbled with age, but his eyes held the sharp gaze of a lawyer. 'Most of the people who came into the office were usually innocent . . . often if they weren't innocent then they would quickly plead guilty without representation and hope it wouldn't be reported in the press or [brought] to anybody's attention.'

A group of lawyers like Offenbach saw the need for a helpline like Switchboard but instead staffed with lawyers who could help callers address this specific issue. They set up the Gay and Lesbian

Legal Advice line, known as GLAD. The organisation, which was much smaller than Switchboard, first operated out of a university room and then a room in Central Station, a gay pub in King's Cross just a stone's throw from the old Switchboard base. The calls, when they came, were always complicated. 'I do remember the saddest ones always came from those who were way out in the country,' said Justin Gau, a barrister who volunteered at GLAD in the 1990s. 'I remember a farmer from Cumbria telephoning to say he'd been caught in a public lavatory, and he lived on his own, but the shame of it was making him suicidal, and what could he do? It's very easy to forget now that being gay right up till the late nineties in certain areas left you absolutely abandoned. And farmers are on their own. If you're a gay farmer living in the middle of nowhere and you're arrested, all your support systems disappear.'[12]

Helplines did what they could to triage cases, but the cause remained: a misdirected, overreaching, homophobic police force. In dredging through this history we could see how crucial Switchboard became. It was at once a nexus and a counsellor, a database and a friend.

Like the tight jeans worn by pretty police, all this persecution could not hold forever. Police officers were living in the dark ages. And, as George Michael pointed out in his satirical pop song, it's better to live outside, in the sunshine. In 1997, the Labour Party came to power. We were newly at secondary school, still living under Section 28 and receiving paltry sex education. Just at the time when we would have benefited from seeing some queer elders, they were still being held out of sight.

Despite this, many queer adults were positive about the new politics and a government led by Tony Blair. His campaign song had been 'Things Can Only Get Better' by D:Ream. Although that sentiment was a low bar, we're told by our LGBTQ+ elders that there was a sense of optimism in the air. The Labour Party had said it was committed to equality (including of gays and lesbians); a campaign to equalise the age of consent for sex was gaining steam, and more and more queer characters were appearing on TV.

Things did slowly change. Blair's government edged closer to fairer human rights protections, passing the Human Rights Act in 1998. This law paved the way for marriage equality, the right to start a 'family', and reforms that recognised trans people, among many other things. More and more individual police officers seemed to care about LGBTQ+ people in a new way, and many log book entries show them recognising the usefulness of Switchboard at the same time.

15 July 1999
Sgt Rob Perkins – Middlesborough Police. Local 15-year-old boy gone missing yesterday. Think it's because of bullying/teasing at school about being gay. Could we post details or offer any help? Didn't take details, but gave number of Pink Paper editorial.

Above and beyond individual cases in the late nineties, the atmosphere between the police and the LGBTQ+ community was about to change – and it would take a nail bomb planted by a neo-Nazi. As well as being a key turning point for the broader LGBTQ+ community, the 1999 attack on the Admiral Duncan gay pub, described in the previous chapter, also affected the relationship between the police and Switchboard. A better relationship was sorely needed, because even before the pub bombing, Switchboard and its volunteers were threatened regularly by homophobes banging on the door, and fascist groups:

17 March 1995

Combat-18 phoned again. I've made a report of this to the local police station, as this seems to be a direct threat to our building.

Volunteers worried about drawing attention to their work had often been reluctant to report intimidation like this to the police. But the horrors of the bomb attack on the Admiral Duncan meant that Switchboard and the police had to work together. In the days after the attack, the then co-chairs of Switchboard, Jeremy Adams and Boo Armstrong, attended the Metropolitan Police headquarters in New Scotland Yard to contribute to briefings. 'Having spent the previous decades [with] the police always being the enemy, always being terrifying, always being the people you were scared of,' said Jeremy, 'to suddenly be asked to be in their rooms and to be asked how they should handle things, was completely extraordinary.'[13]

As Switchboard was at the forefront of taking care of the community in the wake of the bombing, volunteers worked with police officers and other LGBTQ+ organisations to liaise with the families and friends of victims over moving flowers from the bomb site to the gardens in nearby Soho Square. Police recognition of the human dignity of the people affected by such a terrible act of violence didn't fundamentally change the community's relationship with the police, but something had shifted.

Within a few years, officers began to appear at Pride festivals as participants as well as law enforcers. In 2002, two gay officers in uniform even snogged on national television. This was the work of the team behind the fictional police drama *The Bill* – specifically a maverick producer called Paul Marquess. A decade earlier, Marquess had been the young twenty-something who hooked up with a gay cop who told him that his earlier lover, another gay officer, had died by suicide.

By 2001 Marquess was a TV producer who'd worked on the popular soaps *Coronation Street* and *Brookside*. *The Bill* had started in 1983 and had been popular for years, broadcasting episodic police drama twice a week at prime time. By 2001, however, 'the ratings were really bad,' said Marquess. 'But not just that . . . the demographic was very, very old.' Facing a demographic cliff edge, he was tasked with attracting a new audience, one emboldened by changing social attitudes and even the TV sensation *Queer as Folk*, which had revolutionised the depiction of gay characters in 1999. 'It seemed to me like a bit of a win-win that we should do some sort of gay storyline,' he told Adam. When one colleague resisted, Marquess recalled the story of the young gay cop who had taken his own life – and he persisted. He debated with the writers, the PR department at the Metropolitan Police, and even the TV company's lawyer over whether the kiss would attract complaints. Marquess told them that he would either leave the kiss as it was or tell the papers it had been censored. 'Whatever happens today, you will lose, and I will win,' he told them. 'And,' Marquess said, 'they just folded like a pack of cards.'

So the cops got to cop off. Their gay snog was the TV hit of 2002: it brought a lot of welcome press controversy, boosted ratings and, together with the broader changes to the show, won the team a National Television Award, which is voted for by audience members.

Marquess and his team had shown that the police had feelings, too – sometimes gay ones. The nail bomb had showed the police that the LGBTQ+ community needed protection, and were for the most part regular, law-abiding citizens.

Of course, even with such strides in representation, the relationship remained uneasy:

25 October 2001

I'm sad to start this book off with such a negative call – but the caller was calling about police action at toilets in Kent and Essex – where police were claiming 'a member of the public had complained' and were taking our numbers and calling up the registered owner. I'm staggered beyond belief: I thought this sort of police action was a thing of the past . . . Isn't there any REAL crime left in Kent and Essex?

This log book entry from 2001 shows the cyclical nature of police homophobia. Even when laws and attitudes had changed, officers were still acting with prejudice. Over the decades successive reports and inquiries have found police forces to be institutionally homophobic, as well as sexist and racist, all issues that harm their relationship to queer folks. Things changed; things stayed the same.

In 1982, a charity called Galop was founded to oppose the Metropolitan Police's homophobic behaviour towards gay and bi men. Forty years later, in 2022, Louise Casey, a government official and member of the House of Lords, was asked to conduct a review into the standards of behaviour and internal culture of the Met. It was the kind of study that Peter Tatchell had called for in 1991. When Casey reported back in 2023, she confirmed what Galop, Tatchell, Switchboard, and many other organisations and individuals had known for decades: the force was 'institutionally homophobic'.

The review focused on the experiences of police officers and staff, which meant that it avoided asking LGBTQ+ citizens for their experiences of prejudice at the hands of the police. This also led to a major oversight. 'It does not find the Met to be institutionally transphobic – seemingly because it failed to look,' Galop said in a statement in March 2023, continuing:

'TODAY IT'S LOOKING...'

> From the work we do with trans victims of abuse in London, transphobia in the Met Police is even more entrenched and less addressed than homophobia. Trans victims of abuse are treated as the problem – as though they are bringing the abuse and violence they experience on themselves by being who they are. Trans and non-binary people are misgendered, deadnamed, and treated with disregard for their gender identity.[14]

Galop had expressed something that Tash had been feeling deep down for a long time: presenting in a gender non-conforming way could be dangerous. This was shocking to read. But it was more shocking to discover that attitudes do not always progress over time; progress can stall, and even go backwards. Although Galop was still reporting rampant transphobia in the Met in 2023, decades earlier the force had in fact been able to acknowledge the dignity of trans people. This was another chance discovery in the archive as we researched this book.

Buried in government files held at The National Archives, we found documents from the 1990s headed 'Police and the gay and lesbian community'. These files include operational notes on how the Met should work with 'transsexuals and transvestites'. Despite using words that would become archaic for many, the policies are surprisingly inclusive of trans people:

> We must ensure that we treat them with the same respect and dignity as any other member of the public.
> If there is doubt as to a person's sex, they should be asked what sex they consider themselves to be and what sex they would prefer to be treated as.
> If they appear to live predominantly as a woman, they should be treated as such.[15]

We are not suggesting that Met police officers were fully trans-inclusive in 1995, nor even that the force as a whole was not institutionally transphobic, but the note makes it clear that it was possible within the force to see the dignity of trans people. It was hard for us to read these policies in 2023. Adam nearly jumped out of his seat in the archive. He immediately texted a photo of the page to Tash. The news was that the police were capable of thinking inclusively in 1995 . . . and yet almost three decades later the forces were still transphobic. Policies such as these – about respecting the dignity of trans people – would have caused a transphobic backlash if they were issued as new at the time of our research. In fact, in 2025, backed by a Supreme Court ruling, police forces began to issue practice guidance that was the opposite of that Met policy from 1995, meaning trans women had to be treated as men. We felt yet another whiplash in our experience of doing queer history; sometimes the chances of LGBTQ+ freedom, then and now, feel so desperate.

We had to keep finding signs of optimism, signs of how our elders had managed to keep standing up. We found one such sign in the tight handwriting of a man named Mr Oke. In June 1997 Mr Oke wrote to the newly elected prime minister, Tony Blair, to say: 'We need to change attitudes and create an environment of acceptance, where gay and lesbian people are valued . . . The first step in the same is to give all of these people equality in law.'[16]

Across four pages, Mr Oke told Blair several ways that queer people were not valued. He relayed the story of a local gay man who was knifed to death, but the police had dropped the case due to a lack of witnesses (owing to their own fear and shame of being gay). A similar murder happened in Central Park in Plymouth when Tash was growing up there. Tash had just turned ten, in

'TODAY IT'S LOOKING...'

November 1995, when three teenagers tortured and mutilated two gay men, killing one of them, Terry Sweet.[17] The idea that this happened opposite her secondary school long haunted Tash.

Mr Oke also wrote that a public toilet in Scotland was raided, resulting in the arrests of thirteen men, two of whom died by suicide shortly after. He was also concerned for the prospects of young children who were being bullied for being queer – which was a reality for Adam. Mr Oke rightly pointed out that many teenagers died by suicide without anyone knowing why.

Mr Oke sent this letter just as we were entering our teenage years. As young queer people, we were at a greater risk of suicide than the average teenager, but here was a man writing to government on our behalf. Repealing Section 28, Mr Oke contested, was essential. But moreover, 'we need a bill of rights,' he wrote. He even revealed his own suffering:

> As a second-class citizen, I have been beaten up and verbally abused more times than I remember. A few months ago, a gang of six gave me two black eyes, a bloody nose, cuts and bruises, and a jaw so severely damaged that I couldn't open it for three months just because I'm gay. There is so much discrimination against us – unemployment, pension and inheritance rights, property ownership, marital status, and there is no place for it in our society.

Blair's reply to Mr Oke came in August that year in the form of a letter from his office. The response mumbled about the new government's commitments to end harassment and discrimination through a particularly mealy-mouthed explanation of the relationship between UK and EU laws. It also responded to Mr Oke's proposal to scrap Section 28 by simply explaining that it didn't really prohibit schools from exploring sexuality – even though countless teachers were so chilled by the legislation that this is exactly what it did. We don't know what Mr Oke made of this reply – we know nothing about him beyond what he wrote – but we decided that it was insufficient. Irrespective of this, though, Mr Oke's letter is an example of something we discovered in our research that connected us to queer people across the generations. Like Switchboard volunteers working away quietly in the background, Mr Oke was a queer elder who'd been there for us.

Mr Oke had just been living his life, trying to evade queer bashings, and lobbying his elected representatives for social justice. His letter became part of the story of the state; we came to pluck it out of The National Archives and call it 'history'. Our book could be the first time Mr Oke's words have been conceived of in this way; perhaps he might find it strange that we stumbled across his letter in an old government file and assigned it such importance. And sometimes we have felt uneasy to label all this recent history as such, not knowing how it will eventually be seen, whether we'll have got it right. We were using the log books as a springboard into broader histories, different archives, fresh perspectives. We were placing our findings into our own contexts, using our own feelings and experiences to guide us. By the time we were working on this, Adam had cruised for sex and attended saunas like the ones raided by police. How could these experiences not influence our history-gathering?

We were in conversation with our elders. What we were learning from them was the way they allowed themselves to think freely. To Switchboard volunteers, Mr Oke, Phil Collins in the Navy, Terry Stewart the victim of police persecution, if it felt like injustice, smelt like injustice, and tasted like injustice, no matter what the constables and the ministers said, *it was injustice.*

'TODAY IT'S LOOKING...'

As one Switchboard volunteer implied, when the police are employed by a homophobic state, their real power is felt when they live inside our heads:

> 13 July 1988
> Some police do try it on. Man rang tonight having been charged for 'gross indecency'. The bill had told him that 'looking' is an offence under the Sexual Offences Act. Get the message. I shall close my eyes all the way home tonight. Today it's looking, tomorrow it'll be thinking.

That idea terrified us, and it rang true. As we discussed this flippant log book entry, we felt its gravity more and more. Tash had never had a problem following her passions, her desires, her heart, her own ideas. Almost to a fault she had resisted others' impositions, breaking her parents' curfews, betraying the boundaries of romantic relationships, and turning away from men's sexist expectations. Although Tash had shaken off plenty of patriarchal controls, she still stopped herself from being visibly queer often. She didn't cut her long hair and didn't wear some clothes that would be too boyish. She'd been scared to kiss a girlfriend in the street – something straight people can take for granted.

Somehow, something was controlling her queerness. Maybe, we thought, the volunteer who'd worried about the police in our minds was on to something. The question of what was 'too gay' went beyond the law, beyond the police; it spread through society. When we were taunted in the schoolyard or the street, were those voices doing the work of a homophobic police officer? If we absorbed those taunts, whether we were ashamed or just wanted peace, were we arresting ourselves?

Adam's parents had mocked camp gay men, and they told him they didn't like that one of his teenage friends was gay. Their message to Adam was: don't be like that. He wanted to be a good boy. His friend was able to bring his boyfriend home, but Adam knew that if *he* got a boyfriend his parents' reaction would create a very 'disorderly house'. So, he never thought about having a boyfriend.

We came of age as queer people after decriminalisation, after the peak of the HIV crisis, under a government that was bent towards equality, just as the internet was coming online. We were supposed to be the first free generation, but we were not as distant from the lives contained in the log books as we thought.

4
'THIS TROUBLESOME BODY'

How the state chose not to see us

15 May 1997
Caller rang. 16-year-old man. Very gay positive and confident about sexuality. Parents and some friends know and support him. A school friend is threatening to beat him up, as he found out he was interested in him. Caller very afraid and getting low, although still maintains confidence about being gay. He's decided to tell other people about it, maybe even the school, as he's worried an attack could involve more than a black eye. He will probably call back, as he asked if he could. Try to keep his confidence high.

We were worried about an attack, but our confidence was high. Not even the pouring rain stopped us cheering and chanting 'TRANS RIGHTS NOW!' Smiling faces, holding hands, little dogs carried in slings, a distinct absence of corporate logos, and, instead, sassy signs cast high like sails. A sea of bodies marching, marching, marching. Always forwards, forever together.

The occasion was Trans Pride, 8 July 2023. We had met with friends at Trafalgar Square, huddling under umbrellas, and we set off with the crowd. For Tash, the day felt urgent – simultaneously political and personal. That year had been a whirlwind of complex conversations, with too many people speaking flippantly about trans rights. In February a trans teenager called Brianna Ghey had been murdered in a park near Warrington. Tash attended her vigil outside the Department of Education and recorded the one-minute silence, followed by the crowd chanting her name. As the chant stopped, the air fizzed with anger, power, love, and hope, and tears fell down Tash's cheeks. Meanwhile, politicians and media commentators were debating 'the trans issue', legal cases were seeking to block trans women from certain spaces, and an independent review into trans healthcare for children and young people was under way. There was a feeling that the outcome of all this would not be good for trans people.

That feeling was grounded in Britain's long history of stopping queer and trans people from living their own lives with dignity and freedom. From bullies at school to the state refusing to see us as who we were – these were common experiences revealed in calls to Switchboard. As we were thinking about how to write this chapter about the state's historical denial of rights, in the early 2020s, we found ourselves in the eye of a storm over trans rights. We also wanted to explore lesbian mothers' child custody cases, legal reform over the age of consent, and Switchboard's own battle for legal recognition. But in approaching how the state saw queer people, first we had to grapple with the fragility of the trans rights our generation had inherited and how, by 2023, those rights were under threat.

So by the time it came to Trans Pride 2023, Tash knew that they had to stand up and stand out as a person with a fluid sense of their own gender, using they/she pronouns. This meant that Tash felt fine when people who didn't know them used 'she' to refer to Tash, but they came to prefer those who did know them to use 'they' and 'them'. Since you're reading this book that now means you. Because this shift happened as we were writing this book, we wanted to include it here. That's why we've used 'she/her' for Tash up to this point, but from now on will use 'they/them'. Tash had chosen their T-shirt for the march carefully: it was white with an embroidered image of two cartoon people high-fiving, and underneath it read 'Better Together'.

The atmosphere that day at Trans Pride was defiant. Thousands got together in central London to display the same confidence shown by the gay teen who called Switchboard in 1997, captured in the log book entry at the beginning of the chapter. Like him, and like Tash, the trans people at Trans Pride 2023 wanted to be heard, loud and clear. Like all the marchers from the past who have ever chanted for LGBTQ+ rights, they wanted to be seen for who they were. One of the Trans Pride marchers carried a sign saying 'Teachers Against Transphobia', and they reminded us of Ruth, who marched against Section 28 in the 1980s while working as a teacher. 'I was always on a protest,' she laughed during one of her conversations with Tash. 'Whenever there is a protest I'm there with my banners!'

When Ruth attended several marches against Section 28 she took a risk that other teachers did not. They feared for their jobs and careers, their friendships and family relationships. If Section 28 was going to be passed, it could have led to teachers like Ruth being fired even for just saying they were lesbian or gay. Ruth remembered the fever pitch of the hate and fear in 1986–88. 'I marched and shouted and protested,' she said. 'You had to do things like that to keep you going.' Ruth marched in a big pink T-shirt and big earrings – 'because everything was big in the eighties' – and she chanted 'STOP THE CLAUSE!'

Her efforts built solidarity between queer people but ultimately failed to kill the bill. Section 28 became law in 1988, and by 1997 the gay teenager above was calling Switchboard anonymously instead of speaking to a teacher he knew.

Also in 1997, another boy spoke to a BBC reporter for a bleak *Panorama* documentary about homophobic bullying in schools.[1] He asked for his face to be blurred out when the programme aired, for fear of attacks. He was just a couple of years older than us; Adam was thirteen, Tash twelve. As well as the brave boy with the blurred face, the programme featured powerful homophobes such as the politician Ann Widdecombe. Tash watched this documentary in quiet concentration, in the family living room in Plymouth. As the dramatic outro music played, young Tash turned to their mum, tears rolling down their face, and begged, 'Please don't let me be gay.'

It's now clear how this TV programme weighed on Tash in a way it wouldn't have done for children who were going to turn out straight. In conjunction with Tash's earlier unease at being made to wear dresses they hated and later panics about what the local teenagers thought of them snogging girls, this stress was starting to accumulate. It's the reason why queer people find it necessary sometimes to hide themselves – and that only places further stress on them.

The world was tipped against Tash, Adam, and the boy in the documentary. In 1997 the programme reported that 57 per cent of Britons did not think same-sex relationships were acceptable and valid, and only 35 per cent thought they were.

Although things improved through the noughties, by 2023 the British Social Attitudes report found that the proportion of people who characterised themselves as 'not at all prejudiced' against trans people had fallen from 82 per cent to 64 per cent over the four years since 2019.[2] Reflecting this, the gears of the state were shifting against our community, with ministers especially active in questioning trans rights. This was the same year we were marching at Trans Pride in resistance to the decline in support for trans people. For Tash and many others, this resistance came from just existing.

Queer life, in relation to social attitudes and the changing attitude of the state, was a roller coaster. The first season of *The Log Books* podcast came out in 2019, and by 2023 we were working on this book, collecting more interviews with people who'd been vilified or exiled, visiting more archives, trying to understand our own roles as queer people in the context of the histories we were discovering. Our work was connecting with people: in the lockdowns of 2020–21 in particular, isolated queer folks told us the podcast had helped them to feel part of a community, and straight listeners thanked us for helping them to understand the LGBTQ+ people they were close to. Tash was starting to understand themself more as genderfluid, and Adam had been opening up about his sex life while touring his book about poppers. Yet we were living through a time where a declining number of people were willing to *say* they were not prejudiced against trans people. We were historians of a sort, but the history was not over. We were still living through it.

We were trying to reckon with the attitudes that had cradled us, like the survey stats in the *Panorama* documentary and the words of the anti-LGBTQ+ letters sent to MPs during our childhoods that we were discovering in The National Archives. In one of those, a Mrs Armstrong from Berwickshire wrote to her MP in 1995 to say: 'The new word from gays for people like me is homophobic. Is that correct? Well, so be it.'

Mrs Armstrong was asking her elected representative to see her, happily, as a bigot. MPs had been representing people like her for years. In its own way, the state had been seeing queer people as it wanted: as threats to the traditional idea of a family, and therefore a risk to the entire social fabric, warranting legislation that gagged public servants like Ruth. And as we saw in papers at The National Archives, the state diligently recorded the lives of gay and bi men who had sex with each other. During our research we paired the testimonies from our interviews and from the log books with the data: operations, arrests, charges, fines, and imprisonments.

Through the police, the state had been watching queer men enjoying sex. And then Section 28 had come along as a staring contest between bigoted straights and the LGBTQ+ people who just wanted to live their lives. But after marching at Trans Pride 2023 and calling for basic rights such as legal recognition and healthcare (in 2023!), we began to tune in to all the elders who'd been ignored. We went back to the log books, returned to our interview transcripts, looked deeper and further in the archives – and we began to collect all the times that instead of *seeing* queer people, the state had *turned away* from them. This included the lesbian mothers and the campaigners for equal age of consent, whom we will come to in this chapter too. But it's also how we found the private stories of trans people who, in distress, were desperate to be recognised as themselves.

---

25 June 1994

A guy rang from Chelsea. S/He is a TS (still male becoming female). His GP has laughed at him. The practice staff have no understanding of his situation. S/He is terrified of upsetting the consultants at Charing X hospital – she can be removed from the TS program for any minor reason. She has been cut off by her family and has no friends. I told her about other GPs (which was the start of the call) and she is going to try and change her GP. She said she will call back and let us know. I think she really needs to talk.

> There are so many other problems as well – a history of abuse by her grandfather and a lack of understanding, fear and loneliness.

The issues in this entry are common across dozens of volumes of the log books. Every trans person can probably relate to at least one if not all of them. They include mistreatment by medics, being ostracised by those you'd expect to rely on, abuse, the fear of being denied care, and misgendering. Even the Switchboard volunteer didn't know what pronouns to use, and we assume they didn't do the simple thing and ask the caller. But the call came through in 1994, when the political and social needs of trans people were less clear. As one of our interviewees, Chryssy Hunter, put it after completing her PhD on trans folks: '[For] most of the people I spoke to in my research, the most common trope is that they had no language to think about themselves.'

The first thing you have to do if you want other people to see who you are, and to recognise your rights, is to clarify the words and their definitions. This has been an often fraught process with regard to trans people in the UK. Sometimes it pays to be vague – one slogan for the long-running venue the WayOut Club summed it up: 'For everyone who is different.' Over Switchboard's history, the LGBTQ+ communities have gone through various distinctions between gender and sexuality, and even varied experiences of gender itself, as with Tash who in their thirties started to explore words that might help them to define their gender, and in turn their sexuality. That's how they turned up to Trans Pride 2023 as themself, as a person with a fluid gender.

The evolution of language has been essential for trans people to gain both a sense of themselves and a political imperative. But the fact is, as you look through the log books or hear any stories of trans life, there are no clear lines between the gender we experience our bodies to be, the sex we want to have in those bodies, and everything else going on in society. As it happened, when Switchboard was getting going in the 1970s, its focus was on 'homosexuals', sometimes 'gays and lesbians', and this was meant to include experiences of people exploring their gender too. But the context, as Chryssy told us, was that in the seventies the working assumption on the rights of trans people was pretty bleak: 'They didn't have any!'

Rights or no rights, these people existed. The state didn't see trans people for who they were, but Switchboard knew that they needed support. They were seen by Switchboard even when the state ignored them. In the early days, information collated for the purposes of supporting callers who said they were transvestites or transsexuals was maintained in a file labelled 'TV/TS':

> 19 August 1975
> 'AA' rang re transexual (TS) group. The Patricia Sage Transvestite (TV)/Transexual group no longer exists and has split into separate TV and TS groups. 'BA' is now running TV group. 'AA' has taken over the new TS group – he feels it is very necessary that people interested should be referred to him first as experience proves that many supposed TS referrals are in fact TV or just plain nutters.[3]

> 11 March 1976
> 'A' of North London Action Transexual organisation rang. On call for about 30 minutes. They don't want any transvestites – there is no group there for TV. They are a counselling service for transsexuals. Gay News is wrong to list them under TV/TS and they have told them so.[4]

However ham-fisted Switchboard's handling of trans people was, the truth is that volunteers saw trans people when no one else would. 'I think it was a turning point, calling Switchboard and being validated in that moment,' said Finn, a trans person who phoned for help in 1997.

Finn is a warm and gentle person, and was generous with their story over the course of several interviews with Tash, forging a strong bond between them. When Finn called Switchboard, 'I was starting to struggle with my gender identity . . . I knew there was something going on with my sexuality and I knew there was something going on with my gender . . .' Finn, like Tash, had felt that difference from a very young age, but was brought up in a world that didn't have the language to explain it. Switchboard was the one place that could validate their feelings.

Finn turned away from school after an encounter with a teacher. They had read about Section 28 in the newspaper and felt, as a queer teenager, 'outraged and angry and hurt and upset and pissed off'. When their class was given a writing assignment about *Hamlet*, Finn chose instead to write a polemic in favour of abolishing Section 28. The teacher took them outside and together they staged the kind of surreal moment that was only possible during this time, with the state trying to force the teacher to not see Finn. The teacher told Finn that they couldn't talk about Section 28 in school, even though they were at that very moment doing exactly that. She looked pained by the professional gymnastics. As Finn remembered, 'I could tell she was, like, on board.'

The teacher suggested that Finn write about Section 28 outside of school, and she volunteered to look at their work outside of teaching hours; she also offered to help Finn improve their writing, to strengthen their power as a teenaged essayist fighting Section 28. Finn was touched, but even more pissed off than before. 'Instead of . . . taking her up on her offer, and going back and doing my English assignment on *Hamlet*, I was like, "Screw this!"'

After that moment, Finn disengaged. At fifteen they quietly quit school to go in search of places where they felt they could be more useful, and more accepted. We admired Finn's bravery – or adolescent nerve anyway – in walking out of a place that didn't truly see them. Adam stuck with school, desperate to get GCSEs so he could escape to college and then, hopefully, university in a big city. Tash crept around Plymouth as a teenager, drinking alcohol in parks and bus shelters, pushing at the boundaries they could feel tightening around them.

There are plenty of stories of callers who received good support from Switchboard, but, as you might be able to discern from the log book entries quoted so far, volunteers were not always as supportive as they should have been. In fact, the way that Switchboard struggled to accept trans people fully and fairly, sometimes even failed to see them, is a microcosm of the UK's disregard of trans people across this period.

The more we talked to Diana James, the more we knew that her story had to be told here. Every conversation with her gave us new insights into the context of the eighties, the history of Switchboard, and the experiences of people like her. Her story is a clear example of how, when the state refused to see her, most Switchboard volunteers – but not all – could. When Diana called Switchboard in 1985, it was because she was realising she was a lesbian. By 1988 she'd grown in confidence, thanks partly to becoming one of the loud dykes on Lesbian Strength Marches, and she applied to volunteer at Switchboard. When other volunteers interviewed her, she talked about being transgender. Hearing this was a surprise to Tash, because they were not aware that Switchboard had taken on trans volunteers in the eighties.

As it turned out, although Diana saw herself as trans at the time, the term didn't truly capture her experience or identity as an intersex person – but this part of her story was to come years later. In fact, when Diana said she was trans, the volunteer interviewing her looked a little odd for a moment. 'She carried on through the interview,' Diana said, 'and then two weeks later I got a phone call from Lisa Power, who said let's meet up.'

When Diana reached this point in the story, Tash knew that it was going to be a significant part of Switchboard's history, whatever the outcome. Switchboard's log books and financial accounts were not enough to tell the full history of the organisation, and so as Diana laid down her story, Tash felt a duty to record it.

Diana and Lisa had gone out to First Out café in London, and Lisa had put it to Diana straight: it was 1988, and joining Switchboard as a trans woman would not be easy. The organisation did not yet have a trans volunteer. Switchboard was set up to support homosexuals and had only recently (two years prior) renamed itself Lesbian and Gay Switchboard; some within Switchboard were not sure whether trans experience fitted into its mission or its family. Diana remembered what Lisa told her in that café: 'You are the kind of woman we really want. Your knowledge and personality fit in really well. But you might face some difficulties as a volunteer.'

According to Diana, Lisa admitted that some volunteers might not recognise Diana for who she was and might give her the cold shoulder. Lisa told Diana to come and see her if she ever received any abuse by a colleague, and despite the warnings Diana knew what she wanted to do: 'I don't know if at the time I was feeling particularly brave or anything but I said, "No, I want to be a volunteer and I don't see any reason why I shouldn't be. I'm a dyke, I know what I'm about and I think I could be useful."'

The result: four women quit Switchboard because they didn't agree that a trans woman should join their ranks. The internal women's group collapsed. When we heard this story from both Lisa and Diana, we felt a real sadness and shock. Diana was telling us the story in 2019 and the anti-trans rhetoric that would only come to grow in the 2020s was starting to rumble. Tash knew from the log books how underrepresented women volunteers were in Switchboard, but this story was not played out in its pages; here Tash was, sitting there listening to Diana in the basement of Switchboard, half a mile from where this had all happened in the original phone room above Housmans bookshop. The same division over which spaces should permit trans women had continued to replicate and metastatise through various legal and social changes over the following decades. The enduring division was crystallised in the question asked in the legal case *For Women Scotland Ltd v. The Scottish Ministers*. While we worked on this book, the Supreme Court explored the same question that Switchboard had explored four decades prior, and made its landmark 2025 ruling that led organisations to begin segregating trans people from cis people.[5]

After her training Diana worked to re-establish the women's group, and it got going again with the primary function of making sure that women (all women) were heard in the decision-making functions of Switchboard. Switchboard evolved and, much later, in 2014 (two years after Tash joined), it renamed itself as an 'LGBT+' helpline. This long-overdue change led to more and more trans and gender non-conforming people wanting to volunteer.

Broadly speaking, for the first few decades of Switchboard, 'transvestites' and 'transsexuals' were seen as part of the 'lesbian and gay community'. Things shifted significantly in the 1990s and early 2000s, when more and more people defined themselves as 'transgender' or simply 'trans'. Some volunteers at the helpline thought that these folks were a part of the community it served, whereas others argued it should stick to serving just those who identify as lesbian or gay (although some may have identified as lesbian/gay *and* TV/TS . . .). When Switchboard affirmed that it served members of the 'LGBT+' community, it was an acknowledgement that if volunteers were going to listen to anyone who called regarding sexuality and gender identity, they had to be trans-inclusive. It was the only way to see the fullness of a caller, as this log book entry shows:

> 26 January 1996
>
> I took a call from a woman and took her quite seriously although her voice is disconcertingly male. I spent an hour with her. My understanding from her was that she was comfortable with her new female self (even though it was a rapid and unexpected transformation) and her issue was sexuality. She's still attracted to women, so we discussed her being a lesbian, and lesbian sex . . . I feel the caller needs support and reassurance – was angered that her sex change sounded more like the convenience of the doctors than a well thought out decision she was supported to make in her own best interests . . . I asked her about her desire to meet other transexuals or find support in this way, but she was not interested. This is an unusual case, so I think she needs respect and support in coming to terms with a new sexuality.

The volunteer's comment about the caller's voice is one that made us bristle when we first read it, and indeed is why many trans and gender non-conforming people struggle with using a telephone. This call came during a period in the mid- to late-nineties when things for the trans community really began to move. In one log book entry, dated January 1996, one volunteer answered another's question about how to advise a trans caller. 'There are support groups for transgender people, both male-to-female and female-to-male,' reads the entry, before listing the names and contact details of the groups. The volunteer's looping cursive also recommends books by Kate Bornstein and Ray Thompson. We smiled as we read these recommendations in the log books: they were books we had both turned to ourselves. The big picture is that trans folks stopped seeing themselves as a subset of the gay and lesbian community and began to demand that others, especially medics and the state, saw them as themselves. Switchboard knew something was shifting, and as it got wiser about the different types of call from the broader trans community, it created workshops to educate volunteers.

Outside Switchboard, trans people were becoming ever more assertive and organising to fight for their rights. In 1994, a trans woman who had been sacked for undergoing gender reassignment surgery sued her employer for sex discrimination. The case went to tribunal and eventually to the European Court of Justice which, in 1996, found discrimination had occurred. The court made a landmark ruling, extending the scope of sex discrimination to include discrimination against trans people. Zoë Playdon, who is a professor and LGBTQ+ activist, described the judgment, which was against Cornwall County Council, as 'astonishing'. After decades of not being recognised, trans people felt that Advocate General Giuseppe Tesauro had seen them. 'He talked about the fundamental and inalienable value that is equality,' said Playdon on the podcast *Legacy of Kindness* in 2023. 'He shifted it from being simply a legal decision to an ethical and moral decision.'[6]

Such judgments emboldened trans campaigners, who began to call for the power to have official identity documents reissued in their true gender and their chosen names, especially birth certificates, and better healthcare, particularly for medical transition. This is how trans people demanded to be seen.

In the UK they pushed for legal recognition through campaigning organisations such as Press For Change, which had started in 1992, and the Gender Identity Research & Education Society, known as GIRES, which began work in 1997. GIRES was established by Bernard and Terry Reed, the parents of Niki Reed, a trans woman who in 1997 sued a theme park, Chessington World of Adventures,[7] over the abuse and harassment she experienced while working there as a rides technician. Reed's case was significant because, as her lawyer Dinah Rose recalled on *Legacy of Kindness* in 2023, 'at that time, there was very little case law on the employment rights of trans people.'[8]

Judgments such as these put pressure on the new Labour government to hear the demands of trans people, and this pressure can be felt in the files on policy to do with 'transsexuals' in government notes held by The National Archives, which reveal the delicate politics at play. The notes highlight the back-and-forth over the idea of a cross-departmental review into which trans rights could be granted and how. Some voices in this debate inside government failed to see the dignity of trans people. In August 1997 Alastair Campbell, the government's chief press secretary, wrote to Jack Straw, who was the home secretary at the time. A glimpse at Campbell's letter shows that not everyone saw trans people as a political priority:

> My reaction:
> 1. Oh no, not another review!
> 2. Of all the reviews to pick!
> 3. Is this really a review necessary to undertake?

4. This is the kind of story that would run for days during August.
5. Have a nice holiday.⁹

Reading papers like these in the archive, we both felt a weight in our stomachs. Campbell's political intuition was sadly right, of course: the newspapers would have printed stories against Labour's interests in equality. More than this, though, more than a quarter-century later, as we read those words in 2023, political actors were still diminishing the urgency of trans equality, and trans people were still under attack in the media.

As it happened, some ministers took the proposition of a review a little more seriously. In September 1998, minister Geoff Hoon wrote to the deputy prime minister John Prescott to support the idea, but said it should be 'carefully handled'. Hoon's language is reminiscent of the schoolteacher who told teenaged Finn that they could discuss Section 28 quietly, out of school hours. There is a streak of discretion and 'careful handling' that runs through British culture, and it so often works to hold back LGBTQ+ people. Echoing Campbell, Hoon argued that while transsexuals would support the idea of a review, and it might even appease their demands, traditional pro-family voices would view it much more negatively. 'I therefore believe that a low-key approach would be appropriate,' he wrote. This caution, which was characteristic of the Labour government's style at the time, was supported by other high-profile ministers such as Peter Mandelson and David Blunkett.

When the working group got going, it threw open its doors to the campaigners. In a joint submission, various trans rights groups and Liberty, the human rights organisation, wrote:

> For many years the common social, medical and scientific viewpoint on transsexual people was that we sought to

'disappear'. The last few years have seen that idea overturned as transsexual people used both the media and the courtroom to demand their inclusion in society.

. . .

It is important to remember that many transsexual people want to be open about their trans status. All the groups represented here include many who are proud to be transsexual . . . We are primarily seeking an administrative system which will allow us, after undertaking the difficult road of gender transition, to take our place in society, whether or not openly as transsexual people.

By the summer of 2000 the working group had wound up its work and sent a draft report to senior figures in government for comment. Tony Blair supported reform, but worried that things were moving too fast. 'The Prime Minister does not believe that we should publish the report at this time,' his adviser David North wrote to a counterpart at the Home Office. 'He believes that it would merely polarise opinions, and could raise unrealistic expectations of early legislation on the issue.'

Trans people would have to wait. And that waiting continued to cause harm. One of Tash's close friends at school was experiencing high levels of gender dysphoria throughout these years. Remembering this during our research, Tash reread their own teen diaries. They noted page after page of comments about how sad their friend was, but also how neither of them possessed the words or understanding to work out why. They realised the complications of attending an all-girls school only decades later. Twenty years after the fact, these diary entries made so much more sense, and it made Tash feel truly sad that the world hadn't handed them both the words they'd needed.

Although Tash and their friend didn't know it at the time, the movement for people like them to be seen and heard was gaining strength. People and organisations were gunning for change, and that's why they kept taking legal action, as Switchboard volunteers heard on the phones:

> 4 January 2001
>
> Took a call from Katy a TS wanting information on taking legal advice from us on mental health illness issues and taking the hospital to court. Advised that needs specialist advice, Katy was writing everything down for court action. She will ring again.

We don't know if Katy managed to bring a successful case against the hospital, but we know that other trans people had their day in court. In 2002, in a case about birth certificates, the European Court of Human Rights ruled that a trans person's inability to change the sex on their birth certificate was a breach of their rights under Article 8 and Article 12 of the European Convention on Human Rights.[10]

The UK was shown to be increasingly out of line on trans rights, shamed by a European court. Whether or not Blair wanted to, he was going to have to act. This is why his government finally passed the Gender Recognition Act in 2004: a law that created a process through which a trans person could apply to receive a legal document that saw them in their true gender. The act also meant that people with gender dysphoria were given legal recognition as members of the sex that fitted with their gender identity; a person could also apply for a new birth certificate in their true gender identity. Despite the stipulation that two doctors had to approve this process, the Gender Recognition Act was a huge leap forwards.

'THIS TROUBLESOME BODY'

Back in 2023, however, the year a trans teenager was murdered partly because of her gender identity, the basic trans rights on offer were being questioned by senior figures in the Conservative government. Calls to protect gender recognition were high on the agenda of marchers at the Trans Pride that we joined in 2023. It was disorientating to be researching how this reform came into history at the same time as reading headlines implying that it might be scrapped (in 2025 this became even more likely after the Supreme Court's ruling that led to segregation of trans people). Tash felt the hostile atmosphere personally: they knew that, as a gender nonconforming person, the rights they wanted were also on the line.

But we ploughed on. Sometimes all you can do is look to history and seek out new patterns. When we looked in The National Archives, we found the story of policy development, the prime minister's political hesitancy, his spin doctor's snark; but also our elders' tireless campaigning and pushy test cases. And while an official archive is never enough – we had the log books to show us what trans people were going through. We could bring out their stories, just as trans people bring their bodies out on to the streets at Trans Prides. And fortunately we also had Diana, who made history as the first trans volunteer at Switchboard, who laid down the pattern for it to be trans-inclusive – *and* who made us feel our duty to record all this.

Off and on, the state has tried to not see trans people, and people have agitated and fought to be seen. The same is true for another group of people who the state had turned away from: lesbians who dared to be mothers too.

―――――

Judges, ministers of state, spin doctors, and actual medical doctors have all been found consistently failing to recognise the dignity of

Britain's queer citizens. There is a persistent notion that they would really rather not take us seriously. Official records and statements reveal this – and they appear in stark contrast to the usually kind, caring, and open-minded words of the writers of the log books. Even Switchboard volunteers at their most fumbling have managed to respect the identities of LGBTQ+ people.

Page after page in the log books reveal volunteers taking care of women battling to retain custody of their children after leaving their husbands:

> 24 September 1975
> A woman rang to ask if I knew anything about the case of a woman who was living with another woman who was refused custody of her child inspite of medical evidence that the child would have been better off with mother. This was for a case on now (very similar) which she wanted the info to help her with . . .
> PS. Just realised I didn't ask which side she was on. Probably the mother's.

Getting custody of your children after a breakup with their other parent is a private affair, and unless one of the parties is famous it is not newsworthy. For decades, however, hundreds if not thousands of lesbian mothers fought for their right to be seen by courts as a lesbian *and* a mother – a direct challenge to the idea that these two identities were incompatible. As we have seen, the book about Jenny living with Eric and Martin was banned – but the idea of her having two mummies was not even imaginable in a storybook. That story went unwritten at the time that lesbians mothers were fighting for it – as a result of consistent, deep-rooted state-sanctioned homophobia and sexism.

The issue was that lesbians were being deemed 'unfit mothers' by the family courts. In cases where a man and a woman had a child together and the woman left him to be with another woman, the man could acceptably argue in court that as a lesbian she could not be trusted to raise a child and therefore should be denied custody. One homophobic assumption underlying this view was that gay parents raised children to be gay, and judge after judge upheld this argument in English courts. They were not following a law that forced their hand, but rather a social norm – the same one that could not abide Jenny living with Eric and Martin.

This was the attitude that Elaine Fitzgerald had to fight when she left her husband in 1981 and tried to keep custody of their ten-year-old son (she later met her partner Lyn, as described in Chapter 2). 'It was a very difficult time, I have to say,' Elaine told Adam in 2019. 'The most difficult thing for me was having to stand up and to own who I was in a very public way . . . The prize at the end of my bravery was that I would hopefully keep my son.'

It was going to be a bizarre showdown for a family woman who was born in 1945 'just as the war ended' and raised in Leytonstone, east London. At the age of twenty-two, Elaine had married a man, and set up home with him in a house located between that of her sister and that of her best friend. 'We had communal gates,' Elaine remembered. 'We had parties in the garden swimming pool – not a real one, a plastic one. It was a place where people really knew their roots.'

Family was everything, but by the time she reached her midthirties Elaine discovered that she was seen by the court system to want to undermine that very concept. 'It was a great shock to the family and friends,' she remembered with sadness. It was her first time telling the story publicly, and our first time hearing about this issue. Tash in particular could barely contain their anger at the injustice Elaine had faced. It was a primal rage, like the one that had erupted in arguments between teenaged Tash and their parents, or driven them to drink too much and get lost in the countryside.

Our stress as queer people can become too much, and in our cases this research became a way for us to channel it into something productive. We set about asking more people about the problem of lesbian custody, starting with Switchboard volunteers. According to Femi Otitoju, the issue was 'pivotal' for lesbians from the sixties through to the eighties. She told us how women like her had to collect and share the best advice with lesbian mothers, such as leaving the family home with the children before the father found out they were lesbian.[11]

In the early seventies, politically active lesbians had hoped that the rights of lesbian mothers would be incorporated into the campaigns of the Gay Liberation Front, but they were disappointed that the men did not seem interested enough. 'We, the lesbians, began to abandon the GLF dream,' wrote Janet Dixon, an activist, in 1988.[12] 'We gave up expecting the GLF to solve our problems.' Lesbian mothers also felt let down by child-free lesbians.

It seemed that no one saw the needs of lesbian mothers apart from themselves. A group of them formed Action for Lesbian Parents in 1976. There was also a bigger group called Rights of Women, which was a broad-based feminist organisation helping women to navigate the law and campaign for legal equality. It received plenty of referrals via Switchboard, as the log books show:

> 18 July 1984
>
> Please could all the men note (all the women already know, I hope) that the correct org to refer to is RIGHTS OF WOMEN for all 'technical' stuff on lesbian custody . . . RIGHTS OF WOMEN have a lesbian custody specialist worker on staff.

Between 1979 and 1983, a researcher named Julia Anne Brophy collected testimonies from twenty-two mothers like Elaine, covering custody matters for forty-six children. As she assembled her findings into a PhD at the University of Sheffield, Brophy encountered shocking stories of a divorce court welfare officer interrogating lesbian mothers about how they reached orgasm, husbands presenting intercepted phone calls in court to disclose their wives' lesbianism, and a magistrate who lectured lesbians 'about perversion and about wifely duties'.[13] The women describing their contested hearings leave little doubt that it was the worst day of their lives: 'it's so painful to recall'; 'I was so exposed, so defenceless'; 'I was made to feel like an animal.'

Rights of Women continued the job of collecting evidence like that amassed by Brophy, detailing how the system stood against lesbians. It established a Lesbian Custody Group in 1982 to support lesbians who were facing such discrimination in the family courts. And in November 1984, that group published a report titled 'Lesbian Mothers on Trial'.[14] We managed to view this document, from the year of Adam's birth, in Bishopsgate Institute, where it is held as part of a lawyer's archive. Across its sixty-three pages are the findings from a landmark survey of thirty-six lesbian mothers, chapters on how the press maintained the myths about lesbian mothers, and even a set of wonderfully sarcastic cartoons by Sue Beasley and Lyn May. The report built on Brophy's findings, documenting exactly how lesbian mothers faced prejudice in the family courts and how they were assumed to be unfit and unsafe parents. 'From this report it can be seen that there is still extreme prejudice and discrimination towards lesbian mothers,' the report said. 'The courts make the prejudiced, unsubstantiated and speculative assumption that lesbianism will have a negative effect on children.' The authors of 'Lesbian Mothers on Trial' concluded with seventeen recommendations, from court reform to better education to anti-discrimination laws.

In the meantime, lesbian mothers had to battle on with advice from groups such as Switchboard and Rights of Women. In order to find lesbians who needed support from these groups, volunteers like Femi and Lisa made sure they put Switchboard's phone number under women's noses. They needed to know all the publications and places where women might stumble across an advert for a support line. In the case of women who were living as straight, in probably quite conventional family homes not in London, this posed its own challenge. Their lives were far away from some of the radical circles and dyke discos where Switchboard volunteers hung out. Lisa remembered placing an ad in *Woman's Own*, a very popular magazine for women. Not long after the ad ran, Switchboard's phones began to ring.

> Suddenly we started getting calls from married lesbians who were literally sneaking downstairs at one or two in the morning to phone us while the family was asleep. They knew that they were lesbians – quite often they were in love with the woman next door, or something like that, or their best friend or whatever – and they had agreements that they would not tell their husband or leave their husband until the kids had grown up and left.

Their reasoning was diverse, but chief among their concerns was the issue of child custody. 'They were literally just waiting to be able to come out until it would not destroy the family.'[15]

Elaine worried about this too, but there was no way she could continue living in a heterosexual relationship. She knew she could be a lesbian and a good mother – but to demonstrate that, she was going to have to fight the system. In 1981, when Elaine's son was ten, she found herself starting something with another woman. Her brother joked that it was a 'hothouse affair'. For Elaine, it was a revolution. 'My recollections of that particular time was that it was a time where people were coming to terms with lots of things that were happening in the outer world,' she said. 'Anything outside of my own world was quite a shock really. Having this sudden realisation that I was in the wrong life was really scary.'

The affair taught her that she was a lesbian, and that there was no way she could live without seeing herself for who she was. 'I was determined to find the life that I knew I needed to live,' she said. This meant leaving her husband, finding love elsewhere, and continuing to raise her son. 'It was a great shock to the family and friends,' she said. And she worried that her relationship with her son would be severed, with force, due to homophobia and sexism. Her brother helped, by phoning Switchboard. The volunteer knew exactly what to do: they recommended some lawyers with expertise in lesbians retaining custody of their children when they leave their husbands. As a low earner, Elaine received legal aid which paid for a very good lawyer. 'She told me her brother was gay, she wasn't gay herself, but she wasn't going to let anybody take my son away.'

As Brophy's research had shown, they were up against a prejudiced legal system and the odds were against Elaine and her lawyer. One of the things she found the hardest was fortifying herself for having to come out – in court. She knew from other women that judges often asked lesbians about their sex lives, asked how they would feel if their children grew up to be gay/lesbian, and looked down on them from the bench as perverts. Elaine had to walk into a courtroom like that in 1981, and declare herself in public. She prayed that the judge would see her for who she was: a lesbian and a mother, where one of those had no impingement on the other. The stakes could hardly have been higher. 'If ever I've had a difficulty in my life I have to think, *Look what happened there*,' she remembered in 2019.

This line has stayed with us since we recorded Elaine saying it. We talked about it a lot during our research, and why it sounded significant. It revealed Elaine recognising the importance of her own story, of *seeing herself*, which is what we were trying to do with our work, and with all the memories we were gathering from elders. History is not just the wars between states or the great discoveries, it is also the personal trials of every one of us. Elaine knew this, and she was proud to recognise what she'd done. Her kindness and her strength as a lesbian fortified us, too. That is why we were both personally so intrigued to learn how she fought for equality before we were born, for those who were like us in 1981, and even for *us* as we would come to be.

And Elaine won. She and her lawyer convinced the court, and Elaine won the right to continue caring for her son – as a lesbian mother.

More and more lesbians were granted custody in the late eighties and into the nineties, and over the years the courts built a case law that gradually eroded the judiciary's bigotry against lesbian mothers. Various laws passed in the early 2000s made claims that women like Elaine would be unfit mothers impossible to make, and the Equality Act 2010 batched these laws together in even stronger provisions against discrimination. Finally, in law, the British state dignified queer citizens by signalling that they, too, should expect equality.

So many women who had come before Elaine, and indeed many who came after, were unsuccessful. The state did not want to see lesbian mothers for who they were, and we had to record this in our work, continuing on from Brophy's research. One of Brophy's contributors, Lisa, said: 'All of a sudden I was an unfit mother, branded morally dangerous for my child simply because I exhibited the ability to love another woman.' The judge had made the common, homophobic assumption that a child living with a queer parent is likely to be influenced into becoming queer. The flipside is that both of us were raised in heterosexual households but turned out to be as queer as fuck.

We don't know what happened to Lisa or the other women who opened up to Brophy, just as we never found out the full stories of those who had called Switchboard. That unknowing is something to carry through research like this. Day after day we sat in Bishopsgate Institute reading the log books, surrounded by other books and boxes and cabinets, finding only the notes about the women who phoned Switchboard asking where they could turn to. That is the nature of this archive: it's incomplete, even though it runs to thousands of pages. However, in the log books, we had found leads. We'd seen volunteers directing lesbians to named support groups with phone numbers. We'd felt compelled to look deeper and further to find out more. We'd spoken to our contributors – and had been particularly taken aback by Elaine: she'd initially only planned to share the story of how she met her partner Lyn in the olden days but ended up telling us about her greatest trial. All of this investigation led us to find the publications of Rights of Women and the Lesbian Custody Group, and Brophy's heavily researched book – we bought a copy that had been withdrawn from a library.

Just as Tash had been drawn by their curiosity into the crawlspace at Switchboard, we'd been pulled ever deeper into what we'd sensed were important histories. Switchboard's log books held at Bishopsgate are significant, but, we realised, they only scraped the surface of queer history in the years they covered.

Somehow we couldn't hear a story like Elaine's and not feel duty-bound to find more. Our sense of duty to our queer elders grew deeper as we heard more and more stories of the state choosing not to see them. We would see them, we would listen to them, we would record them, and we would share them.

Were we, in some way, making up for previously being unable to see ourselves?

---

7 June 1992
17-year-old in Portsmouth. First sexual experience with man in toilet. A bit confused, excited . . . wants loads of sex, but scared. Will phone back – he wants info on novels, pin-up mags, videos but ran out of 10p's.

This young caller had managed to see himself. He knew what he wanted, but the law in 1992 was against him. The age at which a person could lawfully consent to sex differed depending on the type of sex you wanted to have. One of the ways that the Sexual Offences Act 1967 freed up some men to have sex with each other, while denying permission to others, was that it said the sex had to be between men who had reached the age of twenty-one. (Lesbians were, again, invisible in the eyes of the law, and not 'protected' in the same way.) Young men under twenty-one could choose to vote, smoke, drink beer, join the army, *and* have sex with women – but they were banned from having sex with other men.

This legal paradox led to one of the greatest campaigns for equality in Britain in our lifetimes. It happened right under our noses while we were growing up, and it relied on the bravery of all the young men who came out to the state and demanded to be seen. Finding out more about those young men, and about the campaign, led us down some surprising avenues. First we started by asking Switchboard volunteers like Judith Skinner about calls from this demographic. 'I remember taking calls from boys and young men who were under the then age of consent,' she told Tash. 'There were a lot, a lot of young men who were active on the gay scene who could have been – or their partners, if older, could have been – in trouble.'[16]

One person who could have gotten into trouble was a young man named Harry F. Rey who had his first sexual experience as a teenager in the toilet in an Asda supermarket. 'I think it was over in about five minutes,' he told us for the podcast in 2021,[17] 'but it was something real . . . I wasn't just a kid any more.' Harry said he felt like he was owning his own sexuality, and that felt amazing. 'There was no downside,' he grinned.

This issue led to many debates among Switchboard volunteers about how to support callers who wanted to have sex but were underage in the eyes of the unequal homophobic law. In London, volunteers could send the young men to the London Gay Teenage Group where they could at least meet others like them. The archive of this group, held in Islington's local history centre, contains photo albums of teenaged LGBTQ+ people hanging out and striking silly teenage poses. The snaps are a remarkable record of teenage freedom, because the people who took them saw these teenagers for who they were. They capture a relaxed queer youth experience, which Richard Desmond, who first attended in 1979, recalls. 'It really was just like any other youth group except that all the people there were queer . . . the women played pool and the men sat around talking about music and shows.' It was a chance for queer young people to be together, and as Richard pointed out, 'this was a really radical thing.'

Outside of London, where we grew up, the opportunities for LGBTQ+ teenagers to meet each other were far rarer. The London group made sure that teenagers there were a little less likely than us to feel the stress that straight society places on queer people. The state, by contrast, did not want to see the teenagers like Richard as free queer individuals. The state saw them as criminals.

A survey conducted by Stonewall in 1993 and published as the report 'Arrested Development?' found that the majority of gay men had broken the law.[18] No less than 78 per cent of the 2,088 gay and bisexual men who took the survey had had sex before the law allowed them to.

Switchboard volunteers also had to handle another type of call due to the unequal law: from men over twenty-one who were in sexual relationships with those under, and sometimes with significant age gaps. In law, this was a black-and-white issue: it was illegal. 'I had a friend who'd been put in prison,' Clare Truscott told Tash in 2020, 'and treated as a nonce, you know, as somebody having sex with children.' The friend was in his early twenties, and his boyfriend was nineteen – but this meant Clare's friend was having sex with someone who could not legally consent to it. He was jailed with sex offenders. 'He had a terrible time in prison,' Clare said, her voice softening.[19]

The dynamics of age gaps and power differentials are harder to legislate for than an objective fact like age. Switchboard trod carefully here, knowing that there had been elements of the gay rights movement who pushed for no age of consent, and there were plenty of people who saw it as their 'right' to have sex with children. Switchboard never agreed with that, but it also knew that the law as it stood was unequal. It wanted to support callers, but sometimes it was hard to know the full details of what someone was experiencing – volunteers only had what the caller told them. As Lisa recalled, 'We got . . . calls from people who were being blackmailed by underage men or men who said they were underage, who were then blackmailing them after sex. Sometimes it had been paid-for sex. Sometimes it was just someone they'd picked up in a bar.' She thought for a beat and said, 'That was very difficult.'[20]

Switchboard's belief in young queer people did prove problematic once, when they took on Richard as a volunteer around the same time he started going to the London Gay Teenage Group. He was very eager to help but was just sixteen at the time. 'The rule about Switchboard not having volunteers under eighteen is because of me,' Richard told Tash, decades later. Richard's dad found out that he was volunteering for an organisation with 'gay' in the name and contacted Switchboard to accuse the organisation of corrupting his son. He told them: 'I'm going to contact the *Daily Mail*!'

Switchboard was doing nothing wrong, but it also did not want to attract the attention of the anti-LGBTQ+, hate-filled writers and editors of the *Daily Mail*. Richard's dad's threat caused some panic among the volunteers. 'People were very fond of him [Richard], but actually, we had to put Switchboard first,' said Lisa, who was the one dispatched to ask Richard to leave. 'It was awful because we all felt like we were betraying what we were there for.'

Young Richard accepted the reality and resigned. He and Switchboard agreed that he could return in a few years' time, when his dad had calmed down, if he wanted. Unknown to Switchboard, however, having been prohibited from joining them and serving his community, he was secretly working on smashing through the legal barriers holding back other excitable teenagers. Richard clearly knew he was gay, even as a teenager, and was not afraid to say it. That's why he attended the London Gay Teenage Group. And being a member there was how he heard that a pair of lawyers from the Campaign for Homosexual Equality were looking for a gay teenager to join their fight against the unequal age of consent. Richard jumped at the opportunity. It was 1982, and a plan quickly developed for Richard to sue the British government. If Richard was excited about taking phone calls, you can imagine how his hormones reacted at the chance to take on Margaret Thatcher.

The lawyers, Peter Ashman and Nigel Warner, needed parental consent. Richard knew his dad would not give it, but thought his mum just might. For her, 'I could do no wrong,' Richard remembered. 'So I took mother along to the upstairs bar of the Edward VI, with Nigel Warner and Peter Ashman, and they explained it all in detail, which all went over Mother's head, just as much as it did mine, I suspect. She signed the forms.'

Warner and Ashman explained everything to him, and it meant that Richard had to confess to breaking the law, in official legal documents. 'I was sixteen and I was having sex, and I stood up and I admitted this,' he said, proudly remembering his teenage courage. The documents even included details of Richard's teenage journeys into a local public lavatory 'to find sexual contacts with other men'.[21] They recorded details of how the unequal law made him 'frightened' and placed him under 'psychological strain'. All these facts supported Richard's case, which was put to the European Commission of Human Rights. It argued that the inequality in UK law around the age of consent breached Richard's human rights.

The case flew under the radar, but Richard's lawyers warned him that if they succeeded, he would become notorious – probably something Richard would have welcomed, given his confidence. The commission gave its ruling in 1984, saying that individual

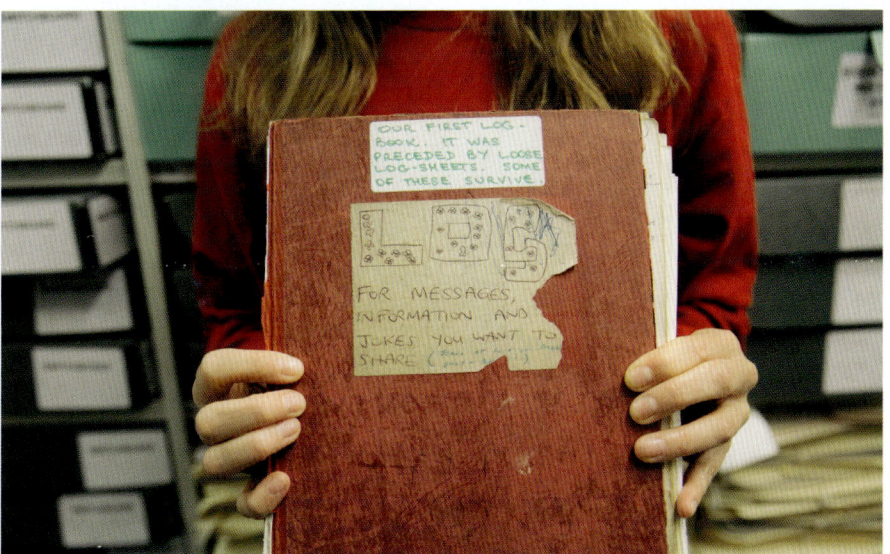

Top left: Tash aged 2.5 years in the summer of 1988, Dartmouth, Devon.

Top right: Adam with his older sister Hannah in their living room, Cleethorpes, 1985.

Bottom: Tash holding Switchboard's first log book, dated 1975.

GAY SWITCHBOARD
01-837 7324

Information and help service for

HOMOSEXUAL
WOMEN & MEN
24 hours a day

Gay Switchboard poster advertising the service, c. 1978.

Top left: Switchboard's phone room above Housmans Bookshop, 1984.
Top right: Andy Piccos taking a call at Switchboard, c. 1978.
Bottom: Lisa Power and other volunteers taking calls in front of the many files that were used to help callers, 1980s.

Top: Switchboard's volunteers at the helpline's 10th birthday celebration, 1984.

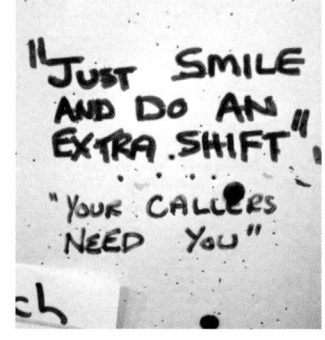

Above: Photograph of Denroy, a Switchboard volunteer, posing with the phone in front of the computers in the phone room, c. 1997.

Right: Volunteer morale boosting in Switchboard's phone room, 1984.

David Seligman, Switchboard co-founder, 1982.

A poster made and distributed by Switchboard to raise awareness about HIV transmission, c. 1991.

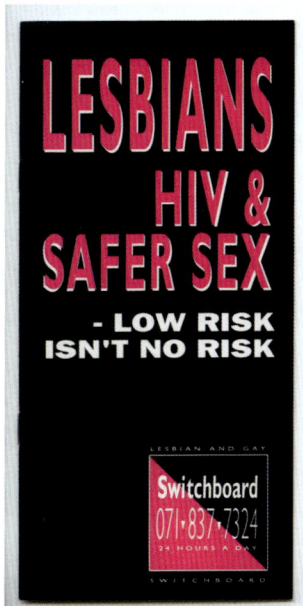

Top left: A4 poster for supporting organisations to display, 1985.

Top right: Leaflet made by Switchboard to raise awareness about HIV among lesbians, c. 1986.

Bottom: Hand-drawn volunteer recruitment leaflet, 1979.

Top: Switchboard volunteers and their banner at Lesbian and Gay Pride in London, 1983.

Bottom left: Femi Otitoju, dressed in homage to Grace Jones at London Pride 1985.

Bottom right: Protest at British Home Stores against the sacking of Tony Whitehead, 7 February 1976. Tony holds the 'Equal Rights' sign.

states were allowed to make their own laws on issues of morality, which included sexuality – the European-wide body could not decide on Richard's claim. The case had essentially failed.

It often takes several attempts to change the law through cases like these. When we made season two of *The Log Books* podcast in 2021, Richard was still unknown as a pioneer, despite being the first person to challenge the unequal age of consent. Tash had known him for seven years as a fellow volunteer, but it wasn't until they sat down in his east London council flat, cup of tea in hand, that he started to reveal the role he had played. Being on the podcast brought him out, and shone a light on his case. 'It's quite odd that forty years later, I'm being reminded of it,' he said. 'It's nice to get some credit for it because I was anonymous then. More importantly, and to be fair, I have to give some credit to my mum because . . . it was her that signed the forms.'[22]

Richard knew that the documents of his case were of historical importance, and so he placed them in the LGBTQ+ archive at Bishopsgate Institute. This meant that other people, including us, could read them. As Richard sipped his tea and told Tash his story, it was clear what it all meant to him, and this in turn helped us to see a pattern of queer people demanding that the state see them on their own terms, from young adults like Richard to trans people and lesbian mothers. This only added extra import to Richard's story, and led us to his archived papers, so we could go deeper than his memory could manage. We knew where to look because Tash was friends with Richard; it's daunting to think about all the other important legal papers that are not archived, all the untold stories and memories that we'll never get to hear.

Despite Richard's courage, the inequality in law remained. The calls to Switchboard kept coming: *I'm seventeen, can I have sex with my boyfriend?* These calls would become a cause of the gay and lesbian movement for well over a decade, moving away from the anonymity of Richard's case and onto the front pages of the newspapers. One of the young men who put his face to that campaign where Richard could not was Hugo Greenhalgh. One night in 1989, Hugo was sixteen years old, walking hand in hand with his first boyfriend in Exeter. 'A police car came by and he dropped my hand,' Hugo said. 'He was right to, just in case . . . [but] that's bonkers, just bizarre – to have two sixteen-year-olds walking hand in hand to be terrified of a police car 'cause they could end up in jail.'

Within a couple of years, Hugo and his new boyfriend Will Parry, along with Ralph Wilde, were spearheading a national campaign to equalise the age of consent. In effect, they'd picked up Richard's baton. The new lobby group Stonewall, founded as part of the backlash to Section 28, took up the campaign, supporting Hugo, Will, and Ralph to sue the British government and tour the country to raise awareness. Politicians fought over the issue in parliament and TV studios; lawyers filed bundles of arguments; Hugo received love and hate. Government files reveal that the issue was hugely complex and controversial, with various factions in office and parliament divided – and Stonewall pressing hard from the outside, knowing that the law bends towards justice eventually. The prime minister John Major was minded to reform the law, but he knew it wouldn't be popular with the Conservative base represented by voters like Mrs Armstrong, who appeared to be more than pleased being labelled homophobic in her letter to her MP in Berwickshire.

We don't know much about Mrs Armstrong, except that her letter made it to Number 10 as an example of the concern of the 'average person' about the prospect of an equal age of consent.

Adam had found the letter in one of John Major's files held at The National Archives and paused to read it carefully, then re-read it.

Adam was just ten years old when Mrs Armstrong wrote her letter, and she was 'appalled' at the idea that when he reached sixteen he'd be able to consent to the sex he wanted. She wrote: 'Apart from all else, boys of 16 haven't sorted their sexuality out for themselves (at best the ones who aren't streetwise haven't). This is one point. Another is, What about AIDS? Aren't the government spending a fortune of taxpayers' money to get across to homosexuals and drug users the fact that this vile disease is almost totally in their minority groups?'

How could Mrs Armstrong know when would have been the right time for Adam to sort his sexuality out for himself? As it happened, the attitude she exemplified contributed to him not 'sorting it out' until he was twenty-nine. (And in fact, hopefully it's never sorted out.) With Adam's freedom and pleasure, finally, came also regret and pain that he'd allowed voices like Mrs Armstrong's to hold him back. Her letter is an example of what campaigns like Stonewall and organisations like Switchboard were up against in trying to convince the state to respect the autonomy of young queer people.

The Conservative prime minister John Major was trapped between furious letter writers like Mrs Armstrong and charming activists like Ian McKellen, dispatched by Stonewall to lobby for equality. In 1993 an aide to the prime minister reminded him of his manifesto pledge that 'racial and sexual discrimination have no place in our society.' The aide argued that Major therefore ought 'to do something for homosexuals'. Short of a piece of legislation directly about them, the aide recommended a 'modest but solid change' in the law – perhaps reform on importuning and entrapment in public toilets, or even slipping a lowered age of consent into the Criminal Justice Bill.

It is a little surreal to think about what you were doing as a child at the time of important legal and political moments that would have an impact on your life. Adam was growing up under a legal system that blocked the 'promotion' of homosexuality and would later block him from consenting to sex even when his straight peers could. In 1993 and 1994, the height of political activism around equalising the age of consent, he was watching *Jurassic Park* over and over and going on a family trip to Disneyland Paris.

Nevertheless, on 21 February 1994, the issue of the age of consent came to a vote in parliament. It was a real test of the country's attitude towards sex and members of the LGBTQ+ community, and it was set as a free vote where MPs could vote in line with their beliefs instead of having to follow their party's policy. A few days before the vote, a Switchboard volunteer had glued an announcement about it onto one of the pages of the log books. They had written in blue and green ink, with underlining and capital letters, to advise all volunteers to remind any relevant caller that there would be a rally outside parliament on the night of the vote. The announcement also requested stewards ('Lots'), leafleteers, and two car owners.

Hugo was one of the campaigners who made it into the public gallery to watch the debate ahead of the vote, along with Lisa Power. They had to sit through hours of stuffy and heated political discourse. 'It was all about sex,' Hugo remembered. 'The arguments were unbelievably offensive . . . from a bunch of dinosaurs, quite frankly.'

The debate was kicked off by Edwina Currie, the Conservative MP for South Derbyshire, who within parliament was leading the campaign for equalisation. The MP for Northampton North, Tony Marlow, was among many of her parliamentary colleagues who stood in direct opposition to her. 'What my honourable friend is seeking to do is to get this House to vote to legalise the buggery of adolescent males,' said Marlow during the debate.[23] 'Does she really think that that's what our constituents have sent us here to do?'

Currie retorted, 'No, our constituents send us here with our brains intact, and we should be using them.'

Nicholas Fairbairn, Conservative MP for Perth and Kinross, said that 'Heterosexual activity is normal, and homosexual activity – putting your penis into another man's arsehole – is a perversion.'

Young Hugo sat in the gallery listening to the MPs calling him a pervert. Others stood up for him. Labour MP Chris Smith, who was openly gay, rose to say, 'Yes, we are different. We have a different sexuality. But that does not make us, in any way, less valid or less worthy as citizens.'

Meanwhile outside parliament the crowd had gathered, singing songs, holding placards and waving flags with the number sixteen to signal their plea for equality. During our research, we found documentary footage from the night of the demo, shot by none other than Will Parry, one of the three young campaigners who'd put their necks on the line in the legal campaign. It was thrilling to know that someone had been documenting these events well before us. Not only did it help our understanding of the history, it also connected us to those who, like us, had felt the urge to preserve and share such stories.

Watching Will's documentary, *Age of Dissent*,[24] we could hear and feel the electric energy of that night in 1994. The people who had assembled in the cold were powered by the push for equality and the recent loss of a beloved community member, the film-maker and artist Derek Jarman, who'd died of AIDS-related illnesses just two days prior to the vote. The LGBTQ+ movement had lost thousands to HIV/AIDS, had lost the battle to stop Section 28, and was now faced with losing the fight for an equal age of consent. 'The debate around the age of consent felt so dominating at the time,' said Monty Moncrieff, a Switchboard volunteer. 'It felt like such an important battle for our communities to win.'

But dinosaurs ruled the Earth. Parliament voted against equalising the law. In Will's footage, his boyfriend Hugo runs out of parliament to tell the crowd what had happened. 'Sixteen is lost!' he declares 'They've just had the vote. The vote's just happened. Sixteen has not happened.'

The crowd boos. 'We've lost sixteen!' they shout.

When Hugo says they lost by twenty-seven votes, Will howls, '*Bastards!*'

Will's anger sent a shiver through us. His cry was so hoarse, so visceral. This was particularly unusual for us because most of our research was paper-based: scribbles in the log books, typed letters and reports, photographs at the most visual. In contrast, Will's film was a *living* history – a history of a time when we had both been alive, in fact – and it screamed at the inequality we had all lived through, even if we didn't know it then. It reminded us of that log book entry from 1975: *Fuck society for twisting people*. Seeing Will and Hugo in the film, and hearing their pain, fuelled our work.

Although the equality campaigners had lost, the parliamentarians continued debating into the night. They next voted on whether the age should lower instead to eighteen. This reform passed, meaning that MPs had voted actively to proceed with inequality. Tony Blair, who was then an MP and three years away from becoming prime minister, said, 'The so-called compromise of eighteen is misguided. What is the rationale behind maintaining the stigma but at a different age? It is an issue not of age but of equality.'[25]

Lisa stood up in the public gallery, yelled 'Thanks for nothing!' and then legged it. Outside she met a crowd that was turning into a riot of anger and defiance. They marched to Downing Street and continued chanting into the night. In voting for inequality, British lawmakers sowed confusion:

> 27 February 1995
> One cold, lonely, quiet, Switchboredish sort of early, pre-dawn vacuously empty night shift I had a call from a worried, concerned man whose brother, aged 20, has just been arrested for bonking a poor innocent (sic) 17-year-old (as if!); looking for reassurance in the legal file that the age of consent really has gone down to 18 I find that there is a curious lack of new information about this most serious of subjects.

> 17 April 1995
> Can we have an update on the Age of Consent legislation? I had a caller who wanted to know the state of play on prosecutions.

The fight for equality had to continue. Hugo, Will, and Ralph were now too old to fight the government, so a younger claimant, Euan Sutherland, joined the legal campaign. The case rumbled through the courts, running in parallel to crucial moments in Adam's sexual development. Adam was legally on course to reach sixteen while inequality still reigned, but of course his body paid no attention to the law. In 1999, aged fifteen, he watched *Queer as Folk*, the landmark television drama depicting gay lives, including that of another fifteen-year-old, a character called Nathan who knew exactly what sex he wanted and went out to a gay club to find it. Like so many queer people, Adam watched *Queer as Folk* alone, in his bedroom, with the volume turned down. The shame and fear of being gay kept Adam silent. His parents, the school environment, and even the law told us we were wrong.

But Euan, the brave teenager fighting the unequal age of consent, knew that we were not. Thank god for Euan. Euan's case, supported by Stonewall, helped to deliver the eventual equalisation of the age of consent in 2001. In that year, Adam finished school, started college, turned sixteen, and started buying lube from a Superdrug in Grimsby. Although some of the gay boys at college were dating (and even shagging – or trying to), Adam didn't. He studied a lot, kept friends at a distance, and wanked his way through the tubes of cheap lube. The whole idea that sex with a man was something he could do was suppressed in his mind. If he had, he would have been a member of the first generation of gay teens to go through this rite of passage without breaking the law.

The Sexual Offences (Amendment) Act 2000, which became law in January 2001 throughout the UK, equalised the age of consent at sixteen for both heterosexual and homosexual acts, regardless of gender.[26] This meant that for the first time sex acts between two women were seen in law: they were no longer invisible. And it meant that the law finally saw young people like Hugo and Richard, who knew what sex they wanted, and recognised their freedom to consent to it lawfully.

―――

The log books primarily contain notes pertaining to calls made to Switchboard. These entries set us down a path of learning about the trans people who had wanted the state to recognise them, the lesbian mothers needing legal advice, and the young queer men wanting to know whether they'd broken the law. Their joint story is one of wanting the state to see them for who they were. As we spotted this pattern and began asking people about it, a few former volunteers hinted at a different story altogether – one about Switchboard itself. Apparently, Switchboard had struggled to register as a charity. It was only when we looked into this, as its own story, that we understood exactly how the homophobic British state apparatus had refused to recognise Switchboard for the life-saving work it was doing. Britain had chosen not to *see* Switchboard.

Switchboard might have preferred to stay away from formal incorporation into the British establishment, with its inherent classism and homophobia, but the volunteers knew that official registration as a charity would bring tax relief and the chance to apply for various funds, meaning more support for front line services. Queer people are often suspected as paedophiles, so being sanctioned by the state would also bring the welcome signal that the organisation was not associated with paedophilia. In 1978, then, the volunteers sought to come out to the British state, and to gain charitable status for what was then Gay Switchboard.

We read their application in The National Archives. Switchboard's attempt to become a charity was such a saga that the archives hold a very chunky file, spanning nine years of correspondence, evidence, and memos. It took several days to read through it all, to write it out as a timeline, to find the important notes, and to understand what had happened.

It should have been a simple case. That Switchboard was doing good work was obvious, no? The volunteers drafted their charitable objectives as being for 'the preservation and protection of good health both mental and physical of homosexual men and women'. As volunteers sent this statement as part of their application to the Charity Commission in 1978, they were handling calls like this one:

> 13 April 1978
> I took a call from a guy aged 21, didn't give name, who is in dire straits. No money. No place or anywhere to go.

They received a response back from the Charity Commission that their service did not constitute charity. One commission official in particular handled Switchboard's claims off and on for almost the full nine-year adventure: Maurice Rao. His papers make it clear that he did not want Switchboard to attain charitable status. Rao and some of his colleagues seemed to look for reasons beyond the letter of what constituted a charity in order to not give Switchboard official recognition.

In one memo, from 9 May 1978, Rao called Switchboard's representative 'argumentative . . . overexcited and emotional'. This is a classic tactic that the British state often uses to deflect the claims of minorities. There is a deep force ingrained in the British establishment that one should be calm and rational in making arguments, and one who is not can be more easily dismissed. This is why New Labour's ministers later cautioned to use 'careful handling' in their equality agenda. Adam integrated this intellectual force into his own character at school, trying to argue with bullies on the grounds of their logic, instead of throwing names or punches back at them. During one debate, Adam made a knock-out argument against another student – who then *actually* punched him. Adam was stunned, but walked away to report the violence instead of retaliating. Although this was probably a good thing to do, it demonstrated how Adam had trained himself to suppress his anger or, at best, channel it into action without really experiencing it. Could that have been the same process that led him to suppress his desires and channel them into wanking rather than sex with partners?

Finding traces of homophobia like Rao's made us reflect: what would we have done? Adam could have become the lawyer, arguing dispassionately for equality. Tash might have punched back, or at least felt the rage that Adam didn't. As it happened, when we read Rao's letters, we both felt angry. Rao had listened to Switchboard volunteers describe how they counselled lonely people contemplating suicide, and he told them that they should not be emotional. How did he dare say that to our elders?

Worse, he denied our number and our need. Although he argued in his correspondence with Switchboard that its provision of information about social activities (such as pubs and clubs) and its compassionate counselling were not technically charitable aims, Rao mostly dismissed the application on the grounds that Switchboard's work concerned homosexuals. In his report of a phone call with Switchboard's representative, he wrote: '[I told him that] I did not regard homosexuals as a charitable class in themselves, and further I did not regard them as being a sufficient section of the community to constitute the public.'

At the very same time as these words were being written down, Switchboard volunteers were being attacked in the street. When two of them, Banks* and Switchboard co-founder David Seligman, next met Rao and his colleagues, they told them that they were the victims of violence. 'Only the other day someone had pushed a cigar up Mr Seligman's nose,' the meeting minutes say, 'and their office received bomb threats every other day.' Seligman and the others were receiving 140,000 calls a year at this point, only four

---

* We can't find this person's first name.

years after the phone line opened – and yet the officials maintained that there just weren't enough homosexuals like Seligman to warrant special help from a charity. The Charity Commission's documents note that the service was 'particularly valuable to provincial callers', but the high numbers and the geographic diversity presented by Switchboard were still not enough to constitute a worthy 'public'. (The Charity Commission's documents present no actual count of homosexuals in the UK, so the officials appear to have been simply guessing that they were few in number.)

But even if millions of people had been subject to the violence Seligman reported, and the calls for help had reached the same number, the people seeking help were homosexuals – and that was the biggest sticking point. On 24 April 1978, a letter from the Charity Commission to Switchboard declared that '[homosexual] acts are regarded in law as immoral and contrary to public policy because they are a deviation from normal sexual behaviour. Thus homosexuals are not a proper beneficial class and I regret that I cannot help you in this matter.'

Rao later wrote, on 20 July 1978, that 'There can be no doubt that the law still regards such acts as contrary to public policy and immoral.' He also added that procuring gay sex remained a criminal offence. In the eyes of the state, as represented by officials at the Charity Commission, Switchboard volunteers were seen as perverts, as bad as paedophiles: one internal handwritten note by an official whose name is indecipherable says that if the case went to the board of the Charity Commission for a decision, the note's author would intervene to block registration. They added: '[homosexuals] have done untold harm by seducing young persons at that moment in their sexual development when they are uncertain, young persons who would have developed normally but for the doubt that bodies such as this create.' This implication that gays were paedophiles proved the existence of the very prejudice that Switchboard volunteers hoped registration would help to stamp out.

Fortunately, Switchboard was not deterred: by the mid-eighties volunteers were taking 250,000 calls a year, and they knew how vital their work was. They stuck to their ideals and poured some new fuel into their rockets, hiring a skilled solicitor called Andrew Phillips. In 1984 he took over the case to get the charity registered. Phillips was also a volunteer at Samaritans; he understood the need for a helpline and could reliably claim to the Charity Commission that there was no real difference between Samaritans and Switchboard, except that the latter still had no legal status.

Phillips looked through the Charity Commission's earlier arguments and went on the warpath. He argued against the claims that homosexuality was contrary to public policy and immoral, claiming that 'the various arguments advanced by you based upon your belief as to the views of "the common man" look strange when set against the fact that Parliament itself (hardly an unimportant judge of the popular will) has in 1967 and since passed major legislation radically altering the law with regard to homosexuality and its expression, and with regard to discrimination generally.' He added that 'there is more than a touch of medievalism' in the Charity Commission's attitudes towards homosexuality. This must have riled Rao. In an internal note to colleagues, Rao wrote, 'no one would be more happy than I to see the end of the saga of this troublesome body.'

Somehow, Phillips managed to move Rao and the commission on to discussing acceptable wording for Switchboard's charitable objects. He and Rao went back and forth over terms like 'distress' and 'despair', with Rao saying they were too imprecise and Phillips saying they were accepted by the commission in the case of

Samaritans. A few redrafts later, however, and by September 1985 the commission wrote to Phillips to say, 'I think we are now very close to agreeing a form of words to express exclusively charitable objects.' This was an enormous advance for Switchboard, especially given the hostile environment of the time, in which parliamentarians under the influence of rabid right-wing newspapers were introducing bills seeking to protect the idea of a 'stable family life' (code for heterosexuality) and 'moral considerations' in sex education. The final application from Switchboard declared the primary aim of the organisation was 'to relieve homosexual persons suffering from mental or emotional disability or despair and to promote their well being by counsel and/or help'. (It stayed this way until 2015 when the beneficiary group was expanded to be 'members of the LGBT+ communities'.)

Nearly nine years after first contacting the Charity Commission, Switchboard submitted this primary object as part of its memorandum of association on 29 December 1986. It was signed by twelve volunteers: Joanne Pollack, Darren Tossell, Martin Williams, Paul Hay, Timothy Bishop, Thomas Haworth, Paul Ashton, Dennis Grainger, Constantinos Leontarakis, Steve Ewart, James McNicholas, and William Meakin. After thirteen years taking care of a community, and nine years fighting for the state to recognise this work, Switchboard was incorporated officially as a charity in February 1987.

―――

Switchboard's private battle for official status had paralleled the battles of trans folks seeking legal recognition, lesbian mothers fighting for custody of their children, and campaigners demanding an equal age of consent. They all wanted to be seen by the state, with dignity and freedom. And they were all powered by anger and a sense of justice, the same as the Trans Pride march we joined in 2023.

There is another way of thinking about this anger. When it comes to LGBTQ+ people like us, there is a theory that we experience something called 'minority stress'.[27] This stress affects members of stigmatised groups, such as people of colour and queer people, and can be caused by things like interpersonal prejudice, state discrimination, and low social support. As we reflected on our own histories, we saw how in Tash the stress came out in loud arguments, heartbreaks, heavy partying; in Adam, self-restraint, avoidance, and work.

But our work in the archives and with the collected memories taught us that we could ease our minority stress by engaging in the struggles of our people and telling their stories from our point of view. We had decided that this was a valid way of 'doing history'. Our work became our witnessing, our reckoning – and it would be powered by the tradition of protest.

'There was strength pulled from each other,' said Diana, of the Lesbian Strength Marches of the 1980s, later the Dyke Marches. These protests were a crucial way for queer women to feel seen on their own terms, she said, and we loved that idea. 'We had our banners, our huge labrys [double-headed axe],' Diana said,

> and we'd shout, scream, beat drums, sing . . . It was a tremendous community thing, and that brought women much more together to realise that there weren't two of us – there were hundreds of us. And we weren't quiet, we weren't meek, we weren't kind. We were *fucking powerful*, and we were going to take our space.

5
'PLEASE BE GENTLE'

How we learnt to care for each other and ourselves

21 December 1989 – 6.45 a.m.
I have just finished a call with a 19-year-old man who has been diagnosed HIV+. His lover hit him and walked out. He is full of self-loathing and can see no point in living. He eventually went off to sleep and I got him to promise to ring back in the next 2 or 3 days to let me know how he is. Please take any message and, of course, be nice to him.

This caller was desperate for someone to care about him. He is one of thousands who phoned Switchboard in crisis during the HIV epidemic in the 1980s. The log books are filled with their desperate cries for help.

In our little coastal towns, we had no idea what was going on. We were just a few years old, and we lived with families that fitted the accepted type in Thatcher's Britain: a married and monogamous heterosexual couple with salaries, a mortgage, a car and two children. Like every residential address in the country, in 1987 each of our cosy family homes received an information leaflet printed with the stark acronym AIDS. The leaflet explained what the disease was, who it affected, and how to avoid it. When the leaflet arrived on Tash's doormat, their mum picked it up, quickly read through, then put it in the bin. She had children to feed that night.

For us, the 1980s were a time of learning to read and trying our first ice creams. AIDS was not affecting our families. But it was hitting the lives of numerous others in our parents' generation. Men like the one above who called Switchboard were going through hell. The queer elders we would come to meet and become friends with later in life – Richard, Julian, Lisa, Femi, Ruth, Diana, and so many more – were suffering. The queer family we would later come to join was under siege.

The story of how HIV tore through the LGBTQ+ community has been told many times. Before we read the log books, we learnt about HIV through films, television, exhibitions, photographs, books, plays – many of them famous. They chronicled how the virus left countless bodies defenceless against illnesses that took away their vitality, their energy, their life. It is a story that starts with young men enjoying their bodies, feeling free, fucking free, and then, at first, one or two dropping away. Night sweats. Purple lesions. Coughs that never stop. This friend, then that one. Hospital visits. Toxic experimental medicines. Dread. Waiting. Rage and protest. Friendships and families torn, sometimes decimated. Then the funerals. So many funerals. Eventually, better drugs, rays of light, weakening virus cells, stronger bodies, time to breathe and time to grieve. These tales are our AIDS memorial, and we must not forget them.

This chapter, however, tells a different story.

As we worked to collect our queer history, we met the people who had survived the HIV epidemic, those spared by the catastrophe. We listened to them speak not only about the horrible days of the past but also how they were faring all these years later. We found ways for their generation and ours to talk about all of this.

We were also reading through Switchboard's log books to learn about how the volunteers had responded to the floods of calls about HIV. We began to see that how Switchboard picked up HIV calls was informed by how the volunteers addressed other challenges too – it was grounded in a deep practice of care.

We also sought to understand how we had been affected by HIV; how despite being at a remove from it, we felt its stain sticking to us.

The clinical psychologist Walt Odets explains in his book *Out of the Shadows* that with regard to HIV we belong to what can be called the middle generation. The first generation are those represented in the log books, people like the caller above, and the survivors we've interviewed. Those people experienced the epidemic first-hand and were exposed to the death, loss, and trauma it caused. Their generation had already felt isolated by growing up at a time when many – probably even most – gay men led secretive, ostracised lives.

Odets, who has spent years talking to members of the LGBTQ+ community, goes on to describe the second, middle generation as those who grew up in the swamp of anxiety and fear about HIV. This rang true for us because, as we were learning about our bodies and sex, we were warned everywhere that HIV would be coming for us. Most of us in this second generation had had no sexual life before AIDS; consequently, we'd seen sex as lethal business. We often feel like survivors of childhood and adolescent trauma.

Odets' third and final generation, the youngest, comprises people who are too young to have been exposed to the early epidemic or to have made the association during childhood between gay men and AIDS. These younger people have known HIV mostly as a liveable condition, and have not experienced the trauma and loss associated with it that the earlier generations have.

As we read the log books, listened to our elders, and read Odets' generational framing, we felt validated to think about how exactly HIV had hit *us*. Our experiences may not have been as overtly horrific as those of our elders, but we had been affected in subtle and insidious ways. The public-health emergency of HIV/AIDS was already burning when a lit match was held to *Jenny Lives with Eric and Martin*. Together they combusted into a blaze of accepted homophobia. The fire spread through politics, the media, and even the classrooms where we spent our days.

Typically when we think of Section 28 we don't think about sex education, but the truth is that the moral panics of HIV/AIDS and *Jenny* combined to educate us about sex in a way that was lacking at best, and dangerously ignorant at worst. So as we learnt about the HIV/AIDS crisis, we began to see, with some surprise, who cared for queer people during our adolescence and who didn't, and how this shaped the poor sex education we received.

As a lesbian who qualified as a teacher in 1988, the height of AIDS and the year Section 28 came in, Ruth Turner felt trapped. 'What could I do?' she asked when Tash interviewed her in 2020. She took her time to remember it all, one arm holding her body. She explained that as her community was being decimated by a virus, Section 28 felt like an extra, human-made blow. 'It legitimated hatred, homophobia, homophobic bullying,' Ruth said, 'and it really impacted on young people's lives.'

One day, Ruth wanted to tell us a story. 'This is an important memory,' she said, 'I can remember it as if it was yesterday.' At school one afternoon, in a school that could have been ours, Ruth had found herself in a conversation about the pastoral curriculum with the head of personal, social and health education. Ruth asked the senior colleague if they should teach the children about HIV/AIDS and same-sex relationships, but her fellow teacher firmly said no. 'I remember her, as clear as day, turning to me and saying, "We can't do that, Ruth, because it's against the law."'

Ruth's heart sank. 'What could I say?' she said to herself years later, each word spoken slowly, as if weighing her down. She knew that she had been silenced. Barely concealing her long-held anger, Ruth said that her colleague's position 'went against everything that we should have stood for as teachers'.

Section 28 confused a generation of teachers about exactly what they could lawfully say about homosexuality and, with it, HIV. Many were probably relieved to sidestep the sticky issue. Others, like Ruth, wanted to respect young people like us, and trust us with knowledge about our own health. In fact, they were blocked from giving us this basic level of care.

Decades later, we could finally speak to our elders and read Switchboard's log books. We could discover how HIV had affected us, as the children who were cradled in the crisis.

———

Like any crisis, and in fact any pandemic, HIV/AIDS blew the lid off society, revealing horrendous truths about how people treat each other. Sometimes these revelations were public: in 1985, the *Sun* newspaper ran a story under the headline 'I'D SHOOT MY SON IF HE HAD AIDS, SAYS VICAR'.[1] You might wonder why that vicar was so cruel, and you might also ask the same of the journalist who wrote the story, and the editors and subeditor who added the headline and printed it. These kinds of careless public actions were ten-a-penny in the eighties and nineties. But often dark truths were intensely private, and we can only know of them through people's memories and unique archives like the log books. On calls to Switchboard, queer folks could offer their true selves. Candid and troubling entries from the log books gave us a uniquely honest perspective on what our elders went through:

3 August 1992 – 0525hrs
A 43-year-old man phoned. Was very drunk. HIV+ and has had PCP [an AIDS-related illness]. his boyfriend walked out on him recently. Although he says he didn't care as he was stealing from him. Was fostered as a child and abused by both foster parents. Wants to remain positive in his attitude and 'stay alive'. Spoke to him for ½ hour, when he said he was going to bed.

This is the kind of log book entry that piled up in our research into the theme of HIV, and meant we needed to take the work slowly, to take care of ourselves. It's difficult to read about this caller's experiences and know that at the time the state was against 'pretended family relationships'. That phrase in Section 28 was talking about the partnership between that caller and his boyfriend – a boyfriend who couldn't support the caller and had been stealing from him. Bigots believed all gay relationships to be this dysfunctional and destructive. In fact, relationships between LGBTQ+ people are no more likely to collapse, nor to involve crime, than those between straight people. The log book entry above also shows that straight relationships are on the hook too, in the horrific childhood treatment the caller endured at the hands of a couple who were supposed to be caring for him. It is a tragedy that he suffered so much, was let down by so many, and then became sick in a way that tarred him. His only hope was Switchboard: however brief, however anonymous, his call may have felt like a true family relationship based on care.

Whether or not we want a conventional relationship, we all want to be loved. Our research into the story of HIV, through the calls made to Switchboard and through our interviews, has uncovered countless stories of love. One of them is that of Richard Desmond, Switchboard's resident leather queen and the teenager who sued the UK government over the unequal age of consent. Richard met a man named Bob in 1982. 'Bob and I were born nine days apart,' he told Tash in an interview in 2020. 'Two ordinary working-class families, his mum liked a drink, my dad liked a drink. We were just in love in a way that only teenagers can be.'

The young couple moved into their first flat with a single bed and some second-hand furniture given to them by relatives. 'It wasn't perfect,' Richard remembered. 'We weren't without problems, is one way of putting it. But it taught me that I was capable of being loved and it taught me about being in relationships.' One foundation stone that Bob laid for Richard was that it was better to be honest all the time, even when it was uncomfortable. 'If I am able to sustain relationships, and I think I proved that, it's because of the lesson Bob taught me.'

Richard and Bob had started the kind of relationship that was later described in law as false. Supposedly it was a truth that gay relationships like Richard and Bob's were unnatural, unbalanced, and weak. And yet their relationship was iron-strong when disaster struck. 'I'd had friends who had become ill, you know,' Richard remembered, as Tash watched his eyes drift off for a moment at the memory. 'It is difficult to remember how gaunt men looked.'

Richard was at work in a record shop in 1985 when he got the call. '[Bob] phoned the shop to tell me that he tested positive, and I thought, "Well that's me done as well."' When Richard did indeed test positive for HIV, he and Bob went through it together, with support from a psychologist. Bob accepted the experimental treatment AZT, which was known to have horrendous side effects but at the time was pitched as the only drug that had the chance of curbing the virus. AZT didn't work, and in Bob it caused anaemia, which led to a stroke. 'It wasn't HIV that killed him,' said Richard.

Tash was used to seeing Richard stand up in big Switchboard meetings and hold forth in discussions about how things should be run. After decades of experience handling calls, Richard always had good ideas, and while Tash was a trustee, they learnt to listen to him in those meetings. Here, however, at home on his soft leather sofa, sitting among his artworks and photographs, Richard was slower to speak, softer. He was more used to listening to stories than telling his own. Bob's picture hung on the wall looking into the room at Richard. 'We were together for nine years and nine months. And he's been dead twenty-seven years this year.'

By the time Tash interviewed him, Richard was living with undetectable traces of HIV in his body, surrounded by evidence of a life well lived. His HIV status of 'undetectable' meant his life expectancy was the same as it would be if he were HIV negative (also, that the virus could not transmit from him to anyone else). Richard had survived the years after Bob died, carrying the grief of losing his partner and many friends. He was a member of the generation of queer people that was decimated by HIV, and also of the smaller group of people who, thanks to drugs, care, and good fortune, survived. He'd come back from the war so he could tell Tash about it. This is how it struck Tash that a huge part of our history project was to collect stories like Richard's, to help those of younger generations understand what he'd been through, but also to shed light on what it meant for us. To draw one lesson from his experience, Richard and Bob's model of reaching out for help when needed, the intervention of the psychologist who supported them, cannot be understated. Many survivors told us that their counsellors and therapists saved their lives in ways that the medicines alone would not have.

Unfortunately, this caller's therapist didn't know how to give the care he needed:

'PLEASE BE GENTLE'

22 October 1985

A caller from a northern clinic reports that his doctor has given him no information at all on the result of his test being positive. He was asked to go to a psychotherapist who gave him a leaflet (from St Stephens) but has only offered to introduce him to somebody else in the town who has AIDS and has come home to die. He is totally depressed, has cancelled his hospital appointments and is still ignorant as to what it means and what he can do. Can others log here their calls that show the general incompetence of the medical profession? It might be useful anecdotal evidence later on.

The sad fact is that during the HIV/AIDS crisis, while some mental health professionals were able and willing to care for those affected, many were not. This pattern was reflected in the healthcare system, too, and while many medical staff worked hard to understand what was happening, to take care of people, there are plenty of log book entries that show this was not always so. Richard and Bob received some good mental health care when they were diagnosed, and they had each other for mutual support as they lived with the virus, but once Bob was gone, Richard needed new care. Twelve weeks after Bob passed away, one night at three in the morning, Richard found himself nearly unable to cope alone with his grief. He called Switchboard. The volunteer sat with him on the line, listened, and consoled him. 'I was blubbing my eyes out and talking about Bob and she said, "You know, it's only twelve weeks, that's not long."'

In their nine years and nine months as boyfriends, Richard hadn't been apart from Bob for more than a few days. Those twelve weeks since losing him felt like the end of the world. The volunteer who helped to give Richard some perspective was Diana

James. Richard didn't know, but she was very familiar with the grief caused by HIV/AIDS. As well as volunteering at Switchboard, she also helped at the London Lighthouse, a centre and hospice for people with HIV/AIDS. She worked tirelessly to care for people like Richard and Bob, helping them to live. 'And she was right,' said Richard, 'we did move on, and all these years on, I can see it made perfect sense.'

Calls like these were never easy. Imagine picking up the phone in the dead of night and facing a desperate caller, smothered in grief and hopelessness, and all you can do is talk and listen. Day after day the phones rang. One caller might need something simple like an explanation of safer sex; the next might have been turned down for a flat due to their HIV status; another might be bereaved like Richard, and contemplating suicide. Many of the volunteers themselves were also testing positive for HIV, getting sick, or worse.

The toll that this took on the volunteer family was immense, and they had to care for each other, too. 'They would come in to do their shift but you would make sure you kept time in that shift to talk to them,' Diana said to Tash decades later. 'Are they not as deserving [of] the care and consideration you would give someone who called? . . . A lot of us did that, and it was a lot of the women in Switchboard who were into helping the guys.' This is a point that is often forgotten, across all the decades of books, television, and films about life with HIV: many women, many lesbians, cared for the men who became poorly, the men who died, and the men who grieved them.

One of those men was Richard, who had joined Switchboard at sixteen but then left because he was too young. Shortly after his call with Diana, he rejoined Switchboard as a volunteer. When Diana told this story to Tash, she smiled and said, 'We're still friends now . . . we know each other from a different level; when you've been through something like that with someone, it takes your knowledge of that person and how you feel about them to a different level.' This was the kind of relationship we were forging with each other and our elders, too, through our research, through listening with care. Tash had known Richard for years as a fellow volunteer, but as a middle-generation queer person who hadn't directly experienced HIV, Tash was still finding their way into the history that Richard had endured. Although we both spoke about this a lot during our work, we still found it hard to imagine the strain of it all. It must have been intensely difficult to balance the self-care with the flood of suffering in the community:

> 1 December 1985
>
> A West Indian caller phoned with STD problem. He had visited Praed Street [clinic] for treatment, where the nurses were hostile and were bandering on about HTLVIII [HIV] and the doctor told him to 'Go back to Africa'. He was obviously very distraught as he is a dancer and relies on his fitness for his income, and this problem has been going on for 1½ months and three visits to various clinics. Does anyone know of any other incidences of this kind of racial abuse at this or any other STD clinic?
>
> [Undated] 1986
>
> Call from distressed 39-year-old who had a tough time at the UCH Dental Hospital. He told them he was gay but only with his partner for 5+ years. Student referred registrar who said he must have HIV test and that student would not treat him whatever the result. So remember: at the dentist lie through your teeth – back into the closet!

7 March 1987

Caller Patrick from York had an antibody positive test with no counselling at all. Had his lover Martin die of AIDS three weeks ago, wouldn't talk to me but knows my name, called at 4:13am on 8 March, hence the incoherent scribble. He could call back at any time. Please be gentle, he's scared stupid.

Among the volunteers' stories chronicled in the log books, the story of a volunteer named Steve is the most prominent. The thing we noticed about Steve was the care he showed for himself. Steve was fighting a war on three fronts: a homophobic society, a repressive government, and a virus inside his own blood. Part of our research method was to take photos of log book entries that we thought would be useful, initially for the podcast. Later we would batch these photos together into themes; HIV was such a big theme that it needed lots of subcategories. On one page from a log book, Adam saw an anonymous note written by one volunteer to the others. Adam took a photo of it as we wanted to know about volunteers' own experiences of HIV, too, without knowing what was yet to come from Steve's story.

In his note, dated 3 February 1987, Steve explained that he had been taking calls in the Switchboard phone room since 1979. At the time of writing the note, he had just recently received a diagnosis of being HIV positive. Here's his anonymous, typed message:

> I'm doing all the right things – phoning Body Positive, seeing the health advisor at the clinic, and so on. The one thing I really want to do right now, I can't, that's to talk to other antibody positive people at Switchboard. The reason I can't is that I don't know who you are.
>
> . . .
>
> How does being AB+ affect the way you see Switchboard?
> How does it affect your phone work?

'PLEASE BE GENTLE'

. . .
I think we've got to do something (And yes, this is my way of dealing with the news)
Please drop me a line c/o Lottie: how can we help ourselves? How can we help if one of us becomes ill?

. . .
Hope to hear from you soon,
Love,
Sorry – no name yet!

Steve was so upset about his diagnosis that he couldn't even reveal it to his comrades at the helpline, apart from Lottie who agreed to receive messages on his behalf and pass them to him.

A little later, Adam found another note from Steve. He'd placed another volunteer notice in the log book, written in thick pink highlighter: 'Can we talk?' Steve's note indicated that he was trying again, suggesting a small group for fellow volunteers who wanted to discuss their feelings about AIDS and dying. Adam read Steve's sign-off – 'Ideas, offers, help, solidarity please, Steve' – and wished he could have reached out, back through the decades.

The only thing Adam could do was notice how these two entries were connected, coming from the same person, and begin to track them as such. Dozens of other entries separated them, written in different hands and inks, but Steve's stood out. They revealed a raw pain, still as acute as the day they were written down. As Adam continued going through the log books, he could only hope that Steve's handwriting would show up again, whether under his own name or via Lottie, the woman who was supporting him. We couldn't trace Lottie, but we knew from Diana and others just how crucial women had been in the response to HIV/AIDS, and how their role had been overlooked.

'I think people thought at first that we were untouched by the AIDS crisis,' Femi said of women, speaking to Tash at the beginning of 2024. Femi shared with Tash how Black lesbians formed networks to take care of each other through the HIV/AIDS era. 'People forget that Black women are just as likely to be involved as having been prostituted, or in bisexual relationships, so we had to find our own way around that too.'

This work included the founding of a lesbian sexual health clinic at the Ambrose King Centre, Royal London Hospital in Whitechapel in east London. The clinic, named after the Black lesbian writer and activist Audre Lorde, was dedicated to lesbians, just as an earlier one had been at the Charing Cross Hospital. Femi also was involved in Zamimass, a collective of radical Black lesbians who organised conferences focused on political consciousness – including how to take care of each other and good sexual health and wellbeing. 'I was doing the lesbian sex and sexual practice workshop and giving out free dildos for women to try,' she told Tash and started to laugh, 'which is really funny 'cause I'd never used a dildo in my life . . . I'm sure I was holding some of the things the wrong way round.'

Even if the dildos were upside down, where else could Black lesbians speak to others like them? This is the point about care in the LGBTQ+ communities: we have to do it ourselves, around kitchen tables or in public meetings we organise. Volunteers like Femi and Diana, Steve and Lottie have shown us this time and again, as have the log books. This level of care stands in stark contrast to the kind of staid and incomplete information that we received at school and at home around the same time period. In fact, Section 28 introduced confusion about whether teachers like Ruth could mention the connection between HIV and gay sex – all because many parents didn't want their children to know about the facts of life. One of the lesser-discussed subsections of Section 28 stated that the prohibition on local authorities promoting homosexuality should not in turn prohibit doing anything to prevent the spread of disease. In order to tackle sexually transmitted infections, especially HIV in the 1980s, you had to talk about gay sex. But teachers were banned from talking about that, by the spirit and the letter of Section 28, and the broader position in public policy that homosexuality was immoral. Censorship, it would seem, is never neat, never sensible.

Many parents uncaringly withdrew their children from any sex education (a right that ended in 2020), but this only led to students asking ignorant questions. During our research Adam interviewed his teacher from Year 6, Mrs Herrick, about the first time he received sex education. She remembered the children whose parents had withdrawn them from the classes and who ended up clueless. 'The questions were unbelievable,' said Mrs Herrick, all those years later. 'I remember one boy saying, "Do boys have periods?" . . . And I always tried to think that, you know, if one boy was asking that there'd be several others who were [thinking] exactly the same thing.'

Mrs Herrick was as jovial as Adam remembered. She was open, intrigued by his questions, and willing to cast her mind back to the middle of her career when she taught a boisterous Year 6 class at Reynolds Junior School in Cleethorpes. Adam could vaguely remember a special lesson when a TV stand was wheeled into the classroom so the children could watch a videotape. This video, Mrs Herrick told him years later, was from a pack of sex education resources made by Channel 4. Adam remembered the cartoon naked people (a man and a woman), but not the fact that in a big family party scene, two women were implied to be in a relationship. Mrs Herrick explained that the treatment seemed so vague as to go over the children's heads.

Addressing questions from Adam's classmates, she remembered, meant having to walk a thin line between giving answers that acknowledged the fact of gay people without 'promoting' their sexuality. 'We answered appropriately,' said Mrs Herrick, recalling the vague terminology that kept her on the right side of public policy. 'Yes,' she'd say if asked about gay couples, 'that is something that happens.' She knew that her pupils wanted to know. 'The questions were there in their minds.'

Mrs Herrick had good cover in the era of Section 28, not only because she was smart enough with words, but also because she was straight. Gay and lesbian teachers found it much more challenging, for several reasons. 'I've never had sex with a woman, so I know nothing about it,' said Tony, a male teacher who taught girls and boys in the 1990s. 'The female member of staff was a lesbian, and I was gay!' Tony and his lesbian colleague managed to put on a straight face and teach their lessons, leading to another challenge: the material itself. When Adam sat down with Tony and his partner Pete, who was also a teacher during the period we were at school, he asked them what they were teaching in the same era that we both received our sex education.

'It was horrific,' remembered Pete, explaining that the intention was to deter the young people from having sex. Pete had to play a video about sexually transmitted infections, which scared students when it could have cared for them. They discussed the way penises fit into vaginas during sex, and how babies are made, but nothing else. 'It should be taught in a context of relationships and values,' said Tony, still sounding disappointed that it wasn't, 'not as a mechanical or medical thing.'

At home, they had their own relationship, a type that couldn't be taught at school. Tony described this period as living under a 'blanket of silence'. Seeing Tony's enduring anger and Pete's sadness, Adam wondered about the male teachers in his own school, whether any of those had been gay like Tony and Pete, and whether they felt stymied in exercising their duty of care. Knowledgeable teachers like Tony and Pete (and Tony's lesbian colleague) could have taken care to give Adam the lessons on gay sex and gay relationships that he couldn't get at home. Tash saw the same chasm when listening to Ruth talk about her struggle as a teacher having to live a lie, especially among canny teenagers. 'You have to be authentic because teenagers see right through you,' Ruth said.

As Tash listened to Ruth, something tripped in their heart. Just at the moment when teenagers like Tash and Adam needed role models like Tony, Pete, and Ruth, role models who could manifest a true duty of care towards them, a repressive state forced them into being someone else. Ruth continued, 'I never truly felt I was authentic, I never truly felt that I took my whole self to school because I couldn't be 100 per cent who I was.'

Tash felt similarly, as captured in their teenage diary. 'I just don't know how long I can go on like this for, I'm just so tired all the time,' they wrote. Listening to Ruth, Tash couldn't help but think about what happened when they'd tried to talk to their own teachers about being queer. When Tash was in Year 9 a new PE teacher joined the school. Tash became convinced this teacher, Miss Morgan, who also became Tash's hockey coach, was gay. Tash joined in with the other students' homophobic joshing against this woman and added to the gossip that she was in a relationship with Miss Smith the history teacher. Tash may have unconsciously needed some kind of connection with these women, but instead of broaching this they were overcome with an attack of teenage bravado. 'You two are gay, right?' Tash blurted to them both. 'Like me?' Miss Morgan could not have answered more quickly. 'Absolutely not!' she said with the full force of a door slamming. Her denial was too loaded; Tash later learnt that the teachers were gay. But at the time, it was impossible to know, and impossible for Tash to process any of this. Instead they were left with a gulf where a connection could have formed, bridging them to their future.

Ruth could have been that teacher. 'It was rotten that I wasn't able to be a strong lesbian role model that I would have wanted to be. I was very personally and professionally conflicted.' Ruth furrowed her brow. 'I don't know whether I helped them enough, maybe just being there, with my short hair and my big earrings and my grey polo shirt. Maybe that was enough. But I feel like I could have done so much more. I could have been so much more helpful.'

Tash had carried decades of anger, hurt, and confusion towards the teachers who had seemed to not care about them, but this conversation with Ruth began to ease that pain. As we both dug into our own histories, we came to understand what the queer teachers must have gone through during the period of our education: the stigma, the fear, the ignorance. 'I think it's quite buried,' Ruth said, bowing her head. 'I think it's quite traumatic.'

We wondered if the conversations we had with folks like Ruth and Richard could help them at all. Although Tash was trained as a listening volunteer at Switchboard and we felt a duty of care towards the people we interviewed, we did not approach them with a counselling framework in mind. But the more that people chose to open up to us, the more we gave them space to reflect, the more we connected across the generations, the more our shared burdens were laid down. Finally, we were caring for each other.

During the HIV crisis, Switchboard could only do so much. Volunteers routinely had to refer callers to lawyers, social workers, charities, and the right clinic or department in the National Health Service. We wanted to hear their stories too, so we spoke to Leigh Chislett, a nurse who started his career as the HIV epidemic was taking hold, just before the virus itself was identified. 'I was this jolly nurse who was always joking,' he told Adam. Leigh's work changed him. In the few years that Adam has known Leigh, he has had a lightness to him, a good sense of humour, and smiling eyes. But underneath all this there was a seething rage born out of how he saw HIV/AIDS patients being treated, and the years and years of working through their pain.

One day on a surgical ward, Leigh remembered, news had spread that one of the patients had AIDS. 'I remember that the relatives [of others] were coming and saying they wanted their families moved. They said they . . . didn't want their families near "anything like that", or with somebody with AIDS. Part of it was fear, part of it was hate. And I remember getting really, really angry during the shift.' He caught others' relatives peeping through a door window at the AIDS patient. 'It was just ghastly,' he said. 'Demeaning and dehumanising.'

Noticing that he had been unusually quiet that day, the ward sister asked Leigh if he was okay. 'I said, "You've just treated that man like an animal in the zoo." I just said, "I've never been so ashamed to be a nurse, let alone a human being."'

On another day, an HIV+ patient offered Leigh some samosas, which he gladly took, and they ate together. 'He suddenly got quite emotional,' said Leigh, 'you know when you can see somebody is trying to fight back the tears.' As the patient sobbed, Leigh panicked that he had done something wrong, but eventually the reason behind the patient's reaction became clear to him. 'He'd felt so isolated, like a leper,' remembered Leigh.[2] Even though he was a nurse, the greatest care that Leigh could show this patient was to accept food from him. To Leigh it was just a samosa, but to the man living with HIV it was a moment of shared humanity. Patients were desperate for connections like this, and called Switchboard for help in finding them:

> 11 September 1985
>
> A caller reports that a man dying of AIDS in St Stephens Hospital would like someone to come and read for him, since he has had no success in finding a Talking Book Service despite numbers supplied by Switchboard and THT [Terrence Higgins Trust]. If anybody knows of any reliable service, or better still, people who would be willing to give a little time to read to him, they can contact the hospital direct, explaining that they are from Switchboard.

Leigh continued looking after people like the man in St Stephen's, spending the rest of his career in HIV and sexual health. He later helped to establish the clinics in Dean Street in Soho, London, which pioneered an inclusive, affirming, and sex-positive form of care. Adam interviewed him in a room in that clinic, in 2020, during the Covid-19 pandemic. They stayed a few metres apart. This is how we spoke to several interviewees during that time. It was a scary time anyway, and it was particularly surreal to be producing a piece of work about one virus that ripped us apart at the same time as having to take precautions against another one doing something similar. Adam left Leigh's office after the interview full of stories, and with Leigh's laugh echoing in his ears, but also with a sense of doom – the streets of Soho were quiet, ghostly. Here we all were again, in the grip of another pandemic.

'PLEASE BE GENTLE'

Leigh had given Adam one more thing: the contact details of an extraordinary man. 'I'm looking for a long-term survivor of HIV,' Adam had said. 'Someone who can tell me what it was like to get diagnosed at the height of the crisis, to live through it, and still be with us today.' Leigh's eyes had lit up. 'George,' he said, immediately.

George Hodson became one of our most important contributors, and a queer elder to both of us. Adam spoke to George on the phone to arrange the interview, noting down his request to arrive with a box of Mr Kipling's pink French Fancies. A few days later Adam descended the stairs to George's basement flat with the cakes, his recorder, and a list of questions. George made himself comfortable, reclining on his sofa as Adam set up a mic close to him.

'Hello, my name is George Hodson,' he said softly, with his three bronze Brussels Griffons wriggling all over him. 'I'm a seventy-one-year-old, out, proud, fairy queer who's lived with HIV, and been blessed to survive, for thirty-five years.'

George unfolded his own story for Adam with control, replete with perfect adjectives and thoughtful structure – not how people usually speak. We later discovered just how much George had prepared, writing and rewriting his stories in dozens of notebooks over the years, waiting for his moment to tell his tale. Most of the usual way that the story of HIV is told covers the people who died from it, and those who cared for them. This is also what we knew of HIV before making the podcast. Medicines had come to suppress the virus, and a prophylactic therapy called PrEP had come to make it impossible to be infected, changing the sex lives of our generation and the younger one. We were not prepared for George's story, not prepared to place ourselves in the shoes of someone who was, at the time we met him, an elderly gay man living alone, still with the virus inside him, struggling to cope with ill-health and debilitating disabilities – having survived, only to be forgotten. He was living with a stoma, making regular hospital visits, suffering confusing changes to the state benefits he relied on, and encountering teenagers on the bus who were visibly disgusted by the 'old man' who sat next to them. They could never have known that he'd already been through hell.

'It was really like a personal tsunami, you know,' George said of his HIV diagnosis, 'being told you were going to die. I don't think you can really have a worse sentence put to you in your life. And then watching your lover, your friends, all die, and just sitting there like a ticking time bomb waiting for your turn to come . . . and it didn't come.'

Although raised in the UK, George was living in Thailand with his partner Sam in 1985 when he found a lump in his belly. 'A doctor told me it was just a cyst or something like that . . . Sam said it didn't look right. We'd done enough reading and visualisation to know what it could be.' He flew to London to see HIV/AIDS specialists, and sure enough they gave him the news that changed the course of his life. George had a beautiful life in Thailand, living in a four-hundred-year-old wooden house, with a well-paid job, a partner, and an orchid garden. Within a week, all that came to an end. He was quickly taken sick, and found himself in the Middlesex Hospital, on the Broderip Ward for AIDS patients. 'The man who was next to me died in the night. I had no friends left in London because I'd been away for so long. I had no money, no job, and no Sam. I was diagnosed with a non-Hodgkins lymphoma, a cancer that is AIDS-defining. It was to be my first cancer.'

George and Sam, who was Thai, were half a world apart. They were desperate to find a way to be together so that Sam could take care of his partner. George had good medical care from the NHS, but he needed support at home during his cancer treatment. They applied to the Home Office for a visa for Sam, but it was refused. 'The lawyer explained to me that because he was from Thailand, officials feared that he was coming with the intention of being a prostitute,' remembered George, barely concealing his enduring rage. 'Knowing that institutions like the Home Office could be so cruel pushed me to one of my darkest places.'

The British state refused to see Sam for who he was: a gay man who made his living teaching deaf children, wanting to take care of his sick partner.

After an intervention from Chris Smith, MP, the Home Office conceded – with conditions. Sam could come, but could neither work nor receive benefits. He and George would have to live on the £34 a week George received from the state. 'Having him hold me at night meant more than money, but still he wanted to work, to earn, to take care of me. He'd been seen as someone who was playing the system, using me to get his papers, and this really undermined his belief in himself.'

Without the dignity of work, Sam did not thrive in London. He, too, was living with HIV. When he and George were both offered AZT, George said no but Sam said yes. As George vividly remembered, Sam 'shrivelled and shrunk' and died within six months. 'I'd seen so many people die but, of course, to see your grand passion die in agony and degradation, as so many of us did in the bad days, was awful.'

Somehow George managed to tell Adam the story of losing Sam. His words landed like pearls, as he spoke with compassion and love amid the pain. It was hard to listen to, much like a Switchboard call. Having never lost a partner, Adam could barely imagine George's suffering. It was never comfortable sitting in the chair and listening to George, never easy to feel the same pain through the stories, never easy to listen despite the love on show. Adam just focused on the French Fancies and getting a good recording. He wondered how George survived Sam's death, then three more cancers himself, then having parts of his own bowels removed, then the Covid pandemic. And George, of course, had an answer: 'I still carry him with me,' he said.

> With this cancer, when I was going through the MRI scan, I visualised and pulled him around me like a kind of suit of armour, if that makes any sense. Those we lost and loved, I still pull them up and bring them to me when I'm in crisis or scared. Those that we love and lose, we don't really lose, they're just our guardian angel . . . so when we need them we can pull their energy and their love and their memories to us, to stabilise us, to strengthen us, to give us equilibrium, to love us still, and to remind us that we need to love ourselves as well.[3]

George died alone at home in May 2023, but we remained connected to him. We carry him within us, just as he carried Sam.

―――

When George told Adam his story over the box of little pink cakes, it felt like a catharsis – for both of them. Just as George had been carrying his grief and developing coping strategies that needed to be shared, Adam had been holding something too. This feeling, which we as members of the middle generation came to identify, was the silent pain of how HIV shaped the world of sex as we came to enter it. We began to see how the laws and guidance around sex education and HIV that came in around the time of the darkest calls to Switchboard, just before we came of an age to need good information, seemed designed to perpetuate the suffering of people like Richard and George into the next generation – ours. Regardless of our gender, HIV was weaponised against the queer sex we wanted.

Tash was turned away by teachers from talking about feelings like this one, which they wrote about in their diary instead:

> I'm unbelievably confused. Argh why is it all like this? I think I fancy her, yeah I do. Oh, I don't know, what is to 'fancy'?

Through Adam's adolescence and twenties, he avoided talking about HIV/AIDS with his parents or anyone else; he just said, truthfully, that he wasn't having sex. He avoided HIV by avoiding sex. This is exactly what some people wanted gay men like him to do. (When Adam told his parents he was gay, in 2014, they didn't know that medicines could give people living with HIV the same life expectancy as those without. They ignorantly warned Adam about HIV/AIDS, as if it was still the death sentence they'd heard about 1987.)

When we were children, the Viscount Buckmaster had stood in parliament and stirred up a furore over *Jenny Lives With Eric and Martin*, the mounting health crisis of AIDS, and his own conflation of homosexuality, incest, and underage sex. These practices, he claimed, were being taught in schools as acceptable. He proposed legislation demanding that sex education promote 'stable family life'.[4]

Already prior to Section 28 being debated and passed, bigots like Buckmaster and the Conservative government enacted laws with at least the subtext of homophobia. In 1986, as Tash turned one and Adam two, the Education (No 2) Act required schools to ensure that sex education included a focus on morality and family. Given that homosexuality was considered immoral as a matter of public policy (as Switchboard had been told by the Charity

Commission), a focus on 'morality' in sex education was code for mandatory heterosexuality. Five years later, we were in primary school when a draft science curriculum proposed for all state-school students included teaching about the 'ways in which healthy functioning of the human body may be affected by diet, lifestyle, bacteria and viruses (including the Human Immunodeficiency Virus . . .)'. This mention of HIV riled many sexually conservative politicians, even including those in opposition to the Conservative government such as Lord Stallard, a Labour peer, socialist, and, like Tash, Catholic.

In the debate about it in the House of Lords in 1992, Stallard objected to the inclusion of HIV in the science curriculum on the grounds that it would be impossible to talk about HIV without talking about sex – and the legislation on sex education required teachers to place sex education in a moral context. The science curriculum would therefore be incompatible with the law on sex education. 'Morality' is always a concept claimed by those who are sexually conservative, as a synonym for things like having few sexual partners, preserving 'virginity', and abstinence. As we learnt from the log books, there is such a thing as a 'sex-positive morality', based on values about *how* people have sex: do they take care of each other? Does it come with self-love?

It seems to us morally suspect that that even though Stallard said he was 'totally committed to the cause of helping those with AIDS', as a Catholic he also stood against homosexual equality. 'The one thing I cannot come to terms with is the concept that homosexuality must be equated with heterosexuality and that homosexual couples must be equated with married couples,' he said in parliament in 2000.[5]

'PLEASE BE GENTLE'

9 December 1998 – 3.30 p.m.
Had a call from a heterosexual man in Scotland wanting to know whether or not gay/lesbian services in Scotland are being funded by the local authority.
It turned out that he is a born again Christian who did not want local authority money spent on promoting homosexuality.
Spent ½ an hour convincing him that his beliefs are unfounded.
He now accepts that Section 28 is stopping teachers from counselling gay teenagers when they need it.

What was this caller basing his views and attitudes on? His religious morality? Or perhaps what he was hearing in the media and from voices like Stallard in parliament. With these voices in public, how were we ever supposed to get sex education that cared about us?

Other voices went further than limiting sex education, and Switchboard volunteers were listening to them, too. In April 1986 one of them pasted a clipping into the log book from the *Health Service Journal*, a publication covering policy and management in the National Health Service. The clipping was a letter from Alan Challoner, secretary of a community health council in North Wales, who asked fellow health workers: 'shouldn't the homosexual act of intercourse by the anus (from which it would seem the whole debacle has stemmed) be made a criminal act?' Challoner also added a dose of stigma on to bisexual people: 'Finally, the potential eruption to severe epidemic proportions seems possible from the currently underestimated importance of the bisexual carrier.'

This is a classic example of biphobia as it is based on the assumption that bisexual people are having lots of careless sex with all sorts of people, that this is categorically bad, and that specifically bisexual people spread disease. It has always been easier for people like Challoner to target the people they hate rather than a virus or a public health system that isn't doing enough.

Whichever Switchboard volunteer had come across this letter (presumably they were a health worker by day, if they read that journal), they accompanied it with a scribbled provocation in blue ink: 'How about a flood of letters from vols?'

Like Steve's pleas for internal support, this entry and others that were not about callers gave us unique access to the volunteers' mindsets. As we turned the pages of the log books, time and again they presented us with valuable insights. These entries were direct, alive, and of the moment – the diary of an unfolding tragedy.

What Switchboard volunteers may not have known at this time is that the prime minister was being lobbied to do something about HIV/AIDS. Margaret Thatcher's press secretary Bernard Ingham seemed to be coming alive to the government's duty of care when he wrote to the prime minister's political aide David Willetts to say: 'There is certainly a feeling abroad that the government is doing too little, and is not treating the issue with sufficient urgency.' Thatcher met with twenty-four editors of provincial newspapers, and, as Ingham noted, they told her that only a government campaign could counteract the fear-mongering of newspapers like the *Sun*.

Switchboard volunteers, of course, were well aware of tabloid sensationalism:

10 March 1985
Married woman rang – obviously very distressed about AIDS. Had brief affair with a straight man 18 months ago and thinks she's carrying the virus and will pass on to husband. Says press coverage has driven her near to suicide. Managed to persuade

her that she had no reason at all to think she had come into contact with virus. She says she'll stop buying The Sun.

Ingham also argued that the government should not be reticent in talking about HIV/AIDS on the grounds of public taste, citing the fact that the wartime government had run a campaign about venereal disease under a more 'morally repressive climate'. The health secretary proposed to send an information leaflet to every household, but Thatcher was reluctant, partly on the grounds of morality. (Whose morality?! There it is again.) In one handwritten note about the draft of the leaflet, Thatcher wrote: 'Do we have to have the section on risky sex? I should have thought it could do immense harm if young teenagers were to read it.'[6]

Her argument was that if young people hear about how to mitigate risky sex, they will engage in risky sex. It is a dangerous, patronising position: instead of helping people to understand the world and potentially save their lives, it is best to assume they are stupid. It is the assumption against telling children and teenagers about queer people, the same one underpinning Section 28, and the same one held by the right-wing newspapers. It was an attitude that was not only held by those in the Conservative Party:

> 10 March 1992
> Woman called from Harwich to say that the Labour PPC [prospective parliamentary candidate] (who apparently has no chance of winning) called Ralph Knight has made homophobic and AIDS-ignorant remarks to the local press and she is trying to get rid of him.

Knight was never elected to parliament, but he did serve in local government. Even though he was expelled from Labour in 1993 following a local campaign,[7] he was probably just unlucky.

The prevailing view was behind him: people living with HIV/AIDS were immoral, due to homosexuality, and children should be protected from them and 'their' disease. In 1992 the government began circulating a document entitled 'A moral framework for sexual education'.[8] It is clear from this document that, in the name of 'morality', the state was not willing to steer young queer people like us (aged seven and six) away from the possibility of suffering like Richard and George, and numerous Switchboard callers, had. The framework was designed to remind schools that homosexual acts under the age of twenty-one were illegal and that Section 28 prohibited local authorities and therefore schools from promoting homosexuality. (As we have seen, Section 28 said that this shouldn't stop them from talking about ways to curb the spread of disease, but many teachers have told us that the ambiguity of what exactly was permitted speech stopped them from saying anything altogether.) The government note in 1992 said: 'There is no place in any school in any circumstance for teaching which advocates homosexual behaviour, which presents it as the norm, or which encourages homosexual experimentation by pupils.'

It is doubtful that public health specialists or gay rights campaigners were advocating that school pupils should be taught how to experiment with homosexuality. As Adam's teacher Mrs Herrick had shown, there were caring ways to acknowledge gays without sending children into a gay nightclub, though conversely, as Ruth told us, even just touching upon the subject felt fatal. This is how, as we grew up, needing information about our bodies and understanding of our desires, we stepped into an uncaring climate, engendered by sexually conservative values. Fortunately, Switchboard was there to field questions from those who were able to call, pooling and sharing information:

'PLEASE BE GENTLE'

13 June 1985

Does ANYONE know of ANY AIDS literature about/aimed at women having sex with bisexual/gay men?
If so PLEASE CAN SWITCHBOARD HAVE/BORROW IT??

7 October 1975

Just having been cured of gonhorrea(?) the doctor at the clinic advised me that since cases of syphilis in the gay world are rising dramatically all gay men should have check ups once every 6 mths. The main reason for this is that cases **without** symptoms are also rising. All one needs is a blood test.

Other queer people were similarly organised into supporting the LGBTQ+ community. Education policy files from the government of the day in 1992 hold letters from the National Organisation of Lesbian & Gay Youth & Community Workers, Gay Men's Health Project in Southampton and many others; they are held in The National Archives. These organisations all opposed the homophobic sex education guidelines, drawing attention to the higher rates of suicide in younger LGBTQ+ people. They argued that there was no evidence that schools were encouraging young people to be gay; nor were there any grounds to the notion that sexual orientation could be taught. The sex education guidelines had to be changed; our young queer lives depended on it. But we were also in great need of something more – the knowledge of how to build healthy, foundational relationships. How could this happen during a time when our potential relationships were still seen as 'pretended'? (Relationships education was eventually introduced and became part of the statute in 2017, three years after Tash found the log books.)

Each one of those organisations opposing the sex education guidelines in 1992 showed far more care than the government was prepared to, and their letters went largely ignored. It is astonishing that within our living memory the basic level of care, of recognising the existence of queer people during a pandemic, was denied.

During our period of research, however, a new outbreak proved this point yet again. In spring 2022, angry lesions and rashes began to show up on the skin of an alarming number of people. The virus mpox, known then as 'monkeypox', was spreading fast, and it seemed particularly concentrated in men who had sex with other men. This was a pretty terrifying time for men like Adam, especially so soon after the peak of the Covid pandemic. A big sore opened up on Adam's lip, which was characteristic of mpox, so he went to get tested in a special temporary clinic, heart pounding, held at arm's length by a terrified medic in a hazmat suit. (The sore was caused by herpes, not mpox.)

What made the outbreak worse was how the government and the NHS only seemed to respond to the needs of the community when sexual health charities lobbied them intensely enough. While some voices in the media blamed gay promiscuity (again) and the NHS dallied over how much money it could spend on issuing the vaccines it held, Adam watched friends getting sick. He cut off his sex life again. The outbreak was uncanny for us, as two people who were deep into looking into the historical facts of the HIV pandemic. It didn't take a lot for us to be filled with fear about mpox, having witnessed what we had about that earlier health disaster, with knowledge of how the press, public, and politicians had failed us as queer people and stunted our wellbeing and our development.

We knew that as younger people we had always wanted more, and better, information. Tash had tried to speak to a teacher before turning to their diary instead. If Adam views the world in the manner of a perpetual student, it started when he chose GCSE media studies at school. He was fascinated by how the press worked and how films tell a story. Like all teenagers, we'd been interested in the truth. The condition of being a teenager is one of feeling that you're discovering a truth for the first time, and often that it is otherwise being withheld from you by adults. This is why groups catering to teenagers are important, like the London Gay Teenage Group that Richard Desmond attended. Adam didn't have a group like that, but GCSE media studies somehow provided something of a similar space. In 2000, aged fifteen, Adam and his media studies classmates were given an assignment to produce a newspaper. Lessons covered journalism, editing, design, photography, and even management. Adam chose to write quietly about books and arts in the middle pages, but two of his closest friends put themselves forward to cover the big story of the day for the front page:

16 Thursday March 2000
PUPILS GET NEW SEX GUIDELINES
by Sarah Draper and Phillip Randell
David Blunkett, the education secretary, will today announce his plans to abolish section 28; this will require schools to promote 'stable relationships' and 'The importance of marriage.'

The story by Sarah and Phillip went on to explain Blunkett's intention to reform the education system we were all inside without upsetting those who shared Section 28's homophobia. Sarah and Phillip reported Blunkett's motivation of reducing teenage pregnancy (which was its own moral panic at the time), and how the policy would ensure pupils were discouraged from early sexual activity and encouraged to see marriage as a pillar of society.

When Adam dug through his schoolwork in his childhood bedroom and found this newspaper during the research for this book, he froze. Just as we were delving into the anti-gay and anti-sex atmosphere of our adolescence, here was evidence that teenagers close to Adam cared – and they weren't the only ones:

> 25 April 1984 – 2.05 a.m.
> After a fascinating talk with a 15 yr old woman from SE London about the trouble she's had at school as a result of writing a pro-gay project, hearing her stories of the reactionary attitudes of teachers, peers at school she gave me some of her poetry: –
> 'When my time is over and I'm no longer
> this old frump
> I hope the world bury me upside down
> So the world can kiss my rump'

The volunteer added 'she'll go far'; another flagged it as 'This month's star entry'. Adam's school friends Sarah and Phillip, just fifteen and fourteen, were the same age as this caller and knew that this was an important story, and that it was all about *us*.

Three years later, Section 28 would in fact be repealed, but in 2002 it was still blocking fifteen-year-olds:

> 26 October 2002
> Call via Get Connected 15 year old male, school found out was gay & informed parents who are fundamental Christians & now verbally abusing him & making him feel suicidal. Many issues in call, lack of access to support, lack of resources (money etc.) to contact services. School very unsupportive citing Section 28 as barrier to tackling abuse.
> . . .

It's one of the rare times I feel frustrated about our service limitations as I really feel I want to take action.

Monty x

What drove the frustration in Monty, the volunteer who took that call, is the same thing that drove Adam into hiding: the hostility in the air, even in the early 2000s, towards LGBTQ+ people, HIV/AIDS, and sex. But Monty wasn't doing nothing. He was listening and voicing his frustrations. Another word for this is 'courage', which the following teacher and her management team had in abundance:

> 30 May 2002
> A teacher from an all girls school in NE England has managed to convince her management team to ignore Section 28 + install antihomophobia structures + policies in her school! She was looking for speakers to come and to talk to the staff. I gave her numbers of local groups/organisations + helpline etc, but can anyone else suggest other organisations? It would be great if we can help support this excellent bit of progress . . .

This teacher got it. She understood that we yearn for information, even when facing down stigma and prejudice. This can also be seen throughout Switchboard's approach in caring for people. In the mid-1980s, Switchboard scrambled to give the best service to panicked callers and had to make countless decisions on the right way to do this. One of them involved safer sex: it quickly became a policy of Switchboard and a practice of any organisation or agency working in the field of HIV/AIDS to recommend that people use condoms and dental dams to cut risk of transmission. 'There were big arguments about whether condom use and safer sex should be mentioned on every call,' said Nick Partridge, who was a volunteer at Switchboard and went on to work for the Terrence Higgins Trust, a charity that campaigns and provides services relating to HIV and sexual health. When Adam interviewed Nick, he remembered that even if a caller had just wanted to know the opening times of a nightclub, 'We would say on every call, "Remember to take your condoms with you."'

Switchboard went even further than just recommending safer sex on calls. In the mid-eighties, prior to the organisation becoming a registered charity, it was printing advice about HIV and safer sex in gay newspapers – before the government had responded to the growing crisis. Switchboard volunteers also produced little info cards with a distinctive logo featuring two safety pins and a pink triangle, leaving them in bars and clubs. They also turned this logo into badges, which Tash loved so much that they had them recreated for Switchboard's forty-fifth birthday, giving them to many of the people we interviewed for the first season of the podcast. For the first time in its history, Switchboard became more than a helpline; it became a public health campaign, too. Crucially, this work used the language of the people it targeted:

> The AIDS virus is transmitted in blood and cum. Don't put yourself at risk. Don't swallow cum or screw without a condom. Help yourself and help others to stay healthy. Keep fit. Make it fun. Keep it safe.

Other ads used the word 'spunk' and raunchy photos of gay sex; some gay bars refused to stock newspapers with these ads, showing that Thatcher was not the only one who was squeamish. When a new batch of info cards landed at the Switchboard building months before the government's information leaflet eventually landed, a volunteer rallied the helpers via the log book:

'PLEASE BE GENTLE'

21 October 1986

Take some, take lots, give them to your friends, leave them where they'll be seen, leave them where they might be appropriate (or where they might not – use your imagination).

Switchboard's decision to care about our sexual health when others wouldn't, or couldn't, had a huge impact. It educated those most at risk of HIV about a complicated virus in ways that they could understand, making the point that the more people know, the safer we all are; and it even helped to cut rates of other sexually transmitted infections such as gonorrhoea and syphilis. 'That was a reflection of a really big change in sex and sex lives,' said Nick.

---

19 January 1984

Tony Konrath [Switchboard volunteer] has rung in to tell us that Woman's Hour is right now, doing a pretty bad scare piece on AIDS. He's ringing them to complain but it may well lead to some calls over the next few days from women and faggots listening and got the willies. Drat!

The epidemic and the decade rolled on, with further media coverage and vile statements in the press and parliament. In 1987 the government finally took action, doing what Switchboard and others had been doing for years: pooling and sharing information about the public health crisis. The government's dramatic and far-reaching information campaign, using the slogan 'Don't Die of Ignorance', involved sending a leaflet to every household in the country. This is the one Tash's mum discarded; Adam's mum couldn't remember it when we asked her. (The campaign also included ads on TV and in cinemas which depicted a tombstone, a volcanic eruption and a doomsaying voiceover.)

Switchboard's number was printed on that leaflet. As the campaign was rolled out, Switchboard volunteers noticed more and more calls from a particular set: people who were not at risk of HIV, especially monogamous heterosexuals. Volunteers called them 'the worried well', and they were divided on whether they posed a problem. On the one hand, Switchboard was a charity with stretched resources and a mission to serve 'gays and lesbians' (or the LGBTQ+ community, as we now might say). On the other, everyone needed to be vigilant in the case of a public health problem, and some heterosexuals were at risk. These log book entries from 1987 demonstrate the drama:

> 1 March 1987
> What's happening to 'Lesbian and Gay' Switchboard. Half the calls tonight from heterosexuals about AIDS and safer sex . . . there all worried after watching the TV programmes (if I had my way I'd ban them all . . . selective advertising is badly needed I feel).

> 5 March 1987
> I am very concerned about the amount of time that we are spending on AIDS calls from Heterosexual callers.
> Although I can appreciate the difficulty of dealing with this problem on a case by case basis, I think the time has come when we need a general policy decision on how we are going to react to this kind of call, especially since we can safely presume a major increase in them.
> [We need a] careful analysis of the now and future implications to SB on both the nature of our work, our clientele and workload.

In a comment appending the 1 March entry, another volunteer provided the opposing view: 'But look how many gays we've

'PLEASE BE GENTLE'

reached by the door-to-door leaflet too . . . in the long term it will be worth it!'

The reason why this debate was so alive in Switchboard was that the volunteers knew they were doing something greater: they were taking care of a community. This took time, and the calls could run long into the night. How can you be with someone through their pain when you can't hold their hand? You listen. You really listen. You let them breathe, you answer their questions, you speak gently, you listen more, you tell them their feelings are valid, you give them space to breathe, and you tell them they can always call again. You love. You care.

But you also need to keep caring for yourself. We were pleased when fresh words from Steve appeared in the log books. 'My dears,' he wrote in 1987, addressing his fellow volunteers, not just the ones who had attended the internal support group he'd set up to support those living with HIV,

> As most of you know, earlier this year, I was diagnosed HIV antibody positive. At the same time, I ended a relationship of seven years standing. Consequently, I've had to take a long hard look at what I want out of life, and what I don't want.
> One of the things I don't want is telephone work at Lesbian and Gay Switchboard, so I'm off.
> Please understand as well that my employment at National AIDS Helpline is almost totally unrelated with my decision to go. I say 'almost', because I'm writing this letter, OK the draft, only hours after finishing a Body Positive training weekend. The training weekend was the hardest work I've done in a long time, and one of the most rewarding things I've ever done. I hadn't realised how isolated I'd been feeling. On the weekend, many, but by no means all people, were HIV+. The diversity of sexualities is something

else I enjoyed. But above all, the care, respect and love at the weekend have convinced me that the way forward for me is to join Body Positive, and if that means leaving Lesbian and Gay Switchboard, so be it.

Two of the things that have affected me most deeply over the weekend: a pair of role plays that focused on counsellors giving each other support around incipient burnout, a situation we'd both recently been in; [and] a session on bereavement and death. I partnered with someone who'd recently lost a friend, his first bereavement due to AIDS (I've lost count of the number of people I've lost). It all gets too much, and I start crying. I'm in the middle of the room full of people crying, being cuddled by a man I've only just met, knowing it's alright to do that, while the workshop carries on around me.

Later, I realise that most of us did just the same. So, it's definitely a move forward for me, although it hurts to go. You've been at Lesbian and Gay Switchboard for nearly eight years, Steve, what do you expect?

See you around, with love, Steve

Adam had to read the letter several times. Steve's was such a sad story, from his diagnosis and his obvious sorrow at having what felt like a death sentence through to his disappointment at not being able to support others like he'd promised. You can't read entries like these and not wonder: *How would I feel?*

That question is partly why the log books are so useful to historians like us. They bring us all into the story, into the grand sweep of history, and simultaneously down into the minutiae of it all. Through 'characters' like Steve, they have also helped us to access raw feelings, as we experienced them seemingly along with our elders, despite the decades separating us.

'PLEASE BE GENTLE'

Steve sounded so lost, so lonely, and so sad that his life plans had been taken from him by the virus. Still, we were buoyed by the level of self-care Steve showed. He recognised what he was going through, and accepted that he needed to take care of himself. This meant he would have to leave the care of callers to the other volunteers. Steve's resignation took a great deal of courage, of course, but mostly a great deal of care. We discussed his story a lot as we produced our podcast episodes about HIV/AIDS, trying to hold Steve's spirit with us, in the way George earlier described holding Sam close to himself.

There is another type of log book entry that shows how the volunteers cared for each other: the tributes to lost volunteers. Here is one from January 1986, which takes up a full page in the log book. It is written by a volunteer known affectionately as Panda:

> Some volunteers will remember Martin Fright, 'The Bear'. I was devastated to hear last week that he has died of AIDS in Paris on the previous Saturday night. He and I were each other's first gay lovers. We met almost exactly ten years ago in those heady and uncomplicated days of The Gay Liberation, which is why I'm writing this. I feel too, that his work for Switchboard should be remembered . . . He was a volunteer in 1977 and 1978 and threw himself wholeheartedly into work for training group and development group as it was then. I think he was training group coordinator at one point and also press officer and speaker's organiser. Those of us who knew him will remember, and miss his energy, humour and care and intelligence. Certainly, he was responsible for encouraging me to join Switchboard and several others too. He only left because he left the country to live first in Florence and then Paris, pissed off with the looming madness of

Thatcherites in Britain. On the phones and in meetings he was marvellously charming and warm to individuals. He was also good at resisting bureaucracies and oppressive institutions in all walks of life. He had a passionate sense of justice, humorous joie de vivre, and was wonderfully internationalist.

The Bear is one of so many volunteers whom we never got to meet and interview, but thanks to Panda's tribute, we can feel that we have a sense of who he was, and how much he cared for the community he served. When Tash first saw this entry, it made them cry, and they ended up including it in the talk they gave in February 2019 which Adam attended. Long before he got sick, The Bear was one of many people who found it too hard to continue Switchboard's work in the face of Thatcher and her followers. Their infamous lack of community spirit and callous disregard specifically for LGBTQ+ equality sealed his fate long before HIV/AIDS did.

It is not hard to see how the weight of facing down ignorance, caring for callers with such limited resources, and grieving lost colleagues could crush volunteers. As Steve knew, Switchboard would only face more and more callers, each one stretching its capacity to care. There seemed to be no end to the discrimination that people living with HIV had to endure:

21 July 1988
Beware. Caller reports that Northampton Special clinic advised him to tell his employer (!) he was HIV +ve. He is now **sacked** and moreover **homeless** as the info was passed on! What can I say? Aaagh!

'PLEASE BE GENTLE'

23 August 1988

Mattia in Brent area getting shit off employed for being gay and HIV+. No joy from negotiations between Frontliners / THT and NALGO [National and Local Government Officers] / employers. Gave solicitor, NALGAY, etc. But if he calls again please give him anything else eg GLAD [Gay Legal Advice], as situation seems appalling. (English not first language.)

19 January 1992

Caller got cut off during call, he has been thrown out of his accommodation because he is HIV+ and was asking about legal rights, I went to get Legal File and when I came back he was gone.

As the 1990s rolled on, the combination of safer sex and better medicines cut the crisis of HIV. This welcome shift did not end the discrimination and stigma that people living with HIV have faced, though it did drastically change their life chances. More and more people lived longer, and the levels of HIV in them reached 'undetectable' status. Meanwhile, the number of calls on the subject of gender identity began to grow. People facing this issue had called Switchboard since day one, but something began to shift in the nineties and early 2000s. New terms and definitions emerged, plus new services, and new claims on rights and healthcare.

9 July 1994

Very long and disturbing call from Sandra, a T/S, tonight: over two hours long. She phoned on Friday night and has since left a message with a woman's abuse centre who did not get back to her. They won't accept her as a woman. She has been abused many times by various people throughout life. Both physically and sexually. No one seems to want to know. Neither Beaumont Society, the Phoenix Centre, or the Gender Dysphoria Trust have been of any help. She feels that we are the **only** people who have listened and **accepted** her.

Not surprisingly, she feels suicidal and sometimes 'cuts' herself.

I gave her some more telephone numbers and encouraged her to call back if necessary. And I believe she will.

She has no friends, and she doesn't trust people easily. And has little, if any, experience of love.

3 September 1994

Sandra phoned again. Things seem to have gone from bad to worse. Charing Cross will not go ahead with treatment because of her depression and anger. Also she has had her disabled allowance stopped. She had taken 4 of her 'hormone' tablets before phoning which were making her feel sick and achey.

She would not let me phone for an ambulance for her. Long periods of silence during the call with her crying on the other end of the phone and me feeling completely unable to help and useless.

Here, another volunteer has added: 'You are not useless, you're fab!'

When we looked back on these entries, we found that we could draw a line between them and those entries about HIV+ callers who needed care. (And some of the callers were trans *and* HIV+.) They all needed a Switchboard volunteer to listen to them, to know that it was worth them continuing to fight the stigma and discrimination they faced.

As we researched this book and looked back through our history, we had to address the lack of care that our elders had experienced. One of the ways that ignorance hits trans people especially hard is the way that even supposedly caring professionals sometimes do not simply believe a person who says how they are suffering. It was hard to look back at this from the 2020s without seeing the exact same thing playing out in the present day. It was distressing to us, as we worked on this book in 2023 and 2024, to feel the same level of contempt from the then Conservative government, more than three decades after Thatcher's. Successive Conservative governments up to 2024 had allowed the NHS gender identity service to all but collapse, and had closed the children's service altogether with no replacement. Despite a period of increasing visibility of trans and gender non-conforming people, ignorance reigned. In 2023 Kemi Badenoch, who held the position of minister for women and equalities under prime minister Rishi Sunak, wrote an article for the *Daily Mail* that was filled with straw man arguments against trans equality, and even against care for trans people.[9] In 2024, her colleague the education minister Gillian Keegan published new guidance to limit (once again) school discussions of sex and gender.[10] In July 2024, Labour came to power again. Soon after, the health secretary Wes Streeting blocked medical treatments for trans children, and in 2025 the prime minister Keir Starmer accepted the Supreme Court's landmark decision that would lead to segregation of trans people.

Seeing these news headlines, living through the mpox outbreak of 2022, and learning about HIV history while researching this book, we felt as though we were strapped to a boomerang. Politicians' ignorant, uncaring approach to queer people in the 2020s struck the same tone as the discourse around HIV/AIDS in the eighties and nineties. Often, in the case of right-wing tabloids such as the *Sun*, this ignorance was wilful. Journalists and columnists seemed to want to spread fear and loathing.

This is how we began to see this story through the lens of care; there was such a stark contrast between the care on show in the log books (including self-care) and the level of disregard that people can be capable of, seemingly whatever the time period. In the eighties, this led to scary levels of misinformation; Switchboard volunteers regularly spoke to callers such as this one:

> 2 June 1985
>
> 2 callers reported that a news item stated that THT said that 1 in 5 gay men in London are infected with AIDS and advise men from elsewhere not to have sex with Londoners. This probably totally distorted what THT actually said (I hope) – beware of callers needing reassurance.

Even the BBC came under fire over its handling of the public health emergency:

> 3 April 1984
>
> Man who works at BBC called – outraged at sensationalist and alarmist nature of AIDS programme. Would like us to put in an official complaint, on basis of huge flood of calls we get, etc, especially as he would like to raise a bit of a stink within the BBC, and this would give him strong ammunition. No doubt the BBC will have a fair idea of our feelings towards that programme but something specific in writing always helps. Can someone organise this?

Entries in the log books are so specific that every single one felt like it was telling us the story anew, deepening our breathing and raising our blood pressure. Likewise, every interviewee we spoke to had their own unique stack of memories. So often they felt like mausoleums, and we were walked through them by our elders. In those interviews, our contributors took care of us as much as we thought we were taking care of them, sparing us some details and the full depth of sadness they were still carrying. As we walked through the grief and loss with our elders, it was like we were being bereaved for the first time. It was especially hard – and bizarre – that we spoke to most of our elders on this topic in the midst of the Covid pandemic. Through masks, at a distance, and sometimes through screens, we were all just trying to take care of each other.

However difficult it was for us as the middle generation to collect our elders' experiences, though, we had to channel our feelings into something productive. We had to find the energy to carry their weight. This could be our way of caring for them. It could be our duty. As we busied ourselves ordering Steve's letters to volunteers and assembling Richard's and George's memories into a timeline, we wondered about the long-term survivors of HIV. They were entering old age. Some, like George, were in fact very elderly and frail already. (George himself, as it turned out, was too weak to go on.)

Thinking about their elderly care was another way we had to reach them. George and Richard are two of the countless people who were kept away from us as we were growing up, due to social fear around HIV and homophobic policies that were supposed to 'protect' us children. There were many more who, like George's Sam and Richard's Bob, died before we would even get the chance to grow up and meet them. So many of our elders are dead. Some are living, but too traumatised or ill to participate in projects like *The Log Books*. The conclusion of all this history is that the LGBTQ+ community is often good at care, but we have also failed so many times. As a matter of public policy, and the bad faith of the press and politicians, children like us were failed; and our generation in turn has failed to establish the kind of LGBTQ+-affirming care homes that our elders like George needed. It is hard to bear this, to look back through the log books and hear all these cries for help.

Nevertheless, we had to try. We had to trawl through the archive and all these histories, to try to understand. It's why we were drawn to stories like Steve's. We realised as we were collating his story across several log book entries that it didn't seem to have an end. We took a breath, and we started to ask about him. We enquired with our contacts and our interviewees, through the network of former volunteers. Someone said that his surname had changed, from the one he wrote in the log books to Craftman, his own preference. This somehow gave us new impetus, just as Steve had given himself a new lease of life by giving up volunteering.

The year was 2020, and we were making season two of the podcast as Covid raged outside. This is when we found Steve, a long-term HIV survivor, alone at home in South Wales. 'I don't half miss physical intimacy,' he told Tash on a video call, his voice wobbly but resolute. Tash found it hard to keep the conversation going, sobbing a little when Steve said through his computer screen, 'I can accept the fact that I won't meet Mr Right for a third time, but Jesus do I miss a cuddle.'

Steve was reluctant to share – not shy or squeamish, but it was hard for him to return to painful memories. He had left Switchboard as an act of self-care, and had emerged from the 1980s and then the 1990s, building up strength and riding on the miraculous medicines as they came in and started to control and reduce his HIV.

Tash asked him to go back to his wartime memories. He obliged, carefully, slowly, pausing to breathe and sometimes weep. 'Working for Switchboard is probably the most worthwhile thing I've done in my life . . . Switchboard had me for eight years, very important years. Basically, those years at Switchboard set me up for life.'

Thirty-three years had passed since he'd left Switchboard. Each one of those years was a year that he didn't expect he would live.

As each one passed, he still thought about Switchboard and his time as a volunteer caring for our community.

As Steve talked, Tash saw his T-shirt and asked him to describe it for the recording. He did so in a way that showed how Switchboard had set him up not only for life, but to live – proud to care for his fellow humans and for himself. 'Throughout the time I've had HIV, one of the important things to me is to humanise it,' said Steve Craftman. 'It's always important, I think, to put a name and a face on HIV. I'm wearing a T-shirt with the slogan "HIV+ long-term survivor". I do my shopping in that.'

6
'WOULD LIKE TO STAY'

The search for a safe place to call home

11 June 1978
Had a call from a 19-year-old TV who had been thrown out of home this evening by his parents who had just 'discovered'. He'd phoned Samaritans. We had a long chat but he will probably phone back tomorrow for long-term advice. Luckily he seemed reasonably together about his situation and was reconciled to spending a night in his Mini.

The house where Adam lived as a teenager revolved around the kitchen table. The daily newspaper was laid out on it, handwritten notes to family members were left there, and there was a rule that all eating in the house had to happen around it. This included boisterous Friday-night dinners with Adam's elder sister Hannah and her three friends when they were all in sixth form. Adam and Hannah's parents loved inviting 'the girls' over for dinner, with CDs playing in the background and a steaming lasagne on the table mat. A few years younger than these young women, Adam enjoyed them too: confident, smart, funny – a true gang. These dinners, and every family meal – meals that Adam would join at the expense of hanging out with his own friends – beat a rhythm through the house. The big wooden table was the heart of it all.

But this table was also the place where something collapsed, on New Year's Day 2003. Hannah, who was home from university for the winter break, had been forced to tell their parents that she was gay. Mum, Dad, Hannah, and Adam sat around the kitchen table and the conversation turned into what Hannah later described as an interrogation: 'I was made to feel, like, crappy, that I'd done something wrong, that I'd committed a crime.' The parents sat on one side of the table and their children on the other, Adam at eighteen and Hannah at twenty-one. With increasing frustration and resentment, the parents grilled Hannah about her feelings, her sex life, and her alleged lies. They seemed to be more worried about what the neighbours were going to think than about Hannah's wellbeing.

Hannah's dad told her, 'I think you'd better go.' These words committed a loud act of violence against Hannah, and a silent, unknown one against her little brother Adam. A shock ran through Adam as he watched his sister stand, back away from the dinner table and walk out of the house. He ran after Hannah, out into the cold air and down the driveway, but she said she had to go. Just like the nineteen-year-old caller above, Hannah had been thrown out of home by her parents who had just 'discovered'.

The memory was still clear in Hannah's mind twenty years later when she told Tash how she had walked straight to her friend's house. 'I remember knocking on her door and I was sobbing, sobbing, sobbing, so, like, upset. And she was like, "Oh my god, have you told your mum and dad?" And I said, "Yeah." And she said, "OK, come in."'

When the dust settled, their parents set new rules. They would keep Hannah in the family, and she was welcome in the house when visiting. But they didn't want to meet her partner, visit her home, or know anything about her personal life. This ugly arrangement made no sense, but Hannah and Adam accepted it. Family meals around the kitchen table would never be the same again, even if all four of them were there. Adam later realised that Hannah had found her ability to come out to her parents through going to university, finding a new living situation, a new life, and through speaking to her partner's parents. They were all changed after that interrogation. Adam was still housed with his mum and dad, but it was no longer a home.

We both began to remember our own stories of housing: our university halls, flat-shares, couch-surfing, and Tash's career as a boomerang teenaged runaway. Unlike Hannah and Adam, teenaged Tash disappeared from home often. Often they told their parents they were staying with friends but actually snuck out to illegal parties in the forest. They would have lived elsewhere if they could have.

As the log book entries about housing sat between us and we shared our own histories and dreams about how to live, our own stories took on new shapes. Even the one about the night Hannah left began to mean something different to Adam, with Hannah cast less as a victim and more as a role model. We realised that both of us (and Hannah) had grown up in housing that reflected the average in ways that we did not, and did not want to. Our parents came of age in the 1960s and 1970s with the expectation of owning a house simply through working to earn money, and bought their first houses in their twenties. The housing they desired overlapped completely with the orthodox notion of a pair of cisgender heterosexual adults and their biological children. And they made it! This was the best way to live, the right way to live, and it was why little Jenny living with Eric and Martin in the storybook was so destabilising to many straight people. We didn't know about little Jenny; the weirdest housing models we heard about growing up were those of divorced parents who lived in separate houses and, in the case of Tash, Uncle Quentin, who shared a flat with his friends.

Tash thought Quentin's housing sounded odd but was too young to know that he was actually modelling a way to live. Adam had a similar experience without realising it. Since Hannah was unwelcome at the family home, Adam visited her in the house she shared with her girlfriend and two other friends. The four of them lived together in madcap harmony, and Adam loved to watch them. He couldn't get a word in edgeways; he remembers over-eating and falling asleep on the living-room floor. When Tash visited Uncle Quentin in his house-share, everyone seemed so cool, so *free*. Eventually Tash left home for university, and their parents didn't hear from them for months.

Our teenage moments might be clichéd, but they also express a truth that we did not feel at home. Tash's parents never kicked them out, but Tash struggled to feel at home in their house in Plymouth. When Adam left home at eighteen, he knew he would always want to find his own place to live. We each eventually landed in London: Tash instantly moved in with two gay friends, forming a queer household. Adam blocked that possibility from himself, still seven years away from sex and a queer life. He didn't know anyone in London and just needed to find somewhere to live so he could start a job. The flat he moved into was not a home for him; the flatmates were a straight couple with their own lives (and loud arguments), and no one was interested in making the flat a home, or even caring for each other. For many reasons, Adam's sexuality remained locked in his bedroom.

Many LGBTQ+ people live in environments where they don't feel comfortable. Many take themselves away, as Tash did, and many more are kicked out against their will. The pages of the log books are filled with stories like ours, and Hannah's, and many that are far more dramatic, and more life-threatening. They are stories of children made homeless in the dead of night, with no money, nor a coat, nor anywhere to go; of teenagers shaking off homophobic parents only to find themselves in abusive relationships; of queer people desperate to find others like them, to find a way to live together.

———

Long before Switchboard volunteers had to advise callers on how to cope with an HIV diagnosis, they were helping them simply to find a place to stay:

> 26 September 1975
> Carl and his mate would be happy to help any lonely person who comes to London by offering temporary accommodation. They are a long-standing affair. Their interests are boating, travelling, etc. They have a large house. He sounds very pleasant.

> 4 July 1975
> Tony (Switchboard volunteer) phoned, offering crash-pad for TONIGHT ONLY – he can't be contacted on the phone but will be in from 11pm onwards.

Almost as soon as the phone lines were open, Switchboard found itself building a register of gay-friendly accommodation. Volunteers created a service specifically to connect spare rooms to the people who needed them. In 1978, Jonathan Izard was one of those people, a gay man who had just moved to London. 'I wasn't just looking for anywhere to live,' he said in an interview in 2019, 'I wanted somewhere that I would be comfortable.'[1]

Jonathan remembered calling Switchboard many times during his search, as new offers were logged with volunteers daily. If yesterday's offer hadn't worked out, today's just might. 'They'd go through the papers and books and say, "Oh there's something here in SE15", which meant nothing to me,' he said. 'They would come out with places that I'd never heard of, like Rotherhithe and

Woolwich and Croydon. So there was an awful lot of sifting through the information, jotting it down while they spoke.'

Armed with several addresses and transport instructions, Jonathan set out to far-flung parts of London to try to find his new home. Given the technology available, it may have been the most efficient system at the time, though it wasn't always fruitful. 'Eight or nine times out of ten,' he said, '[I'd] come away thinking "You must be joking!"'

Switchboard did try to make the accommodation service the best it could be by collecting as much context as possible from the people offering rooms, with volunteers creating information cards. One such 'accommodation offered' card from July 1975 says that a fifty-year-old man living in Chelsea was offering a double bedroom for one man, aged eighteen to twenty-five for ten pounds weekly rent including food; he had requested that the tenant be 'not effeminate'. That note is probably the reason why the card was taped into the log book rather than staying in the designated accommodation file: to start a debate among volunteers about whether such requests should be accepted. When Adam showed this card to Jonathan during his interview, he became quiet. 'That makes me quite angry,' he murmured, with tears in his eyes. 'Very cruel, very unfair.'

At the time of the interview, Adam simply recorded Jonathan's reaction. Adam had spent years perfecting what he felt was professional objectivity, but was actually personal distance too. Thinking as a producer, he'd have said that the sadness and anger in Jonathan's voice made for good tape, but over the course of further research into these stories over the years, and reflecting on his own life, Adam felt more and more empathy with him. Listening again to the tape while writing this book, Adam thought back to when he landed in that first shared flat in London, aged twenty-two. It was still years before he would come out as gay, or even know much about queer-friendly households full stop. If things had been different, he might have found a flat via Facebook groups for queer flat-sharers, or ticked the LGBT box on the flatmate finding service SpareRoom.co.uk.

Instead, he moved in with the awkward straight couple in Rotherhithe. Worrying about what they thought of him, Adam tried to seem 'not effeminate'. One day he suggested that they hang their own pictures instead of tolerating the landlord's bland watercolour prints of harbours, but one of the flatmates said it was best to keep the house 'neutral'. Adam didn't push it. Instead, he allowed more parts of his character to be kept under the floorboards in the one space where they should have been seen. The prints were anything but neutral, of course, just as the 'average family homes' we had grown up in were anything but neutral. It was probably from that moment that Adam began to dream about his ideal home, and who would be in it.

The distant owner of that Rotherhithe flat happily collected the rent, and later asked them all to leave so he could sell the property for more than he'd bought it for. Adam's search for housing began again, but he was unaware of what he really needed; the model he desired was rare and unseen. He managed to land in a rented flat with the possibility of the long term, thanks to it being owned by a charitable trust rather than a private landlord, though he was still not connected to queer life as a consequence of being disconnected from his queer body, and under the influence of his parents' rejection of his sister.

The first place Tash lived while at university was a huge shared house. They were the only queer person and it took them a week or so to come out. When they did, they were told by one of their Christian housemates that they were going to go to hell. A house, then, but certainly not a home. When Tash was twenty-four they moved to London and lived in more than eight places over fourteen years, always with queer people and sometimes with partners. One was a warehouse in east London where the internal walls didn't meet the ceilings. Tash could see their breath in the winter, and black mould blotched the bathroom walls. But it was full of queers, and they loved it.

Just as in nightlife, in social clubs, and in love, living with similar people is a form of community. The need to find similar people to live with comes across loud and clear in the log books, and also through other services that were even more tailored, as in the case of the Black Lesbian and Gay Centre newsletter which ran ads like these ones in April 1987:[2]

> *** ACCOMODATION ***
> Blackgay couple require Blackgay man to share house in Forest Gate. Own large room, £35 pw plus a third of the bills. £100 deposit. Non-smoker preferred.
>
> North London, N4, woman preferred to share mixed house, being transformed into flats. Own room £160 pcm, including bills.

Some queer people of colour found it doubly hard to find safe housing. It happened to a Black man called Roy Bryan, who later joined Switchboard as a volunteer in 1998. As he searched for a gay-friendly household in the early nineties, Switchboard sent him to a place with a spare room in Wimbledon on a rainy Sunday. 'When I got there, they told me it was gone,' said Roy in an interview with Tash. 'And I'm sure it was because he didn't like the look of me because I was Black.'

Tash went to Lisa Power to ask how Switchboard's accommodation service tried to filter out racist landlords and house-shares before sending people like Roy to them. Lisa explained that it was so important to get it right that Switchboard added a question to volunteer interviews, to ensure they were recruiting the right people to the helpline: 'What would you do if someone rang up and said they only wanted to let to white people?' Lisa said, 'The number of people who thought, because we're a helping service who wanted to do their best, that that's alright, was horrific. It was illegal for a start. More people fell over that question than I think any other, in the interview sessions.'

Queer people of colour were (and are) under attack from the intersecting prejudices of racism, homophobia, biphobia, transphobia, sexism, and misogynoir. This is why they may have found even less success with Switchboard's accommodation service than Jonathan, and why some volunteers always pushed for diversity in recruitment. They wanted Switchboard to be a place where any LGBTQ+ person could go, regardless of (indeed especially because of) their background. They knew that they'd keep getting calls like this one:

> 17 November 1975
> Roger, a Dutch Indonesian, 25, has been suddenly evicted from his Romford lodging. I have given likely places to him to check out for accom. but he has to be out by 18/11/75. I have told him should he find nothing he should phone us back and we could think about referring him to one of our crash pads for 2/3 days to help him look around. He has been looking but he says his Indonesian background has caused people to reject him, because he looks to be 'coloured.'

Words like this, that were either racially offensive at the time or have come to be so, often appear in the pages of the log books. They give us all an insight into how language was used to subjugate people who were not white. When Roy had his experience of racial discrimination in Wimbledon, he called Switchboard back to tell them – and the volunteer removed the listing.

In 1983 a dedicated charity, Stonewall Housing, was founded to serve the needs of LGBTQ+ people experiencing homelessness, but for other housing needs Switchboard had been there since 1974. Even in the early days it was working wonders:

> 20 January 1976
>
> I don't know about the rest of you but often when talking to others about Switchboard I find when mentioning accom. that people often say that Switchboard found them to accom at which they are now living – amazing when one considers that we have only been operating the files for the past 6 months on this scale – sad also to find many people do not know about the accom files. PLEASE MENTION THIS SERVICE WHENEVER POSSIBLE WE ALWAYS NEED MORE ACCOM.

Another volunteer, David Seligman, added:

> Truly amazing! Wonderful! Fantastic! Superb! Sincerely beautiful! Extraordinarily delightful! Super! Wonderful! Marvellous!

David's palpable pride at the work that he and other Switchboard volunteers were doing was surpassed only by the scale of the need. It wasn't only the runaways who needed support, but often their parents, too. Indeed, a number of log book entries reveal parents calling with shame, anger, and homophobia, trying to find the missing teenage child they had rejected. However, most of the time when a parent called Switchboard, it seemed to be out of genuine concern:

27 August 1975

A woman called Mrs MacCallum phoned very worried about her possibly gay son who is down in London. If he phones in to GS could we try and ensure that he phones her to reassure her that he is OK. His name is Sam.

23 September 1975

Carwyn, 15 years old, looks 18, 6ft, fair hair, medium length. Knows gay scene. Has run away from home. Parents are looking for him. Please ring Parents Enquiry immediately if you know where this man is. Apparently he's quite together – ie, passes for 18 in his head as well.

While some queer people run away from the house they share with family, others feel the urge to run away from their home country. Their stories are told in the log books, although not always with much detail. There are myriad reasons why a person moves from one country to another, but what is evident in the log books is the number of migrants who called for help because they were already in the UK and wanted to continue building their home. Sometimes they wanted legal advice or support with the citizenship process, and Switchboard could help with that, or refer them on to other organisations. In the 1980s, the Black Lesbian and Gay Centre helped with this too, as can be seen in this ad from their newsletter in 1987:

SATURDAY 25 APRIL
LESBIAN AND GAY IMMIGRATION GROUP
are meeting at the Hampden Community Centre, 150 Ossulton [*sic*] St, London NW1. Nearest tube Euston/King's Cross. The meeting starts at 2 pm. The group is particularly looking for

people who work in law centres, advice centres or community groups who have skills and advice to offer. For more information please write to LGIG, BM WELCOME, London WC1W 3XX.

Most calls to Switchboard from migrants, however, would be looking for a person who could help them to stay, with a wink and a nod:

1 August 1984
Caller is Spanish and wants to find a sympathetic male who will marry her. She is a lesbian. She knows the ins and outs of this, pardon the metaphor. No disparagement intended. She's seeing a lawyer about a visa and work. Would like to stay. This is deliberately vague, but you know what I mean.

Volunteers knew exactly what callers like these were asking for, and also knew that it was a delicate subject given that it was and is illegal to marry someone falsely. Diana James and other volunteers had to be vigilant: 'Are they a police officer calling up to check us out about giving advice about breaking the law, circumventing the immigration laws?' This fear made it hard to counsel some callers, and in any case Switchboard did not want to give legal advice or act as a matchmaking service for 'lavender marriages'. 'Sometimes you were at the end of the call, putting the phone down, thinking, [*That was*] *really awful*,' Diana told Tash in 2020, 'because you couldn't help someone you really wanted to.' Tash had also taken calls where they were left feeling helpless, hand still holding the receiver minutes after it had been put down. Trying to still help, somehow.

Still, the calls kept coming. Regardless of the law, the fact is that many LGBTQ+ people have subverted the traditional institution of marriage in this way. That subversion is probably as old as the institution of marriage itself, as even in the past marriage was about cementing the status of a household.

Queer people have always shared the knowledge needed to do such things in order to survive. That is why there are so many log book entries about it:

28 March 1990
Don Watkins phoned to say he has a friend (male) from Sierra Leone, who will be deported in 1 month unless he can marry a woman with an easy passport. He is prepared to pay for such a marriage if you know of any women who may be interested.

Sometimes the volunteers themselves asked for help:

6 June 1991
Would any women be interested in a mutually convenient arrangement with the interested male being a 23 year old Jamaican, who is my partner? He has had enough of studying and therefore marriage should be the way ahead.

3 March 1990
My boyfriend's about to get sent home to the States. He married one year ago to obtain residency but now, after a year, when he has to obtain the full visa, his wife is chickening out. She's threatening to call the Home Office to try and wash her hands of him. Has anyone been in this, or a similar situation? We've been to the JCWI, the Joint Council for the Welfare of Immigrants, and they can only give legal facts. I'd so much appreciate anyone who might have advice or know of someone in the know.

The legal jeopardy of those seeking a lavender marriage was only matched by the need that the person had. Either they wanted to avoid returning to their home country, or they wanted to stay in the UK because it was now their home, or both. With borders and passports and immigration law, it was never simple.

In 2020, Adam interviewed a woman who wanted to be known as 'Louise' – she had broken the law to help a gay migrant stay in the UK.[3] They were part of the same radical queer friendship network in London, and the man, 'David', wanted to avoid returning to his home country where he would be drafted into a brutal military. Louise and David concocted a backstory for their fake relationship and they tied the knot at the registry office surrounded by their queer friends. 'I don't know how the registrar didn't realise there was something amiss,' remembered Louise, her voice lifting with laughter at the memory of that special day, ''cause the assembled crew was like something out of the bar scene of *Star Wars*. They were just extraordinary. People dressed in drag, feathers, ballroom gowns, and it was packed.'

It gave such a cosy feeling to Adam, as he listened to Louise's story, to know that all these friends came together to help David, their gay brother, to give him the chance to build a safer space for himself in the UK. It made Adam think about all the times he and friends had come together for dinner, people from all over the world, supporting each other with community, advice, hummus, and maybe a bed for the night.

A few months after the wild wedding day, Louise and David found themselves under investigation by the Home Office. They lied through their teeth, passed the test, and stayed married for twenty-five years – even after David got his permanent residency. He and Louise only divorced so that David could marry his actual partner, after same-sex marriage became legal. As she relayed this to Adam, Louise seemed proud but also careful, and she had checked with David to see whether he was happy for her to speak about it. 'The bond I have with David now is probably unlike any other I have,' said Louise, her voice true, her memory warm like a fireplace still glowing at the end of the day. 'He's eternally grateful to me. He feels I saved his life.'

The desire to move to a place where you feel safe and more able to be yourself as an LGBTQ+ person can be compelling. It was something experienced by one of Tash's oldest queer friends, Layla Ahmad, who arrived in the UK illegally in 2001, aged seventeen. 'There was no future in Somalia,' she told Tash in 2023. Not only was her home country torn apart by war, she did not feel safe and welcome as a lesbian. Layla's brother paid $28,000 to a smuggler to help Layla to travel on false papers to the UK.

'Oh my god, it was a bit scary,' said Layla, her eyebrows raising and eyes widening. 'He gave me fake Italian ID. And I remember taking the journey on my own. I didn't speak any language or anything. All I was told was that when you reach a certain area, like in Heathrow [Airport] or something, just flush the ID. And then go and say, "I want to seek asylum" . . . And that's exactly what I did.'

Layla was taken to an asylum centre in Bristol where she began the formal application process. 'I had a mission,' she remembered. This is how Layla began to build her life in Bristol, wearing trousers for the first time in her life, resisting the family members who tried to control her, and, eventually, finding other queer women to love and be loved by.

People like to feel rooted. It is why we buy houses and flats to live in, and why we invest love and money in making them into a home. We want safe spaces, away from our hostile families or home countries. But for some LGBTQ+ people, the place where they live is not always safe. There is only so much you can do to stop the prejudice of other people from infiltrating your space. Catherine Lee was a PE teacher during the years of Section 28, and of our own education. Even though she created her own home, as a lesbian Catherine was not safe there.

In 1993, Catherine was hiding her sexuality from her school colleagues, but she was working in a job she loved, earning a salary, and was free to duck into a lesbian bar at the weekend. She earned £604 per month and used this to pay a mortgage on a house in Garston-under-the-Bridge in Liverpool, close to the school where she taught. 'This was the first place I lived where I could lock the door for the night,' Catherine wrote in her book, *Pretended*, about her years as a teacher under Section 28:

> My previous places were shared digs with other teachers, and their friends, other halves or one-night stands would regularly come and go. [The house I bought] was my first adult place of safety: a home where I could watch [the lesbian film] *Lianna* without keeping the volume low or quickly changing the channel if someone else walked in.

Reading these words reminded Tash of how they'd crept downstairs as a teen in the early hours to watch *The L Word* at volume level 1, nose so close to the TV it was almost touching, jumping at the smallest noise in the house.

Catherine continued:

> I put my lesbian books on my pine shelves. The green and white spines of the Virago books and the black and white stripes of the Women's Press books appeared to shout in celebration that I could at last be myself.

Catherine's house was a bargain, at £19,000. Not long after stacking her books and hanging her pictures, Catherine soon realised why it was so cheap. Children from her school shouted outside the house, 'She's a lez' and 'Dirty dyke'. One evening she heard a thud at the living-room window, then another. Her home had been egged by the hostile teenagers. 'Two evenings later, alone in the house, I hear the letterbox snap,' Catherine wrote in her diary. 'On my porch mat is a lit firework, sizzling and spinning. I grab it, open the door and throw it as far as I can down the street, to whoops and howls of laughter from the boys.' Another day, her car was vandalised.

Catherine went to the police but they did nothing to stop the hate crimes she was enduring. They advised her to move house. Instead, Catherine began parking her car in front of the police station and walking the mile and a half home. Every day. 'This was symptomatic of the complete absence of self-worth I had at the time,' she wrote in *Pretended*. 'Five years into Section 28, living a lie at work and facing harassment outside my home, I believed this was the inevitable price of being gay.'

As Catherine's story and the log books show us, queer people are desperate to secure safe housing for themselves, on their own terms. No one should feel isolated and fearful at home.

Some queer people, especially throughout the years covered by the log books, were more alternative in their approach to housing, adopting different living structures and economic models. The log books don't really cover this part of LGBTQ+ life, given that most housing calls were addressing callers' urgent needs for a bed for the night. But while Switchboard volunteers were handling these calls, many of them were living alternatively.

After joining Switchboard in 1977, Andy Piccos moved in with Lisa Power and Jonathan Walters from 1981, until Lisa moved out in 1984. They were living in short-life housing, essentially licensed squats – buildings that the council owned and were planning to do up. Around this time, Islington Council launched a cooperative housing 'homesteading' scheme which was open to people already living in short-life housing. Jonathan, Andy, and Don Tyler (another Switchboard volunteer) worked with others to set up a housing cooperative for lesbians and gay men: Islington Gay Housing Co-Op. Through the council's homesteading scheme they were given three houses that were to be developed into eight flats; co-op members were issued with council tenancies for their future flats. 'It was a glorious house,' said Andy, when Tash interviewed him in 2024.

This is how Andy and his friends set about creating a queer home: as council tenants. A housing corporation and council funds covered the cost of making the building safe and watertight. They created the 'shell' flats within the buildings, each containing basic electrics, a cold water tap, and a toilet. With tight budgets, the group worked with an architect to design their individual living spaces. Tash was blown away by this; it felt to them like it had been plucked out of a radical queer future. 'Being able to decide how your flat should be laid out doesn't happen to many people unless they have a lot of money,' said Andy. 'We were very proud of ourselves for coming in within our budget and not having to increase our loans, as some co-ops were having to do.' Their council rents were set at the flats' shell-rate, as everything else was seen as tenants' improvements and therefore not eligible when calculating the council rent. Once the loans were paid off, the flats would be charged at the shell-rate. 'We created really affordable housing!' said Andy.

And so Andy, Jonathan, and friends came to live on the top of a hill in a double-fronted house with great views over London, with interconnected queer lives. The dream didn't last forever, though.

'Suddenly we were getting cracks,' he explained, his face animated, 'The house, our queer house, top of the hill, end of terrace, fell *up* the hill!' After eight years of creating the shared home that should have been theirs for a lifetime, they were going to have to move out. 'I was just so upset,' said Andy, his head gently shaking at the terrible luck, at the sadness of it all. It reminded Tash of the warehouse they had lived in with queer friends in Dalston, one of whom had lived there for seven years. Their collective queer warehouse dream was literally demolished when the landlord ended their tenancy, kicking them out. The landlord knocked through their shoddy walls and turned the place into fancy flats, each of which was then rented out for three times the price they had paid collectively. (Tash and their friends did, however, manage to sneak into the property, just before the new flats were built, to have a party and give their queer home a proper send-off).

The political ground was shifting at this time, too, and councils were changing their relationship to housing. Soon after Margaret Thatcher came to power, her government passed the Housing Act 1980, which gave council tenants the right to buy their homes from local authorities. Many took up the chance, and the next decade saw a huge transfer of homes from the state into private hands. By 1987 more than a million council houses in the UK had been sold to their tenants.[4] Although the policy was pitched as a way to empower and enrich those on lower incomes, in reality it created structural problems that over time transformed housing into a commodity.

Just like the cracks that appeared in Andy's council-owned queer co-op, the chronic flaws in the housing sector would come to affect subsequent generations more and more acutely. By 2007–09, as Adam and Tash were arriving in London, irresponsible bankers who had been lending money to people who couldn't afford it had pushed house prices up and caused a global crash. The upshot was that for people in their twenties, like us, housing became more expensive relative to earnings, and ownership was held much further from our reach than it had been for our parents' generation. Councils still had a legal duty to provide housing, but as they owned fewer homes, London councils were actually having to rent back many of the homes they'd sold off under Thatcher's scheme. A report in 2014 by London Assembly member Tom Copley found that at least 36 per cent of the homes sold by councils across London were being let by private landlords, who began charging higher and higher rents. Substantial numbers of these former council homes were let to tenants who were supported by housing benefit. This meant that the policy, according to Copley, was 'possibly unrivalled in representing such poor value for money to both taxpayers and local authorities'.[5] (The son of Thatcher's housing minister Ian Gow came to own at least forty ex-council homes as a private landlord, according to a newspaper investigation in 2013.)[6]

Back in the eighties, Andy's co-op had to take the council to court as the cracks were due to the council's structural work, not the tenants' improvements. The council decided to take possession of the building and offered them alternative council housing. The co-op continued in a form for a while, but some members ended up buying their flats, and the co-op collapsed. Collective living, collective ownership, a collective home – all these things vanished. Andy, who worked for a housing charity and who believed in alternative forms of cohabiting, was devastated. He couldn't afford to buy his flat, and so he was moved into another council property that didn't feel like the communal home he'd once had.

'It took me five years to unpack,' he said; but by the time Tash interviewed him, he had made a home in his new flat. As he opened the door to Tash, they were greeted with a flood of pink interiors and a beaming Andy declaring, 'It's BARBIE-GEDDON! Do you like?'

Although Tash was familiar with Andy's face from the Switchboard archive, this was the first time they had met him. They burst into the biggest smile and laughed at the sight of him surrounded by the fluorescent pink nettings that were draped everywhere. As they climbed the stairs, the smell of incense filled the air. The flat was full to the brim with Andy's life, not a spare spot of space anywhere. As a single-income householder whose income has been far outstripped by the cost of commercial housing, if it weren't for the long-term housing provided by his local council, Andy would probably have found himself moving again and again over the years, and further away from the home that was his community in London.

The idea of collective queer housing had taken root in the late sixties and seventies within the radical circles of the Gay Liberation Front, the anti-racism movement, and the women's movement. One of the most significant queer housing co-ops is situated on Railton Road in Brixton, London, which for decades has been a home for activists and artists. It's where Marc Thompson, one of our interviewees, lives, and it is where we both interviewed him for the podcast and the book. Artist and photographer Ajamu X also lives on Railton Road. Both Marc and Ajamu featured in Jason Okundaye's landmark book *Revolutionary Acts*. 'I think what is missing when talking about a Black queer history is that loads of us lived in housing co-ops,' Ajamu told Okundaye. Okundaye noted that this was how such artists became more exposed not only to each other but to a wealth of creative, intellectual, and social groups, individuals, and cultures.

The housing co-op on Railton Road was (and is) remarkable, taking in multiple houses divided into flats, and even including houses on the parallel street Mayall Road. This led to the creation of a huge shared garden through the knocking down of the dividers. The residents of the co-op created 'our own little village', according to the character Marie from a play about the co-op, *On Railton Road*, written by Ian Giles and Louis Rembges. The show was developed through research including interviews with residents, and it tells a semi-dramatised version of how the misfits who created the co-op came together, plotted radical political acts, and founded a home. The play was aptly staged at the Museum of the Home in November 2023, and we went to see it with Railton Road resident and lifelong queer activist Jonathan Blake. In one moment, the character Atom proposes to knock down the garden walls. 'Instead of separate gardens,' she says,

> we would have a shared space between all occupants here on this road, turning it into a new house for us all to live in and grow,
> To stay and become cold, only to get warm again,
> To shelter from rain and snow,
> To bask and bathe in the sun.
> To share food and stories.
> To plant flowers and new ideas with roots strong enough to stay long after we are gone.
> To nurse, and to be nursed in return.
> So that anyone can see, from inside or from above, if Aliens. Aliens flew by and looked down, at us, at this road, Aliens and straight people of the future and the sky can see that on Railton Road at least, we made a utopia.[7]

Atom's beautiful speech captures the spirit not just of Railton Road, but of all those queer people who created alternative homes during the years of the log books. The seventies and eighties especially were times of squats in run-down urban areas, and authorities that either turned a blind eye to unusual queer home set-ups or had housing policies that were flexible enough to accommodate them. Watching the play was a surreal experience: here was a historical model of living, staged and celebrated, feeling at once dated and progressive. We sat in the audience as members of the middle generation, wishing that the model had been brought to life in buildings up and down the country, not just in a handful of properties.

Alternative housing is something that came up in our research with those who lived as queer adults through those years – and yet something that seemed impossible by the time that our generation came of age and sought to create forever homes.

When Adam went to interview a man named Graham McKerrow, he found himself captivated by his story of a house in Stockwell, London. By the time of this interview, Adam was well into his queer life, with new loved ones and pictures that were far from 'neutral'. Graham's was the kind of household that Adam now dreamt of creating, but he would once again be confronted by the fact that it would now be impossible.

Graham had lived in flat-shares across London for years, but by the early nineties he and his boyfriend Marc wanted to do something different. 'We wanted a big house with lots of people,' he told Adam, who nodded, feeling the same feeling across the decades. 'We wanted a sense of community.'

Those were the days when banks sold mortgages without proof of income. 'You could self-certify,' said Graham, grinning, surprised, as if remembering a key ingredient in a special recipe. 'You didn't have to prove what your salary was, you could just say what it was.'

The year was 1992, when an average house cost just 3.21 times the average salary.[8] Graham and Marc found a big house in Stockwell and told a fib about their income in order to get a mortgage for it: they knew they could rent out the bedrooms to friends and collectively cover the mortgage. The house was a mess: dry rot, wet rot, and every other kind of rot. But within a few months they were able to take on their first housemate. 'Part of the attraction of living in a communal household is that you get all of those different inputs,' he said, 'which makes life so interesting.'

Graham and Marc and the community lived in that shared house in Stockwell for twenty-nine years. They enjoyed countless garden parties, Christmases, birthdays, elections, heartbreaks, and family meals. Graham mentioning the group Christmases struck a chord with Adam. For nine Christmases in a row, his parents were shunning his sister Hannah, creating a dilemma for the two queer siblings: whether to spend Christmas with their parents at the 'family home', or with just Adam visiting Hannah's home with her partner. Each Christmas saw Adam forced to choose between family members, because his parents saw his sister's life as not valid in the family home.

Adam first met Graham in the Stockwell house in 2020. It was in the summer when people were meeting carefully with facemasks due to the Covid pandemic. The house was spacious enough for Adam to sit more than two metres away from Graham and record him for the podcast. *They must be rich*, Adam thought. He noticed that Marc was pottering about packing boxes. Graham explained that they were moving to a house in Deal, Kent, to be near the sea. When Adam went to interview Graham again for this book, the sale of the Stockwell house had enabled him and Marc to buy a flat in Pimlico in London too. They now split their time between the two homes in London and Kent.

'WOULD LIKE TO STAY'

In 2024, Adam sat in Graham's Pimlico flat, not far from Tate Britain and the River Thames, and listened to his elder tell the story. Not long after that interview, Adam and a friend wandered one day along the banks of the same river. They didn't have a planned route but somehow found themselves on the north bank at Wapping, across from the building in Rotherhithe where Adam had lived when he first moved to London. Adam couldn't take his eyes off it, remembering the 'neutral' artwork and the pre-queer 'neutral' twenty-two-year-old he was when he lived there. The younger Adam had no idea what his life would hold – that he could live a queer life making the work he wanted, a life filled with loved ones. It was better than anything he could have imagined, and yet the younger Adam might have dreamt of more stable housing, or a more comfortable life. These thoughts moved him to tears, and he turned to his friend for a hug. They were both approaching forty and in the same situation, the same demographic, the same misfortune to want to live unconventionally. The hug felt like the home they both dreamt of.

Although Adam and the friends he would have liked to create a home with had many more social freedoms than their queer ancestors, their incomes were not high enough to meet the cost of home ownership in London. What's more, many of their incomes were earned from insecure freelance labour that wasn't (and isn't) valued enough to be stable. Having a life partner might have helped, but that wasn't on Adam's path. Charities were rightly focused on people experiencing homelessness. With no public policies for truly affordable housing, no generational asset transfer, and no winning lottery ticket, by the time that Adam had seen enough models of his desired way to live, it was beyond his reach.

In Pimlico, Adam sat across from Graham in the lovely flat, beside the busy bookshelves and Graham's sculptures, and felt proud to know him. But Adam also felt sadness, and a pinch of envy, about the generational economic difference. If we recognise the huge value in creating homes as Graham and Marc did, or the Brixton housing co-op, why does it have to be so hard and so rare? Why do we value living with friends less than living with a partner? Why do we allow the caprices of a market to limit the life options of those queer people who simply want to live alternatively? How, exactly, over the four decades since 1974, did LGBTQ+ housing change so much?

The way we live says a lot about who we are and what we need. Some of us have a partner and we need them to be close. Some of us want to raise children. Some of us want to live off-grid, settling for an abandoned warehouse or a van in a field. With LGBTQ+ people this point is especially true. Our bodies set us out to live a life that is different from the average, dominant ways of living. They used to say that the personal is political, and when it comes to LGBTQ+ people this could not be truer. The lesbian separatists of the seventies and eighties provided the best example.

> 15 July 1975
>
> I've had several women callers asking for accommodation which we can't offer, as most of you already know if you use the files – I suggest that an advertisement is put in Spare Rib or TO (Time Out???) designed specifically for women. It is not enough to write an ad and put 'women + men' – changing the order of the words obviously doesn't win us any attention from women – and especially lesbian – separatists. I think that a separate advertisement would work, and is necessary. Something on the lines of an appeal to women with rooms/space to help those other

women who have contacted us and desperately want to live with other women/lesbians. I've written a note to the development group but wanted to bring this to everyone's attention.

By the time of this log book entry in 1975, lots of lesbians were living in this way, and the Switchboard volunteer who made that note knew that they would have to work extra hard to ensure they were serving that part of the community.

Suzanne Ciechomski lived in a lesbian separatist household in Coventry in the late 1970s, shortly after coming out aged twenty.[9] 'It was a kind of a political movement at the time,' said Suzanne in an interview with Adam in 2019, 'of women who wanted to kind of get away from a male-dominated world.' She spoke fondly of her years in that house, explaining how it helped her to find herself as a woman and a lesbian, and of course, even though it is a cliché, how to cook a good lentil soup. Lesbian separatist households were often vegetarian, according to Janet Dixon, who lived in one and wrote, 'I stopped eating meat in case the chunk of sizzling corpse I was about to sit down to had come from a male animal.' Janet's account of how she and other lesbians quit the male-dominated Gay Liberation Front and struck out as separatists is lively;[10] she explains proudly how she fixed cistern valves, hung three-inch steel angle brackets, and ditched using tampons because she thought of them as 'cotton-wool pricks', attending to the problems presented by living in a squat in the eighties with 'a pioneering spirit'. The whole point of houses like Janet's and Suzanne's was to live independently of men while creating a new way for women to relate to each other. This meant that the lesbian separatists tried to live their politics, and so their squatted homes doubled as workplaces, nurseries, and refuges from male domestic violence. According to Suzanne, residents also spoke truthfully about power dynamics, their feelings, and their sexual fantasies. '[It] felt liberating,' said Suzanne, 'but it wasn't always easy.'

In parts of east London, women-only squats were a significant presence. By the late seventies, an estimated fifty such households were scattered throughout the streets close to Broadway Market, according to Christine Wall, a professor who studied these housing models and stories.[11] After reading Wall's research, Tash walked to Broadway Market, down the streets that were namechecked: Amhurst Road, Landsdowne Drive, Brownlow Road. They had walked down them countless times in their fifteen years living in east London, but now each road took on a new meaning. Wall found that the total number of squats around Broadway Market, including the mixed-sex ones, reached as many as 250. They were part of a wider network of squatters all over London who supported each other with understanding their rights and sharing techniques for building such households. Squatting became harder in the 2000s with various reforms, and then eventually became a criminal offence in 2012.

Alternative housing models are immensely valuable to the individuals who live inside them, but they also send a signal to everyone else: there is another way. Houses like Suzanne's, squats like Janet's, and communal homes like Graham's provide a *model* that other LGBTQ+ people might follow. The problem is that the rest of the world is sometimes not willing to accept such alternatives, and people can use violence and hatred to reject them, even though they have nothing to do with them. In the seventies and eighties, lesbian separatist homes were frequently vandalised with graffitied words like DYKE. And in 1972, a gay commune in Athlone Road in Brixton was attacked with bricks and broken bottles by local schoolchildren.

'WOULD LIKE TO STAY'

The story of this commune has become somewhat legendary within the LGBTQ+ community, and it involved a teenager who would later become one of Switchboard's volunteers: Julian Hows. Julian was just sixteen years old at the time and attending the Tulse Hill Comprehensive School for Boys when a bunch of drag queens moved into the nearby house at 9 Athlone Road. The neighbours saw their tights and skirts hanging on the washing line and started yelling homophobic abuse, and the kids at the local school got involved in the abuse, too. They were Julian's classmates, so he reported the violence to the headmaster. The school did nothing to stop the pupils, and so the drag queens took the matter into their own hands.

Recruiting the school insider Julian and a bunch of queens from other gay communes in west London, one day they all dragged up and went into the school grounds to hand out a leaflet that asserted their right to live as they wished, communally, peacefully, and with dignity:

> We are gay men living in Athlone Road. We do, and dress, and have sex and are what we want to be, which is nice for us and doesn't affect you.
>
> We start no trouble, no arguments, no violence. Since we moved in we have had shouts, bricks, two of us have been hit with bottles, most of the windows and the door have been broken in.
>
> We've also had a lot of support. We know a lot of you are on our side. We are not being driven out by a few confused, uptight people trying to look big.
>
> From now on any trouble and we'll answer back. We're not going to use the school or the police. We don't believe in them any more than you do.

We'll do it ourselves and there are a lot of us. We have a lot of friends. Today there are dozens, next time there'll be hundreds. We believe in talking, in friendship and understanding each other and we'll talk anywhere – on your ground or ours. But we won't talk to those who attack us. We will attack back and there are a large number of us. We are very strong because we love each other.

These gay men were facing down the full force of toxic masculinity and mandatory heterosexuality. The school reported them to the police. Officers turned up, as did the pupils' parents. There was uproar and mayhem, with Julian even threatening to out the teachers he knew to be secretly gay . . . Sadly but understandably, the radical collective withdrew from the fight. They moved out of the house and went to live elsewhere.

For his part, Julian was expelled from the school via a letter that explained he was 'a corrupting influence on the younger pupils'. The headmaster refused to give him a reference to join another school, so at sixteen his education was effectively over. 'I ran away from home and went off to join the circus,' he told us, breaking out into his ragged smoker's laugh.

We remember Julian telling us this story in the first interview we did with him. The thing that struck us both was that even though Julian was thirty years older than us, he was able to run away and find his people. There were several reasons for this, of course: Julian's teenage bravado was one, and another was his location, having grown up in London. Running away to the radical queer commune meant not having to go far – just a short ride on the Tube. We were quite far from much queer life (that we knew of), and there was nothing like those London communes in the Plymouth of Tash's youth or the Cleethorpes or Grimsby of

Adam's. There is no assumption here that Julian had an easy adolescence, but it was noticeable that he seemed to have more options to find a new home than we did as teenagers.

The story of 9 Athlone Road reveals how threatening a queer household can seemingly be to some, and how violent the enforcement of heterosexuality and gender conformity can be. We all want to be safe in our homes to live as we please, not harming anyone else. In 1972, in Athlone Road, two years before Switchboard started, this dream was dispelled.

The dream does persist through the log books, however, with callers looking for a home, and in our interviews. Another contributor, Anson Mackay, told us how they pushed down their gender non-conformity for years when living in various cities – Edinburgh, Manchester, and London – even when they were perceived as a gay man on the clubbing scene. 'I was much more gender non-conforming at home,' they said in an interview in 2023, sitting on their sofa aged fifty-six, wondering aloud about the impact of hiding their non-binary identity away for forty years. 'Visibly outside it might never come back,' Anson said. 'But inside is definitely changed.'

Tash has felt similar to Anson. They didn't have the words to be able to express themself at home among their family, or at their girls' school, where teachers spoke about girl power and how women could build the future – Tash wanted these things but didn't feel as though they necessarily felt like theirs, too. This pressure around gender also occurs in the most subtle of ways: one summer Adam attended a cricket club because he knew that people wanted him to do a sport, but he'd already learnt that football, rugby, tennis, and hockey weren't for him. He poured his body into a tracksuit and turned up at the cricket club with the other boys, longing to disappear and read a book instead. In the end, he did. Reading and studying didn't seem to carry the weight of having to be the right gender. Safer to be mostly alone.

This is why queer housing is important to queer people: our spaces help us to be who we are. They help us to take care of each other and to love each other. After a breakup with a partner they shared a home with, Tash moved into the spare room of two queer friends (a couple). These friends opened their home to Tash, and that home helped Tash to heal. In times of crisis, they are where we retreat to and where we organise.

Countless community efforts started in the home, because it is where we have the safety to dream and to plot. Kath Gillespie Sells, who started Regard to support LGBTQ+ people living with disabilities, used her home to stock all the photocopied newsletters for the organisation before they were stapled, stuffed into envelopes, stamped and sent out. The co-founders of Sisterwrite, the feminist bookshop, shared squats with other women close to Broadway Market, using these spaces to live rent-free while running an incredible operation which would not have earned them enough money to afford housing.[12] The telephone helpline for Black people with HIV/AIDS, Blackliners, was started by Arnold Gordon and Dawn Hill in Arnold's flat in Brixton in 1989.

The reverse is also true, however, in that the buildings of community organisations can *become* a home to those who flow through them. The Black Lesbian and Gay Centre, for example, went from being a project in 1982 to an actual physical centre underneath a railway arch in Peckham, south London, in 1991. 'It was *our* railway arch,' said Yvonne Taylor, a DJ and co-founder of the Sistermatic club night, who spoke about the centre on the podcast *Black and Gay, Back in the Day*, in 2022.[13] 'We could go and talk, just play pool . . . do everyday things that you might want to do. Loved it. Absolutely loved it.'

The idea of a community space that feels like a home is also true of Switchboard. Although its building wasn't open to the public, countless volunteers over the years have described Switchboard as being like a home to them. By this they have meant that it was a space to be themselves, a space to support and be supported, and a place where the difficulties of life are processed. In fact, before Julian was a volunteer, he ran to Switchboard for cover. The year was 1978 and it was his final day working at Earls Court Tube station. To mark the special nature of the day, he wore the London Transport uniform that was made for women. This lark got him on the television news, but the car that the broadcasters promised would take him home safely didn't show up. Julian worried about travelling in public in clothes meant for women, so he called Switchboard. The volunteers broke the rules by allowing a caller into the building for safety, for shelter, for a home.[14]

Reading between the lines in the log books, too, reveals how callers felt 'at home' on a call to a fellow queer person, and volunteers also knew that in the phone room they were creating something of a home for themselves. Evidence of this was captured in the log books, as volunteers picked up their pens to make the most domestic of notes:

17 April 1995
No milk, no biscuits, no proper towels in the loos – it's enough to make a grown woman weep . . . Jennifer

1995/6
How about a joint Switchboard resolution?
Let's all wash up our mugs!!!
Radical or what?
Phil x

13 December 1975

There seems to be rather a lot of semen on the sheets (as opposed to seamen in the bed). Would it be possible for those on the point of discharging onto communal bedding to remember that others have to use it [here another volunteer has annotated: WHO REUSES SEMEN?] either restrain themselves or interpose some absorbative material twixt their dripping member and the bedclothes. I hope this won't be taken as coercive or exemplifying my inhuman, bureaucratic tendencies. [Another volunteer has added: NOTHING COULD. YOU DO IT SO WELL YOURSELF.]

18 December 1997

The Tellytubby cake that Richard Desmond made and left for vols to eat was fabulous. Thanks. Ian Johns.

27 August 1982

Finally – the ultimate in sophistication – folks we have a teapot!! (3 teabags are enough and you get 4 cups+ out of it!!)

Switchboard, much like our interviewees, also had its own housing situation to sort out in the eighties. In 1984, on its tenth anniversary and amid fears that 5 Caledonian Road might be demolished due to development planned in the area, Switchboard decided to launch a campaign to raise £100,000 to purchase its own property. The campaign was aptly called 'Put Your Money Where Our Mouth Is' and it was a success: in October 1988 Switchboard became the owner of a building half a mile up the road, nearer to Angel. They then raised further funds to convert the building to meet their needs, eventually moving there in 1993. Diana volunteered for Switchboard across these years and, in a book celebrating sixty years of 5 Caledonian Road, she noted the importance of the charity's first low-rent home: 'Switchboard might have existed but not as it is . . . Switchboard has saved lives, so if 5 Cally Road hadn't been there to help set Switchboard up, or give it a place, how many lives would we have lost?'[15]

As we made the podcast and interviewed our elders, one very pressing theme emerged about housing: as a cohort, they seemed to have done better than our generation, the middle generation, will. In fact, many lived in large homes which they owned and decorated beautifully, having somehow made financial successes of themselves despite the odds. This was pretty jarring to us, and forced us to reflect on our own positions, as queer people working and living in our thirties, trying to create the homes and lifestyles we desired under testing economic conditions. People of our generation who have bought a home have mostly had a two-income household, with higher-than-average salaries and/or with money from biological family members from the older generation. Tash could only buy a flat at thirty-seven after their Uncle Kim passed away and left some money to them.

In many ways our identity-based freedoms were greater than those of the elders we interviewed, but our economic chances were poorer – simply because of how much housing costs have outstripped income growth for our generation. In 1968 housing costs constituted 9 per cent of average disposable incomes for households in the poorest quarter of the population; this had risen to 26 per cent by 2015.[16] Between 1986 and 2021 home ownership rates for thirty- to thirty-four-year-olds fell by 20 percentage points (compared to just 3 percentage points in the USA).[17] A study by the Office for National Statistics in 2023 found that while earnings had doubled since 1997, house prices had increased by four and a half times.[18] And in the period from 2002 to 2023 in England and Wales, the ratio of house price to income nearly doubled from 4.81 to 8. In London, where lots of queer people want to make a home, it more than doubled, from 6.74 to 12.66.[19]

This is how, on every economic measure, it has become harder for the children of Section 28, whatever their gender identity or sexuality, to establish a home than it was for our elders.

There were stark economic differences between our generations, but when we visited the homes of the elders we interviewed, the economic differences between them, too, crystallised. Some of them, such as Femi and Lisa, had managed to build financially successful careers out of ethics forged in their LGBTQ+ community work as Switchboard volunteers, leading to good housing options. In contrast, due to long-term disability and ill-health from HIV complications, George Hodson had been unable to work and so had lived for decades in a flat owned by the council and rented to him at a very low rate; long-term Switchboard volunteer Richard Desmond lived in a similar model. It was a good but grim deal – many councils handed such leases to men who, like George, were living with HIV and not expected to live very long. During our research into our elders and their housing arrangements, we found so many disquieting situations like this one. It became apparent that many of them faced a difficult housing future, too. George provided the best example, not least because he himself was depressingly aware of his own impending struggle. When Adam first interviewed him in 2020, George had said, 'If I take a fall this afternoon I'm going to be shipped off to a homophobic care home 'cause I have no money, no choice, no savings, and that's very scary.'

Adam listened as George described his flourishing years sharing homes with friends and lovers in San Francisco, and proudly living alone in a flat he bought with his own salary, decorated with collages he had made and knick-knacks he had collected. Decades later, Adam had to observe George's poverty and related housing insecurity. George's life mirrored something of how calls to Switchboard changed over its first forty years, too. In the seventies and eighties, the volunteers primarily served people in their teens, twenties, and thirties. As these callers got older, many of them became more isolated and called Switchboard again, not for pub and nightclub recommendations this time but for help with fears like George's.

George was terrified of having to live in a nursing home surrounded by strangers who would expect him to hide his sexuality, after decades of living freely with it. 'I can't be who I want to be in my final days,' he said, thinking of that prospect. George knew that he was not alone: thousands of elderly LGBTQ+ people, and HIV survivors like him, were facing the same fate. 'We're really in a difficult situation 'cause we have no savings, so we'll be sent to these awful places where we can't be ourselves.' George's greatest fear was having to hide his sexuality and spend his final days listening to Vera Lynn on a loop.

Such concerns came to life for those LGBTQ+ people who, like Noel Glynn, did indeed have to move into a care home. Noel's story is an example of how the dominant housing model intersects with enduring homophobia, with devastating effects for LGBTQ+ people, especially in our older years. Noel moved into a care home with dementia in 2018. His partner of fifty years, Ted Brown, stayed in their house in Brixton, round the corner from the Railton Road co-op, which is where Tash interviewed him in 2023. Staff and other residents in the care home behaved in ways towards Noel that substantiated George's fears. According to Ted, Noel was called a 'dirty fag', slapped, and spat on; Ted also found bruises and cigarette burns on his partner. On visiting Noel, Ted was asked who he was in relation to Noel, time and time again. The staff in the home could not entertain the idea that these two elderly men could be partners. Tash felt so full of anger and emotion sat in Ted's kitchen, the home he had shared with Noel, listening to him. As a seasoned gay rights activist, Ted was not short on perseverance, but he did not expect his own later years to require him to endure such homophobia. Ted was invited to a consultation about Noel's needs, but was assumed to be his father. 'I'm saying this is an example of homophobia because the minimum information those people would have had about me and Noel, would have been at least our names,' he told Tash. 'My surname is Brown. His surname is Glynn [which the care home misspelt]. They might have had our ages. He was seventy-six. I was sixty-nine. He's white, I'm Black. There is no way they could have mistaken him for my father. It was like a slap in the face!'

After losing Noel, and suffering such indignities, Ted began working with Clare Truscott on a campaign called Not Going Into the Care Closet, with three aims to reform care homes for older LGBTQ+ people: to make noise, stop the abuse, and ensure the abuse is treated as a crime. They worked on it with Opening Doors London, a charity supporting elderly LGBTQ+ folks, but the charity closed in 2024 due to a lack of funding.

A small number of LGBTQ+-affirming care homes opened in the 2010s and 2020s, and a small private retirement community was established in Vauxhall with a loan from the Mayor of London, but none of these schemes came close to meeting the housing needs of an entire generation of queer elders and survivors. For the most part, they were pitched at well above what the average elder could afford. Adam listened to George ask for help, and felt helpless. 'I'm trying to raise awareness in the community that we need to be looked after,' said George, looking at Adam, expecting the brains and the strength of his middle generation to find a way to take care of their elders, to house them, to celebrate them – and to find the millions of pounds needed to do this. Later, in writing this book, Adam realised why George's pleas reverberated so loudly with him that day: because he felt a stronger sense of duty to solve the long-term housing and care needs for George than for his mum. Her circumstances were much easier than George's, and a sense of duty hooked into Adam.

———

Recording our elders' memories of housing was a way for us to keep their dream alive, for our own generation and for future ones. Adam was surprised to see anew his yearning for shared and communal living, set against examples from the past that were now impossible; Tash discovered how a feeling of comfort can come from living with fellow queer people, and yet even this was still held away from too many. Our research started off trying to capture how Switchboard supported runaways and flat-hunters in its early decades, but instead we found a battlefield – dominant economics and lifestyles versus queer people who don't fit either. Through speaking to our elders, we realised there is so much more at stake than whether we have a roof over our heads. There is the physical thing of housing, that is, somewhere to live, and the means to stay; and there is the emotional thing of the home, the place where we feel safe, secure, and loved. This is why our elders' stories of housing became so personal to us: they comprised a chronicle of living in a world that has been built for healthy, able-bodied people who live in couples pooling two high incomes. This all clashed with many of the earlier visions for radical queer ways of living, which have withered.

Typical economic behaviour compounded society's typical view of what makes a valid family to make it more and more difficult for queer people to feel at home. This combination of factors has shaped the options we have for how to live. We cannot always realise the homes we need in order to house our love for each other. But through the force of this love, queer people have always been at the forefront of defining family in our own unique ways.

7
'FATALLY DISRUPTIVE'

How queer people redefined the family

19 July 1995
Took a call from a woman who has been married 25 years & last year found out her husband was gay & then this year admitted to him she was lesbian. Both of them wanted to know how to break the news to their kids of 24, 20 & 19.

Life comes at you fast. We smiled at the image of the role of the parent being subverted in the entry above, the caller and her husband trying to work out how to come out to their kids. The woman who made that call was not alone. Thousands of log book entries reveal family surprises like hers.

As these records contain stories of people in their intimate crisis moments, they reveal an arresting truth: even if there is a model way to live, no one follows it. And the thing about LGBTQ+ people is that by definition they exist outside the model:

4 April 1976
There is no where one can get LEGALLY married is there? Caller reports that in Germany, Holland, Denmark + Sweden a relationship can be used to prevent one being sent back to one's own country.

27 October 1994
A woman rang in asking for info about artificial insemination/ parenting. I said that I'd leave addresses on the log for her as she said she'd ring back later. I referred her to the **Lesbian Alternative**

<u>**Insemination Group**</u>. I couldn't find the addresses of Donor Insemination (AID) Group. Are they still going? Other addresses which might be useful. Lewisham Lesbian Mothers Group.

Long before we began to dream about how we might configure our lives as queer adults, our elders were trying out all sorts of families. This was especially gratifying to us – as we read those log books, we also began trying to understand why we felt so far outside the family model that our parents had brought us into.

We had to make ourselves into a history project. We headed to Tash's old haunts in Plymouth and Adam's in Cleethorpes and Grimsby. Tash sat for dinner in the same room where Adam's parents had interrogated his sister about her sexuality all those years ago. We even got to step inside the house that Tash had grown up in, sold by their parents long ago. The current owner saw us lurking outside, as Tash told Adam a story about their teenage bedroom. The owner opened the front door and invited us to look around. It turned out she'd recently put it on the market and assumed we were interested in buying it. We also interviewed each other's parents and sisters. We went to work on each other's pasts together, as historians, as friends, as two children of Section 28, as family. We had to think about the straight, cisgender families of our pasts, but also the families that we, as queer adults, were creating. This was a project about the future as much as it was about history.

As we grew up in our average houses in our average nuclear families, television producers tried to reflect our lives back to us. From 1991 to 1999 the BBC aired a sitcom called *2point4 Children* – named after the statistical average family size at the time – and we both watched it with our own family members. The show chronicled the travails of a chaotic family, filled with the apparently comedic value of seeing characters conform to stereotypes: the busybody mum, the feckless dad, the dramatic teenage daughter, and her mischievous younger brother.

On paper, and in the census, our families were the same as the statistical average, and the supposedly desirable model. And the thing about the idea of an average 'family' is that it tells queer people they're not welcome. As we worked on the podcast we heard about something that happened to Tony Whitehead, a former Switchboard volunteer. In 1976 he was working for British Home Stores (BHS), a department store chain with a branch in Worthing. One day he was featured in a TV documentary where he was seen kissing another man. The day after the broadcast, Tony's employer summoned him to the company headquarters. He entered a room filled with a panel of men in suits. 'I was just grilled, interrogated, verbally beaten, for quite a long time,' Tony told Adam in 2019. 'What it seemed to hinge on was that, they were saying, "BHS is a family firm, therefore you being publicly identified in the media as gay could bring us into disrepute, and damage our family-friendly reputation."' BHS was a shop selling things for the homes of British families, but those homes had no room for gay people.

Reprimanded, Tony returned to work but was shunted around different branches so frequently that he chose to do what the bosses must have wanted all along: he quit. Tony's cause was taken up by activists who staged demos and generated press coverage. But the powerful idea of the 'family' was unshaken: a few years later our lawmakers began the process to protect whatever idea was in the heads of the BHS execs, codifying it into Section 28. Family, most commonly in legal jargon and the census, is defined as 'individuals related by blood, marriage, or adoption'. This is the traditional idea of family, and it is a blueprint for life that was impressed upon us from childhood. Teenaged Tash and their mum would often have arguments about how Tash seemed to care more about their friends than their family; Tash resented their dad working in the Navy and living elsewhere, leaving behind Tash, their mum, and little sister Livi. As we wrote this, Tash realised they were the same age (thirty-eight) as their mum was when she was raising fourteen-year-old Tash. It must have been exhausting. Tash loved their family, and there was no denying that their family loved them back, but teenaged Tash had definitely sought something different. Tash longed for a world where they could see themself in the faith they were brought up in, in the teachers at their school, and in their friends around them. But they also needed help in understanding what was happening for them with their gender. There was no blueprint for that anywhere. Tash was left struggling, lost for words, and in need of something more.

In another part of the country, the completely average family that Adam was raised in buckled when he was eighteen. His sister had just come out, and Adam witnessed their parents' reaction place a heavy strain on the family.

Through log book entries about lesbians hunting for sperm donors or Switchboard volunteers referring to each other as family, we have seen the history of how the concept of family has changed through the lived experiences of queer people. While the traditional family grows through procreation, queer family grows through affiliation and liberation. As we were researching the subject of family in the log books, we even met several LGBTQ+ people who had formed relationships like uncle and nephew, with responsibilities but without blood ties. These relationships had grown with intention, care, acceptance, and love. Those attributes were supposed to be true of the traditional family, and yet such families couldn't seem to hold queer people well:

'FATALLY DISRUPTIVE'

4 December 1998

Just taken a call from a (possibly drunk) Irish guy calling about this 17 year old son who he thinks is gay. This man needs serious challenging. He wasn't particularly argumentative, didn't shout & didn't sound aggressive but he was a Catholic ex-squaddie & v. homophobic (something wrong with our brain, wrong, god doesn't want it – the usual) Good luck if you get him. He's an arse.

This volunteer's note rang out loud and clear to Tash who took their first holy communion at eight years old, wearing a costume that looked like a wedding dress and veil. Their parents kept the photos, and Tash retained the metallic taste of the cheap wine. Tash was Catholic, attending church every Sunday and catechism every Friday, plus Catholic camp in the summer. By 2019, as they sat down with a former Switchboard volunteer for a podcast interview, Tash had long left the church behind, but something said by Rebecca Swenson tied Tash's throat into a knot. 'I just remember lots of church services at the time where there'd be a special prayer at the end for anyone who thought they might be gay,' said Rebecca, 'and given that I was the only person in the congregation under the age of eighty, it was clear who they were talking about.'

Tash first met Rebecca when they joined Switchboard and was struck by her gentle and considered manner. This was unusual in a charity filled with louder characters such as Lisa and Julian, and it turned out that Rebecca had been surviving the loud voices for a long time. Her vicar had told her congregation that if any of them thought they might be gay they had better pray to god for forgiveness. 'It was quite horrible,' said Rebecca. 'It was really striking with the venom he said it.'

Tash could see how hard this memory was for Rebecca all those years later. 'There was no one else . . . it could only have been about *me*. Having that kind of spotlight shone on you was frightening, it was oppressive and you don't shake [it] off easily. That feeling of being bad, or feeling different.'

Listening to Rebecca and finding log book entries like the one describing the Catholic ex-squaddie dad made Tash reflect on their own upbringing. It made them think about attending church with their Irish Catholic Nana. Tash was showered with love by their Nana; Nana taught them poker and, most importantly, introduced them to the TV soap *Neighbours*. Tash and Nana were their own family-within-a-family, but sadly she died when Tash was fourteen, just as Tash was starting to discover part of their true self. Tash never got the chance to tell their Nana who they really were. And then, in a religious studies lesson, Tash learnt how the Catholic Church stood against abortion, euthanasia, and homosexuality. Hit by a realisation that they disagreed with their church, Tash felt sick about it. They went home crying, and shouted at their mum, 'How could you have brought me up in this religion? I've just found out what it really means. How can I stand up and say I'm a proud Catholic?'

Leaving your religion is like leaving your family. For Tash, it was another reason to feel less at home in the family. They started to shut out their relatives, and in turn became more and more isolated.

> 4 October 1983
> Can we be very supportive to a young lad phoning from Bishops Stortford who just wants to talk to someone who is gay – can we please ensure that he receives positive gay models (& I don't mean the sort from Gay News!) and not stereotypical

commercially-scene oriented ones either. He's only 17, isolated, living at home, all his friends are straight & have girl friends & he knows he's gay and at present has no-one . . .

Experiences of isolation are not unique to being queer. Any teenager, caught in a hazy, hormonal headfuck, is just trying to work it all out. This is something that almost everyone can relate to – the feeling of being different to your parents. They don't like your music, they don't accept your choice of career, they don't want your faith to be different to theirs, they vote the wrong way . . . With queer people like the seventeen-year-old caller above, there is an extra element to this difference, and we have both felt it in our families: *They do not understand who I am.* Sexuality isn't everything about a person, but we do believe that it is a huge part of how a person approaches the world – especially when it is alternative to the sexuality of most others around them. Ditto gender identity: if how you feel does not match how other people perceive you, this difference can consume you and how you experience a home life.

The above log book entry also struck us for another reason: the volunteer impressed the importance of the 'young lad' receiving positive gay models, outside of the stereotypes. It made us think about what it means to be 'gay' or 'queer', outside of an individual's sexuality and gender identity. Stereotypes are based on assumptions, often about subcultures, like the many captured by volunteers in the log books: the nightlife, the protests, the sexual promiscuity, the radical housing. These are all things that are attributed to queerness, but what happens if you don't feel aligned with these behaviours? Tash's friend from school who was struggling with dysphoria started their journey to transition not long after they finished school. The world perceives them as a cis man and their relationship with their wife as heteronormative, but Tash's friend is trans and their wife is bisexual. It's hard to know if these are the sort of role models the volunteer was talking about in that log book entry, or if they both felt isolated in their own way.

> 11 April 1984
>
> I had a call from a woman in Lewes who knows she's gay but is feeling very mixed up & isolated – has contacted local gay group without too much success & just needs to chat to other lesbians for support . . . just needs enough confidence to carry on trying to meet other women!

Like Tash, this caller had friends but didn't know anyone who was gay, and she too was left isolated. Actually, in Tash's case this wasn't strictly true, as Tash had their sister all along. Livi was just eleven when Tash told her they thought they might be gay. Livi was the first person Tash told, and she met Tash with love and understanding, even saying that she thought she might be gay too. (She wasn't, she just thought some of Tash's friends were really pretty, but it made Tash smile.) Tash felt like they had no one because what they needed was someone who was queer.

In fact, Tash had gay family members, but their sexuality felt hidden. No one talked about how Great-Uncle Fred had relationships with men until Tash broke the silence by coming out. And then their Papa (grandfather) said it was his family's 'fault', having also produced Fred and a string of 'spinster women' who lived with other women.

Similarly, Adam's family included a great-uncle who was quite possibly gay, a fact that had been long buried until adult Adam began asking questions. As we read through the log books, we saw the ghosts of our own queer blood ancestors flickering back to life, at a distance, in silence. They had never been allowed to guide us, or even model a way of living. When Adam's sister Hannah came out, she was pushed out of the family home. All these queers in the family didn't fit the model. Is that why they were held away from us?

———

Between December 1986 and February 1987, a volunteer at Switchboard pasted a series of clippings into the log books. They were photocopies of transcripts from debates under way in the House of Lords. In one, the speaker was Frank Pakenham, who as a minister under Labour governments had championed rehabilitation for offenders and even helped with the partial decriminalisation of homosexuality in 1967. But he was also a traditionalist: he was a Christian who served in Britain's legislature by hereditary right as the seventh Earl of Longford. He hated the idea that 'heterosexuality and homosexuality should be placed on precisely the same footing'. Core to Lord Longford's belief was that this would undermine the traditional conception of family.

The speech caught the eye of a Switchboard volunteer who spotted that it needed archiving, highlighting passages in which Longford opposes council libraries stocking books such as *Jenny Lives with Eric and Martin*. The context of Longford's speech was the parliamentary debate that led to the passage of Section 28, banning public bodies from 'promoting homosexuality':[1]

> Of course the promotion of homosexuality goes hand in hand with a good deal of promotion of promiscuity of all kinds, aimed in quite a few cases at very young children. It is revolting stuff.
>
> . . .

> Can any country claiming to be Christian spend public money on the active propagation of actual homosexual practices?
>
> . . .
>
> We are talking of actual sexual relationships and behaviour. These are being promoted now in some areas as an alternative to fidelity in marriage and family life.
>
> . . .
>
> The tragedy of such people is that they cannot enjoy family life and they cannot have children.
>
> . . .
>
> In so far as an attempt is being made to expand homosexualism throughout this community, the outcome can only be fatally disruptive for the family . . . I am not saying that the promotion of acts of homosexuality should necessarily be made illegal . . . I say only that it should not be financed by public bodies in a country that still claims to be Christian.

We were still in nappies, but already this unelected lord was questioning our ability to form family bonds. (Later, Tash, who already felt angry at the church, read this speech and wrote in their research notes, 'Fuck you, Lord!') Ruth Turner, who was not yet a Switchboard volunteer at the time of the speech, remembered the atmosphere like this: 'We were being described in such pernicious language as perverts and people that were going to break up the normal nuclear family.' People like Lord Longford did not believe that people become queer as part of their nature; he thought that we were pure heterosexuals liable to corruption by the sleazy influence of homosexuality. That threat could only be resisted by the solidity and safety of the nuclear family.

And yet this is the exact model that we did not belong in.

'FATALLY DISRUPTIVE'

For Adam the family felt like a place of love and support, and in many ways it was, but it was built on his parents' firm ideas about how a person should live. They shielded him and his sister from other, more troubled family members. They criticised their own friends' ways and occasionally judged strangers harshly. The effect was an atmosphere of 'them and us'. *We do things a certain way*, they seemed to say; *we're not like the others.*

Most people recognise that their parents are just regular people with flaws well before Adam did, at eighteen. When his sister came out as gay, the boundary of the family was shifted by their parents, and Hannah was asked to live some of her life outside of it. This set Hannah and Adam on their own path, not just because both were queer and their parents were heterosexual, but because suddenly it was clear that the children had a different idea of family to the one their parents had built. Hannah and Adam had to leave that family, physically and emotionally. It took years: they all stayed in contact with their parents, but both siblings also built new families through their twenties and thirties. Sometimes, you just have to go.

> 1 August 1992
> Liam in SE London has just phoned on a reverse charge call. He is **15** and has been kicked out of his home by his parents because his boyfriend's parents told Liam's parents that he is gay. He was kicked out 2 days ago with a bag of clothes and no money. He's staying with his boyfriend tonite (He's also 15 years old). Luckily his boyfriend's parents are away for a few days. However Liam has got to be from there when they return on Tuesday 4 August. He has rung his parents in the hope of them speaking to him but they just put the phone down on him. He is desperate, has no relatives in London, no gay friends etc where he can go. I have

advised him to go to the Council Social Services and to tell them he is homeless first thing Monday morning. He's also worried about his gayness, we had a chat to put him at his ease. I suggested to him that if Social Services do not help him he should ring again here and seek further advice. He's very sensible, very hurt and very vulnerable. Treat him with intelligence and respect and try to help him.

When Lord Longford opined in parliament that 'the tragedy of such people is that they cannot enjoy family life', he was talking about this boy Liam. He was talking about Hannah. He was also talking about people like our contributor Marc Thompson, who, as Lord Longford spoke, had been recently diagnosed with the novel HIV. 'I will never have children,' thought Marc to himself as he walked out of the clinic. With no way to remove or even reduce the virus at that time, parents could easily pass it on to their children. And in any case, Marc thought he wouldn't live much longer: an HIV diagnosis was like a death sentence. The unelected lord was right: Marc would not enjoy a family life.

Longford was also talking about us. He was trying to bring about a law that would hide homosexuality from us. Otherwise, he said, 'the outcome can only be fatally disruptive for the family'. Of course, it was in fact bigotry like his that meant we couldn't enjoy a family life. It was a lack of love and understanding like Adam's parents showed that was 'fatally disruptive' for the family. Everywhere, teenagers kept leaving, and the calls to Switchboard kept coming:

12 November 1998

Have just taken a call from a TS who is living at home with parents in what seems to be an awful situation. Wants to find somewhere else to live/stay **Tonight**. Has rung back several times but mother keeps cutting off the calls.

'FATALLY DISRUPTIVE'

> Caller's parents are stopping her from wearing womens clothes & living as a woman which her GP has told her to do for 12–11 months. Parents are very abusive & not accepting her choice – are screening all of her calls.
> Also needs T/S referrals

For teenagers who run away from home and call Switchboard, it is often a matter of life or death. Everyone knows that teenagers are dramatic, but it is also true that lives are often threatened by family members who are homophobic, biphobic, or transphobic. It's all just words and looks, until it's not. When we made the first season of the podcast in 2019, we spoke to Carla Ecola who had founded The Outside Project to support LGTBQ+ people experiencing homelessness. In taking in people like the callers above, Carla pointed out, 'Family rejection means we don't have that safety net. We move away from our homes to try to be around other LGBTQI+ people, so people from small towns will go to big cities, quite unprepared for the cultural change, financially unprepared.'[2]

For so many queer people, this has ended in homelessness. Could we really expect the young person who made the following call to stay at home?

> 8 January 1984
> Oh what a night! I had a call from a guy called Ian in Leeds. Straightforward call – gave him Leeds S/bd & GYM, and had a chat to him. He called back an hour later – his stepfather had listened to the whole call on the extension & had a furious row with him when the call finished. Ian was in a state (but he had unplugged the extension!) and he had to wait until his mother came home from work (she's a nurse on the night-shift), so I talked him through for 3 hours. He will be calling back and needs **lots** of support. He's got guts but is very scared and isolated, so be nice.

When Adam read this log book entry, from the year of his birth, he felt the same isolation that the caller had felt. That was because he had experienced it too; Adam also had furious rows with his parents, in his case about his sister. Tash was scared too, like the caller, but couldn't hold their feelings in, coming out at fifteen. Both Tash's parents listened intently, their dad said, 'I thought so', and then the conversation was over. Tash never questioned the love their parents had for them, but at that moment neither of them knew what Tash needed, nor did Tash have the words to ask for it. This is how society pushed us out of the type of family that was held up as the standard. Our families were the type of nuclear family that hurt so many people who felt they could only turn to Switchboard. They, like us, were pulled elsewhere, towards a huge, extended queer family.

Tash started to build their queer family when at university in Bristol. They worked nights and weekends at the Queenshilling gay bar, got elected to the managing committee of the university LGBT society (as it was then), and formed deep bonds with two people who became lifelong friends. First, Jonny. It was the closest Tash had ever felt to falling in love with a friend, but fortunately without all the complexities of sexual desire. They became inseparable and quickly moved in together as flatmates. Suddenly, a new home and a new family. It was liberating. Soon after, Tash met Layla. They quickly worked out their queer connections, and a deep friendship began to develop. Jonny and Layla made Tash feel strongly that they belonged. They found home in each other, although their lives had been vastly different. For a start, as we saw in the last chapter, Layla had migrated to the UK from Somalia using a false passport, and was in the process of removing the influence that Islam had held over her. This helped her to bond with Tash, who was still distancing themself from Christianity. They spent days discussing the hold of religion, around the time that callers like this one were reaching out to Switchboard:

> 20 November 2002
>
> Had a lengthy call from a young Islamic woman, originally from Iran. Has come out to her mother, who has become incredibly hostile. Her father lives back in Iran and is threatening to come over and kill her. She is naturally very fearful especially as her visa is only valid for another 12 months. Have found some support groups and the Naz Project for her and given them to her. I have told her that she can ring us anytime that she wants to. It is not an easy call to take as one's own anger and annoyance and sheer frustration bubbles to the surface, really found it difficult not to introduce my own agenda, but a really worthwhile call.

It wasn't until Tash sat down with Layla in 2024 to interview her for the book that Layla went into the deep details of her childhood, now able, with the gifts of time and therapy, to process it properly. Like the above caller, Layla was brought up in a strict Islamic household and had moved to the UK when she was a teenager. As Layla started to dig deep into her lived experience, she realised that there were aspects of herself that she had deeply denied: her Blackness and specifically her Somalian, Islamic heritage. 'I think I was deliberately avoiding it,' she said. Tash remembered times walking in the street with Layla when they would have to quickly change direction, or how Layla would refuse to get into taxis if she thought the driver was Somalian. 'My family had been really hard with me,' she said, adding that she saw some other people of colour as an extension of her family. 'I was like, I don't want to be judged,' she said, 'so I'm going to avoid.' Layla's family knew she was in Bristol, which was also where her brother lived, and she knew they were trying to find her and take her away from her burgeoning queer family, back to Somalia.

After Layla moved to London, she started to integrate herself more into the Black queer community. She joined a new family, Sisters Uncut, a feminist direct action group that opposed cuts to UK government services for domestic violence victims. 'Black sisters of colour . . . really took me under their wing,' she said. 'I think my life has changed after that . . . just to feeling very proud.' It is a feeling that previous volunteer Femi explained to us like this: 'Family is something cultural, as well as being something biological. And that connects me to my ethnicity . . . It's given me confidence, culture, a sense of belonging.'

There is also a special bond between queer people inside what might look like traditional families. Adam and Hannah have their own queer sibling connection as well as being blood siblings. When she came out to Adam, she said that their parents might not accept it. He didn't believe it, but in any case he knew he would support her. When Hannah did leave the family home, she remembered later, 'I just felt horrendous because I'd left him with Mum and Dad stewing in the situation.' Hannah spoke to Tash in 2023 and expressed how awful an environment it would have been for Adam. She knew for a fact that he was in there defending her, saying, 'It's Hannah, come on, you know Hannah. She's still Hannah. She's still the same person.' This was hard for Adam, for years, but it strengthened the siblings' bond.

And the log books document some other beautiful moments inside what might look like a traditional 'family' set-up:

'FATALLY DISRUPTIVE'

> 6 June 1985
> Young man from Leeds, who rang last night to say his girlfriend had found him dressing up in her clothes, and who had walked out on him, rang again tonight to tell us she has issued him with an ultimatum: if he is going into TV, it's got be full time, and she will help with the hairdo and makeup. He has accepted her terms and her offer of help. Happy ending.

Being given the freedom by a family member to explore your identity and gender expression is a powerful moment, but this exploration can often start when we are much younger, with no one actually wise to it. This is how Tash started to imagine themself as Jason Donovan, or just simply 'Jase'. Tash's mum thought it was sweet, and Tash was certainly more helpful as Jase, but what was happening for Tash was much deeper than role-play. Often we don't realise the impacts of these early moments until we are much older.

> 18 August 1975
> Had a really good call from a woman asking where her husband can meet gay people to talk to etc. because he's in a state & she doesn't like him being unhappy – a really nice person, wow!

Hopefully this gay husband went off to a bunch of bars, discos, or clubs, and found his tribe; the couple may even have stayed together, each developing their own separate romantic and/or sexual relationships. It is clear, at the least, that she knew he needed to build a queer family. Tash's Great-Uncle Fred had managed to do that: living in a house with another gay man, making it a space for various queer housemates over the years. Adam thought going to university in a big city would help him to find new friends, although at that stage he was looking for people who liked thinking and studying, and wasn't seeking people who liked being gay. Later, when he came out at twenty-nine, he began to build a new set of friends altogether. Most of them were met through sex, but also queer nightlife, book events, and film festivals. Once, at a straight wedding, he gravitated towards three other gay guests, and the four of them became besties.

All these folks were so different from his earlier friendships, and the family life he had, and even Hannah. Like Jonny and Layla were for Tash, Adam's new friendships would be the ones to help him through the dark periods to come.

This is the power of queer family: they understand you because they go through the same, or similar, things as you. This is how Steph Fuller, whom we met in Chapter 2, became best friends with Sarah, who, like Steph, is also trans.

Steph grew up in a terraced house in Kent. In the family cellar was a dressing-up box full of old clothes, including a blue dress that Steph loved to wear, before she realised she was trans. 'It was really, really important to me, and I didn't know why.'

Every 5 November, all the local houses would make a big bonfire on the disused railway line behind their gardens, topped by a dummy representing Guy Fawkes, stuffed with old clothes and newspapers. One year, Steph's family added her favourite blue dress to the pyre. 'I was devastated,' Steph told Tash in 2023, still feeling upset about it. Her family had not understood something basic about Steph, and hadn't thought to ask her. 'I'd never told anybody that actually, [dressing up] isn't just a game to me, because I didn't know it wasn't. But I knew somehow this really mattered to me. And they burnt it. And I was honestly devastated . . . it was really symbolic. To me, that really meant something.'

Tash had first met Steph when they were co-chair of Switchboard, and the board of trustees hired Steph to run the charity. They came to know each other well and went through a lot as they navigated the complexities of leading a charity together. It was in these moments when Steph shared her personal stories that Tash felt their bond strengthening, and a care for Steph as a friend deepening. Steph's family could not have understood, could not have seen what she saw in the blue dress, could not have empathised fully with her as she stepped into hospital for her gender-affirming surgery. 'I didn't have anyone to support me except for Sarah,' she said.

Steph and Sarah met in the clubs and became really close friends. When Steph was in hospital, Sarah visited Steph every day; she took Steph home when she was discharged. For the first two weeks of Steph's twelve-week recovery, she couldn't do anything for herself, so Sarah moved in with her. 'I just don't think you could put a price on a friend like that,' she said. 'There is such an incredible act of kindness. And understanding, I guess . . . I don't know if I'd have recovered so well, had it not been for her.'

This is the kind of bond that callers were looking for when they called Switchboard. They may have asked for bar recommendations or the contact details of a social club; they may have wanted to party with fellow lesbians or play chess with other gay nerds. But really they were also looking for the unspoken bond that can exist between queer people.

The experiences that we go through as queer people have a huge impact on the families we build and join. In fact, after we finished the third and final full season of the podcast, Tash came to realise that the longest relationship they'd had had been with Switchboard!

Veteran volunteer Lisa Power had said the same thing of herself.

'Just like any good family, any good childhood, we regret things,' said Lisa of her days in the charity. 'There were a lot of interpersonal rows which were very stupid. There were also walloping political rows about race, gender.' When Lisa added that the rows had contributed to her own personal development, and the evolution of the charity, Tash knew exactly what she meant. Through their twenties and into their thirties, Tash had grown up in Switchboard. Tash was shaped by the calls they took, leading them to know the value in sharing the stories of the log books with the wider world. And Tash had learnt more about who they were and what they believed through the people they met – people like Lisa, Diana, Julian, Femi, Ruth, and Richard – and the conversations they shared. It wasn't until Tash started to have these conversations that they were able to really start to unpick their feelings around family. These elders helped Tash to have the long overdue conversations with their mum, and later their dad, that they had so desperately needed as a kid.

When Tash first began to visit Ruth in her home, to interview her for the podcast, they were moved by how much Ruth seemed to be at peace. She was an example of an older queer person who was single, child-free, and filling her life. In Ruth's case, this meant lots of courses, political canvassing, gardening, and being a Switchboard volunteer. It sounds simple but Ruth's life was stable, and this struck Tash because they observed it at a time when lots of their friends were achieving stability through marriage and children. Plus, Ruth was whip-smart and wise and just the person Tash needed in their chosen family. They came to be like auntie and nibling.

Ruth listened to Tash, time and again. She listened to Tash talk about the latest drama at Switchboard, or their worries about how to make the podcast a success, and also about the horror of having to go to straight weddings in churches. When Tash shared their feelings against the vicar talking about the special love between a man and a woman, and how flames of anger roiled inside them, Ruth nodded calmly and said she understood completely. 'I find it deeply uncomfortable,' she said during one conversation. 'And I've had to sit on my hands and not say anything. And exactly as you say, you look around, and nobody else thinks that there's anything strange about it.'

This is one of the many reasons why many people from the LGBTQ+ family want to be married: to change the face of the institution, to rewrite the language, and to put lie to the claim that our families are 'pretended'. As the log books show, although not in great number, callers were keen to expand these traditions:

> 1 January 1990
> A woman phoned asking about lesbian marriages in the Netherlands, and how to go about it. I didn't know, and couldn't find any info in our files.
> I directed her to Amsterdam Switchboard, and to Lesbian + Gay Christian Movement. Do we have any listings for lesbian/gay marriages/partnerships.

Another volunteer responded:

> Dudley Cave (vol) is often willing to conduct services for same-sex partners at Golders Green Unitarian Church. See Christians on file. (These have no legal significance)

Gathering family members through life is something that queer people have a somewhat unique experience of. We thought about all the older people who called Switchboard because they were lonely, and didn't have any family members to care for them. We thought about the contributors who'd been mistreated by social services and the care sector, such as Noel Glynn. And we thought about George, who developed a friendship with Adam after initially giving interviews for the podcast. Adam found a connection with George, who was a storyteller and an artist, who had a sharp tongue and a way of looking at life both sardonically and with a sense of wonder. They were like uncle and nephew, but they called each other 'Prof' and 'Rose'. Adam reminded George of his early gay days when his friends in San Francisco called him Rose (on account of being English), so George let Adam resurrect that name; George called Adam Prof because he'd written a book. When Prof visited Rose in the spring, the older man pressed fresh canary-yellow mimosa cuttings into his hand. Rose was always as interested in Prof's sexy nights out as Prof was interested in Rose's stories from decades ago. Prof had to help Rose access his computer files and delete old emails. Rose gave Prof artworks he'd made, and Prof brought cakes and books round. They were a family of sorts.

But Adam was also still close to his sister Hannah. In fact, she and her partner had asked him to change the shape of their own family, forever.

---

7 July 1995

Caller from BBC Radio Glasgow – a programme on lesbian parenting is on tonight & they will be giving out our number so be prepared! Ho-hum . . . just realised there's no-one [on] duty til tomorrow 11am though.

23 January 2003

A woman from Newcastle rang to find out how to go about becoming artificially inseminated. I couldn't find anything on the system.

[Here another volunteer has written: *Look under 'Pregnant' or 'Pregnancy']

In the 1970s, the lesbian separatists didn't know what to do about baby-making. Sperm banks and fertility clinics refused to acknowledge lesbian couples. Even local GPs were unsympathetic, as a rule, and the British Medical Association had considered a ban on lesbians using artificial insemination by sperm donors. The doctors narrowly voted against the proposed ban, but not on the basis of a woman's right to choose. Instead, they just acknowledged how a ban would be impractical to enforce. Perhaps they knew a truth that women were sharing among themselves anyway. 'People realised that fertility is actually quite a low-tech issue,' said Marguerite Maclaughlin, in 2022, remembering taking lesbians' calls to Switchboard about this issue. 'All you needed was a cooperative man.'

As the log book entries above show, Switchboard became a repository of requests, but clearly it wasn't the charity's remit to put sperm into egg. Instead, the volunteers gave general advice about how to do it, and where they could get specific support. For all this they relied on publications such as the *Lesbian Self Insemination Pamphlet*. This little publication was printed in 1980 by the Feminist Self Insemination Group, a group of lesbian feminists who met in 1978 to discuss the process of what they termed 'self insemination', and their journeys through that. On one of Tash's visits to see Ruth, they were handed a copy of this pamphlet among a stash of zines, books, and leaflets all on the same topic. On the bright yellow cover of the one about self-insemination, Ruth had written her own name and, on the inside, the date she obtained it, June 1983.

The pamphlet was full of practical tips about planning self-insemination, including such things as temperature and ovulation, as well as tracts about the lack of support from doctors and wider society. Ruth had written notes between the columns and highlighted sections in green. One of her highlighted sections in particular struck Tash:

> Most women (if any at all) do not have a clear choice about whether or not to have a child. Patriarchal society has established, and continuously reinforces, the rearing of children as almost the only function through which a woman makes herself visible and gains an identity. This idea that having a child makes a woman real robs us of our right to choose our particular struggle towards a self-defined identity.

The words 'self-defined identity' landed strongly with Ruth, back in 1983. Next to them she had written 'want'.

The pamphlet came alive in anecdotes from women. 'I felt like a spy as I handed over twelve pound notes and got in exchange a large brown envelope . . . teaspoonful of sperm in it.'

Another story featured a couple called Lucy and Ann. In 1978, after lots of conversations, they decided that they would try to get pregnant by a stranger from a bar. 'The picking of men was degrading,' they wrote. Ann detailed the anxiety she felt in the waiting process, mixed in with the complexities of being a lesbian woman, 'furious again at the way we are denied'. Later she struck a note of optimism:

> . . . there is a group of men who were aware, and angry enough to offer biological fatherhood. My child's conception depends on the political commitment of a group of men, as well as my own. I feel really pleased that I'll be able to say that to my child and to my friends. I think it is a good way to introduce my child to sexual politics – to how men and women can work together without oppressing each other.

'FATALLY DISRUPTIVE'

The women who made this pamphlet were driven by feminist politics. One of them, a separatist, even became upset when she gave birth to a boy and didn't know how to proceed with her choice to live separately from men. From this extreme example of misandry down to more subtle feelings, the pamphlet, like the log books, tracks the feelings of these lesbians as they navigated a complex and often inaccessible journey to create a family. It felt even more pertinent to Tash as several of their friends were embarking on this same journey themselves. Thirty years after this pamphlet was published, queer people were still having to fillet fertility information to make it fit for them, experiencing prejudice and financial obstacles when accessing IVF.

The pamphlet ended with this quote, highlighted by Ruth with her green marker pen in 1983:

> Children can live/belong in groups or communities of women more easily if they are freed from the expectation of nuclear family living and from the expectations of blood ties.

Next to this Ruth had scrawled, 'imposition of feminist ideologies on children'. Although Ruth was clearly thinking through this issue in the eighties, she was also training and eventually working as a teacher. It wasn't until 1996 when she made the time to start volunteering at Switchboard, and by this time calls from lesbians about insemination were very common. The babies and toddlers and teens made in this way were growing in number.

'I remember enjoying explaining that I had two mums to my friends and to strangers when I was a child and loving the shock that it often caused,' said Ruby, in 2022. One of her mums had hatched a plan with a friend who would loan her husband out. As the husband and the mum-to-be were trying to make a baby, the mum-to-be fell in love with a woman who would become her partner. Ruby was born in 1990 to this family with two mums. She knew all along who her biological father was, and it wasn't always easy for her to get her young head around. 'It didn't come without struggles,' she said. 'I remember the odd kid being rude at school if they didn't know what to say to me.'

But Ruby had a warm, loving childhood. 'The best thing about having two mums is that I was never unsure of how much I was loved and wanted,' she said. 'There are no accidents with gay babies. Every single one is desired and planned meticulously. They have to be, or else they don't happen.'

9 December 1992

ONE LAST MESSAGE FROM ME (I don't usually write in here at all!) – a (lesbian) friend of mine is trying to become pregnant and is looking for gay men who would like to be donors, with minimal involvement. If there is anyone out there who's interested + willing, could you ring me. Thanks!

In 2018, Adam's sister Hannah and her partner Sam asked if he would be 'interested and willing' to help them out. They said they wanted to raise a little person and, as a couple of lesbians, they needed some sperm. Of course, Sam would be the one to get pregnant. She and Hannah had taken their time to think it all through and decide how to approach Adam. At first, the whole thing was really just a conversation about their thoughts and feelings. The three of them made a shared live document for questions and answers. Adam wanted to say yes, but he had never wanted to have children himself, and so he needed a plan for the 'minimal involvement' that the volunteer above referred to. However they made a child, Adam would be in its life as an uncle. He just didn't want to accidentally find himself raising a child like some metro gay in a bad comedy movie.

'FATALLY DISRUPTIVE'

This required an agreement document that they all signed up to: even though it would have no weight in law, it was useful to state everyone's intentions and expectations. Adam began to take regular health tests and share the results with them. And when Sam ovulated, Adam travelled from his home in London to theirs in York for a night or two. They tried the home method for more than a year: Adam made deposits into a plastic cup, and Hannah transferred them into Sam. This method works for some, but the chances are low. In fact, they found it difficult to get pregnant. It took four and a half long years, involving lots of train journeys, medical tests, financial outlay, and awkward moments that siblings wouldn't normally have. Adam wanted to help, and had to keep his eyes on the prize when it came to fitting his schedule and sex life around ovulation or clinic timetables – which wasn't easy. Abandoning the home method, they switched to the clinic, first for in utero insemination (IUI) and then for in vitro fertilisation (IVF) – finally this worked. In January 2023, they told Adam that Sam was pregnant. After so long trying, it didn't feel real.

By this point, the expectant mums had been through so much. So many tests and procedures, and, of course, all the emotional ups and downs. The system was a lot better than the one from Ruth's pamphlet, and even the era of Ruby's mums, and yet it still contained inequalities. For example, through their original home method, Adam would have had default parental responsibility, creating a need for Hannah and Sam to get a civil partnership. A man and a woman do not need to be married or have a civil partnership in order to put their names on the birth certificate if they get pregnant at home, but a couple like Hannah and Sam do. They were happy to be registered in a civil partnership, but it created an extra hurdle in what was already not an easy process. Hannah,

Sam, and Adam were still fighting to be seen by the state in a way that was fair, just as their queer elders had.

Ruby's mums faced a similar obstacle. A year after Ruby's birth in 1990, the UK's 1991 census was sent to every household in the country. The census logo was a simple line drawing of a house with three faces within it, one depicting a man, another a woman, and the third a child. Under the logo it said: 'Census 1991: It counts because you count'. In fact, Ruby and her mums were not counted.

We know this piece of history thanks to a woman whom we are going to call 'Vicky'. She is not part of Ruby's family but their histories overlap. Vicky was angry that the census had no way of counting lesbians in couples as who they were. We found Vicky's words deep in the census files at The National Archives.[3] On 9 September 1991, Vicky wrote to the prime minister John Major to share her frustration and to ask, 'Can we be counted too?':

> Dear Mr Major,
>
> I read in the Daily Express that you are looking into the issue of Lesbian and Gay rights. Do you not think that your work in this area would be greatly improved if you had reliable statistics on the Lesbian and Gay population? Then your policies could be soundly based on statistical facts instead of on speculation and supposition?
>
> Are you aware that the Lesbian and Gay population have been counted on the 1991 Census form in such a way that they appear heterosexual? Many Lesbian and Gay people tried to be counted on the 1991 Census as 'Lesbians' and 'Gays'. They were told that they had the right to put 'Lesbian' and 'Gay' on the form but would not be counted as such.
>
> Lesbian and Gay people who have ticked 'Living together as a couple' on the Census form will not be counted as a same-sex

'FATALLY DISRUPTIVE'

couple but will have their status changed to 'unrelated'.

What I would like to know is if there is anything you can do to ensure that Lesbian and Gay people are properly represented on the next Census form?

As the next Census form is 10 years away and government policies are going to be based on these statistics, is there anything that can be done to correct the fact that Lesbian and Gay people have not been counted as such on the current form? If the three main parties could agree a policy on counting Lesbian and Gay people then this would not have to become a party political issue and you wouldn't have to worry about losing votes at the election.

Yours sincerely,

Vicky

Vicky's next two pages are filled with spiky questions for the prime minister:

What percentage of the population are Lesbian and Gay?

How many people who have been obliged to identify themselves as 'single/married/divorced or widowed' are in fact Lesbian and Gay people possibly in long-term relationships with members of their own sex?

We read Vicky's letter with both shock and delight. Tash even took to Google Earth to look at houses in the area where Vicky lived, to try to imagine the place where she had sat writing in defence of our lives. Like Mr Oke's letter that called for an end to police persecution and Section 28, this felt personal to us. It felt like reading something more true, more clear, than any of the census reports. Vicky's letter told a story, like the ones in the log books, of someone trying to catch us before we slipped through the cracks. Like us, Vicky was a number on that census, but in the moment when we read her letter, she came to life, the scratch of her pen a distant noise in our ears. We knew we had to place this letter firmly in the telling of our histories.

Vicky also told the prime minister that lesbian mothers were forced to be invisible, hiding their sexuality for fear of losing their children. In the census logo depicting three people in a 'family unit', Vicky cannily saw an opportunity. She reproduced the logo several times, each time with a different set of labels, such as 'lesbian mother, lesbian, child', or 'lesbian mother, children', or 'lesbian, father, child', and of course 'heterosexual father, heterosexual mother, gay/lesbian child'.

Next to the child that Vicky imagined would grow up to be queer, she wrote, 'Does anybody care how this child feels?' Vicky didn't know Tash (aged five), Adam (aged six) or Hannah (aged ten), but she was thinking of us anyway. She wrote:

> 1 in 10 children may be lesbian or gay being bought [sic] up in heterosexual households. Lesbians in particular are presented with no images whatsoever in the media/books/school/peer groups which might help them to come to terms with the way they really are. Gay male children tend to be presented with negative images.

The correspondence continued when Vicky received a response on 15 November 1991, from Eric J. Thompson, the director of statistics at the Office of Population Census and Surveys. Thompson told Vicky that the question of whether gay people, including coupled ones living together, could be counted was 'not a simple one, nor is it one on which a view has been expressed by the Government or by Parliament'. We wondered how Vicky felt receiving this message from a statistician telling her that her life was not simple, and that the people in power hadn't considered her.

However, as curious statisticians, Thompson's teams had run a test in 1989 in the planning for the 1991 census. Looking at 7,500 households, they found that only one household had a cohabiting same-sex couple. Further analysis found 'about 40 examples per 600,000 population, ie about 1 person in 8,000'. Either way, these numbers were low – perhaps due to respondents hiding themselves, poor methodology, couples not living together, or a combination of these factors. Twenty years later, at the time of the 2021 Census, one person in every 125 was recorded as living in a same-sex couple (476,000 in total, from the 59,597,300 people recorded in the census). Although those two decades saw lots of social change around same-sex couples, including people declaring themselves more openly, we suspected that somehow the earlier statistical research had still under-counted. The state wasn't seeing us, even when it looked.

Vicky had been trying to draw attention to the way the census questions themselves failed to create room for different definitions of family. She was on to something, as constrained definitions harmed and even shamed so many people. Thompson, who privately lived with his male partner, the gay rights campaigner Anthony Grey, left open the scientific question about whether gay couples would be counted in a future census but also wondered 'whether an explicit question on this topic might be regarded by some people (whether gay or not) as too intrusive to be acceptable on a census form'.

As in the case of the Charity Commission rejecting Switchboard's claim about its charitable intentions (described in Chapter 4), another state body, this time the Office of Population Census and Surveys, was telling a queer person: you don't really count, you're not valid.

In finding such letters, from people like Vicky and Mr Oke, we were able to fill in the gaps, find what we had been looking for without realising: the people who were standing up for us. The ones who were shouting loudly, not on the streets where we're often taught to look, but by putting pen to paper. They'd been shouting all this time, and now we could finally hear them.

---

22 April 1995

Caller Mike from Cambridge rang wanting support, advice, information about how he and partner may FOSTER CHILDREN

. . .

They are in contact with ALBERT KENNEDY TRUST but wanted to know if there was any additional info
ANY THOUGHTS?

This caller was about to face an uphill battle. Assuming he was in a gay relationship, it was not impossible to foster, but he would experience a lot of prejudice in the process. Many councils at this time were placing children with gay and lesbian foster parents. On 2 August 1990, Waltham Forest Council in London voted to formalise their policy in favour of gay and lesbian foster parents. They planned to include welcoming statements to gays and lesbians in their fosterer recruitment campaigns. The council was run by Labour, but one Tory councillor who opposed the policy said, 'homosexuality is an abomination'. According to a report in the Black Lesbian and Gay Centre Project newsletter,[4] this Conservative, Laurie Braham, said that placing children with a gay couple could 'put them at risk of becoming HIV positive'. A local group of Conservatives based in Chingford even drew up a legal challenge to the policy, citing Section 28.

Nevertheless, some councils, including Waltham Forest, persisted in attracting gays and lesbians into fostering. Perhaps Switchboard recommended those councils to people like the above caller. In 1991, another gay couple, Tony and Pete, moved in with each other (we first met them as teachers giving sex education, in Chapter 4). Although they worked with children, they didn't think about raising them themselves. Through the nineties, they saw more and more gay couples fostering, and in 1994 John Major's government issued a national policy on gay foster and adoptive parents. Tony and Pete's view on that policy was that the government was trying to claim it was doing something on the grounds of equality when in reality it was just cynically widening the pool of adopters to help ease a burdened care system. In any case, they were still not thinking about it for themselves.

By 2002, though, something had shifted for Tony. In the log books we didn't find any calls from gay men who, like him, came to want children. Aside from one or two high-profile families that made it into the tabloids, adoptive gay couples were not very visible. But we knew they existed, and it was essential for our project that we capture Tony and Pete's story as an example. Tony had grown fond of the idea of raising children, and one day he saw a recruitment ad on a bus shelter, from Southwark Council. Tony remembered that the ad 'indicated they were prepared to consider adopters of all races, all genders and all sexualities'. He decided to give them a run for their money. He put the idea to Pete on a holiday in Manchester over a pile of shellfish.

'I was pretty gobsmacked,' said Pete, when he told the story to Adam in 2021. He'd never thought about children. As a gay man he'd assumed it to be out of the equation. With the shellfish between them, Tony told him that if they were going to have children, they'd both really need to want that. Pete thought about it, and they agreed to go for it. After an eighteen-month process, Tony and Pete became the second gay couple in Southwark to be approved as adopters. This did not mean the rest of the process was easy. As various social workers considered them, one told them she rejected them because the child she was looking to place needed a mother. 'OK, that's a dead stop then,' Tony remembered thinking.

Another pair of social workers with a child to place came up from Dover to visit Tony and Pete at home one Friday afternoon. 'I think really they had no intention of taking us seriously,' said Tony. 'They mainly just wanted to see a gay couple, wanted to see what's going on and have a look at our bathroom furnishings.' The social workers poked around their home and then asked, 'Who is going to be the mother?'

The social workers' preconceived ideas of what makes a mother and what makes a father reflected common views at this time. Adam listened to Tony and Pete talk calmly about these views, and wondered how it had been for them to face down such prejudice. They seemed so calm about it all those years later; not accepting, just unfazed. Adam thought that they must have worried that they'd experience the same prejudice from other parents and various other people, but they seemed resolute, willing to quietly protect themselves and the family they hoped to create. In fact, when he remembered the bigoted social workers who asked who the mother would be, Tony recalled that he felt a bolt of anger inside him, strong enough to shake the social workers with it.

'There's two men,' Pete told the social worker. 'If you mean who is going to do the "motherly" things – the feeding, the tucking up in bed – well, it's both of us.' In any case, like with Ruby's mums, they would love their children and care for them.

Fortunately, one council did place some children with Tony and Pete: two little brothers who had been moved around from adult to adult, whom they had been encouraged to call Mum and Dad. None of those families had lasted, so Tony and Pete didn't try to make the boys call them their dads. In the end, it happened anyway. One day when the boys' friends were over, Tony heard one of his sons casually say, 'Oh, that's my dad.' The boys had chosen them, and they stayed.

Tony and Pete were already a family, however the census counted them. Now they were dads, too, and the four of them were a new type of family all over again. They showed what LGBTQ+ people often show when they create a family: intention. Whether it is a couple, or an uncle and nephew, or lesbian parents, nothing happens by accident, everything is fought for. 'You don't get many straight people who want to adopt,' said Tony. 'They start off wanting their own children and for various reasons they can't have them and then they adopt. And that was never true of us. It was never second best, it was always first best.'

This idea is also what was going through Hannah and Sam's minds when they asked Adam for sperm. It took meticulous planning and a lot of time, but they knew that their baby would be wanted. He grew inside Sam for seven months and then, due to various medical complications, had to be born early. The new baby was so, so tiny. At first he lived in an incubator in the hospital. Adam visited him on his second day, seeing his sister's eyes filled with worry even as she tried to smile. The hospital was very quiet, and Adam's nephew was covered in tubes and dressings, but there he was, little, and pink, and breathing. Adam thought, *This baby wants to be alive.*

He grew and grew. He came home with Mummy and Mamma, and became strong. So strong, in fact, that he sprouted an explosion of upright blond hair. His mummies planned stories to tell him, mixed in with lionesses and a jungle party, about their special family, a true family built with love. As Hannah put it, 'Our son will always know that Uncle Ad played a super-important role in his creation.' Like Ruby, like Tony and Pete's sons, this little boy would know that he was wanted, *really* wanted.

Tash's sister Livi and her husband Nick also had children who were *really* wanted. Livi was diagnosed with endometriosis at a young age and told that it was likely she'd have trouble conceiving. When Livi had her first child, Rosie, Tash was the first family member to hold Rosie and kiss Livi's head. Livi had always fought for Tash's rights and always tried to understand, even as a kid, what Tash was feeling. She grew up listening to Tash, and the impact of that rang out in every part of her life as a teacher, parent, and queer ally. Livi grew into as much a part of deconstructing this world's '2.4 children' as we did – you can get married and have two kids (Rosie and Freddie) like she has, but it's how you raise them, how you hold them, that matters. Livi held Tash in a way that has always felt like family.

From day one, Adam's nephew and Rosie and Freddie were growing up under very different circumstances to Adam and Tash. Every day they see queer family members and their special bonds. When Rosie was five, she heard a boy on the playground saying that only boys could marry girls, and she told him, 'No, anyone can marry anyone.'

We were like Vicky, looking around for people like us, hoping we'd all be counted. That's why Tash had asked their teacher if she was gay, and why her denial felt so painful. As we looked into the history of queer families, Tash realised how much anger they had been carrying about them having been made invisible. When they read Lord Longford's words that 'the tragedy of such people is that they cannot enjoy family life and they cannot have children', Tash thought: *Why would I want anything close to what you would define as 'family life' anyway?* They had been raised as a woman and taught by society that their 'biological clock is ticking', which only ever made them angry. It was only through the writing of this book, and the reflection it offered, that this anger calmed. Tash realised they had been so busy saying *FUCK YOU* to the world that they hadn't actually spent any time thinking about what they wanted when it came to kids and a family.

Meanwhile, Tash's Uncle Quentin had been watching them since they were little, knowing they were different somehow. 'I wasn't sure, but I wanted to be there for you,' Quentin told Tash much later, in 2024. Quentin had been married to a woman, and Tash had assumed him to be straight, but he later came out as bisexual and queer. 'I've always felt incredibly protective towards you,' he told Tash, reflecting on the bond they shared even before Tash knew it. He said he knew how hard it was to negotiate a way through life, 'particularly when you don't have somebody, someone to look up to, someone you can go to for help'.

Isn't that family? Somehow these bonds will never be explicable or counted, but as pages and pages of the log books show, they are always there. Switchboard volunteers created their own family, and then bonds with the callers, and then, with that support, callers themselves built their own families.

And in 1993, three Switchboard volunteers did their own thing. In one page of the log book someone pasted a jolly card featuring teddy bears in pyjamas, bouncing beach balls, and all the colours of the rainbow. The text on the card announces the birth of a baby boy, and lists the names of three volunteers, whom we'll call Peter, Kim, and Valerie:

5 August 1993

Dear Switchboard,

Although I have just resigned as a vol, (after some 8 years off and on), would you mind sticking the enclosed card in the Log Book. Our baby arrived early this morning. Valerie is also an ex-vol.

Best wishes

Peter

P.S. Mothers + baby are doing fine – he has blond hair & blue eyes & is looking forward to going on the Pride March next year!

When we read this entry, it hit us: Switchboard volunteers had been creating a record for all to see that captured and showed what family really could mean. From the stories and voices of those who have lived it but, more than that, thrived in it. Switchboard volunteers created their own registry, their own queer census – and we were adding to it. Our very own queer family tree.

8
'MULTIPLE PARADOX NET FILES'

How technology changed the way we connect

20 February 1976
Has any body heard details about a 'Gay Conservatives Group' which is being formed? Surely this is a contradiction in terms . . . ?
Bit like an RAC pedestrian group.
[In the hand of another volunteer:]
People can regard themselves as Gay Conservatives, or Christian Marxists even. Even if these are contradictions, so what?
[And yet another, finally answering the original question:]
It's listed in the card under Conservative Group.

Always, so many voices. The stirrers, the debaters, the indexers. The log books are a racket, hundreds of volunteers down the decades, writing in different inks, various tones, and a riot of diverse hands. Although rich, the log books were a very basic technology. Those scruffy pages were the only thing the volunteers had, if they wanted to record something of the call they'd just taken. A volunteer would open the log book, pick up a cheap pen, and jot down a few notes before the phone began to ring again.

We loved the log books for their nature of being dashed out in a hurry. Entries were hyper-specific to a person, a place, a time – but they were just a snapshot. Taken as a vast collection, the log books are broad and sweeping. This characteristic is understandable of course, but it did leave us wanting. Our desire for depth led us to build our own layers on top of the log books: first the podcast, then this book. We had to figure out the best ways to keep deepening our understanding of Switchboard, its volunteers and callers, and the hours they'd all lived through.

Using the technology of audio was the obvious first answer: our subject was phone calls, or conversations without visuals. To bring the log books to life for the podcast we wanted to hear all sorts of voices reading the entries. We also decided that we needed voices from those who had lived through the experiences chronicled on the pages. This is how, day after day, we came to jump on to video calls with some people and trail our mic cables around the sofas of others as they took a seat.

No two recording sessions were alike. Tash's interview with Steve Craftman, the long-term survivor of HIV whom we met in Chapter 5, was particularly memorable. We'd never imagined that we'd be able to speak to him. In the end, the interview took place under strict lockdown conditions in 2020, both Steve and Tash alone in their separate homes, conversing through their screens, a red light pulsing gently as Steve's words made it into Tash's digital recording.

When Adam arrived in George's basement flat with a box of cakes and a mic, George announced that he would lay out, to comfort his ailing body and to be in the best position to speak. Adam figured out how to rig the mic around him, so that George could gesture freely and look through the window at the sky – allowing him to find the right words to describe the beauty of his gay love for his late partner Sam – and such that Adam could monitor the recorder to ensure it was collecting the memories.

Becoming active in the process of recording and creating this archive made us more sensitive to the role that technology had played in Switchboard's operations. Volunteers organised their work with log books, index cards, box files, maps, and pins, whereas we used shared online documents, Zoom H4n recorders, transcription software, group chats, and zip files. We became conscious of the constraints and opportunities, the similarities and differences, of the technology options we all respectively had.

The fact that the volunteers used pen and paper had a huge influence on the entries they wrote. We were intrigued by how every log book entry was produced by an individual. Each volunteer is trained in the same way, but when they came to write their log book entries they revealed aspects of their personalities. The log books recorded something of the caller, but also something of the volunteer. In reading volunteers' little texts, we saw the world through their eyes. Their frustrations, their squabbles, their loves, their biases, and all their experiences – these were all locked into their writing. There is something special in how text does that. And perhaps that was what we needed to do, too; after making our podcast, which was like a documentary, we wanted to reframe the log books more through our own experiences, our stories, our ideas. Writing a book felt like the best way to do that. We'd be writing text that added another layer to the voices of our interviewees, which, in turn, sat on the layer of the text of the log books. In writing ourselves, we'd be able to editorialise better, explore deeper, and make our own connections.

As the children of the first internet generation, our lives were already so different from those of our elders. Our young lives were transformed by going online. As we thought more deeply about *why* we were doing all of this, we started to see the significance of different technologies in the story. If tech had changed our lives, how had it altered Switchboard's course, too? When John Lindsay spent a night in 1974 writing out his listings for gay bars, could he have imagined being able to share them with the world with a single click in a viral video? If we thought the log books and our podcast had recorded history, what were we now doing, as writers?

We were again thinking about history – this time, how it gets recorded, and why.

———

Switchboard started with one phone in a room above a bookshop. The first volunteers advertised the phone number, and then they picked up the phone whenever it rang out. This technology was already prosaic in 1974, and the rest of the tech that got Switchboard going was even more basic: paper and pens, maps and pins, folders and binders, a card index, and copies of *Gay News*. Within a few years, the sum of these parts had supported hundreds of thousands of people. After only six and a half years, at 12.58 p.m. on 27 October 1982, Switchboard answered its one millionth call.

Those who named the service 'Switchboard' (or 'Gay Switchboard') knew exactly what was needed: a centralised connector for the community. And so it was proven, as year after year callers enlisted volunteers in their search for others like them:

26 February 1976
John phoned to say he is setting up a group for Bisexuals, married, counselling and supportive. Regular meetings 6–9pm Wednesday and Thursdays.

10 June 1995
Guy phoned wanting info about gay interest things on the internet. I know nothing about this high-tech stuff, but are there any basic bits of info we can give to callers? I know that a friend of mine fixed up a date and had a holiday romance in Chicago via the internet, so it must be good.

Before digital technology properly arrived, Switchboard's earliest information-management system was a box of handwritten cards, constantly indexed and updated by the likes of Ali Bucknell and John Lindsay. Switchboard seemed to attract organisational nerds like Ali and John, both co-founders, and therefore always managed to evolve by adding new technologies as they became available and affordable:

29 September 1983

The arrival of

THE COMPUTER

is imminent (arriving 2 Oct)

Computer Working Party urgently needs people who are willing to familiarise themselves with the system (see below)[†], and then act as trainers for other vols.

[†] The system: Apricot 10mb hard disk, with Ricoh daisy wheel printer, software, initially Superwriter, Supercalc and Cardbox.

PLEASE: anyone familiar with use of microcomputers who hasn't yet 'come out' please reveal her/his presence to us. Just pop a little note in my pigeonhole.

15 May 1992

The Compaq now has extra main memory up from 2 MEG to 6 MEG & main storage up from 40 MEG to 145 MEG.*

7 July 1995

More computer news

The menu system is in place and ready to be used. We seem to have solved the multiple paradox net files error, except for on the accommodation services section. We'll get that bit fixed now. 4 machines are on in the phone room; the fifth should be ready next week. There is a basic guide to using the system in all of the

---

* The laptop we used to produce our podcast in 2019–21 is 30,000–100,000 times more powerful than Switchboard's first computer in 1983.

clipboards and pinned to the walls in the phone room. There's a proper users' manual under production. Cheers.

The computers were just another thing that volunteers could be trained in. Although they were not essential for the front-line service, they were very useful for internal tasks such as producing training manuals.

16 March 1994
Computer training
On Sunday 20 Mar, from 2–6pm (with a tea break) there will be a short introductory course about using the office computers.
This will cover an idiot's guide on how to use the basic programs for producing written materials. Windows, Word for Windows, and MS Publisher.

And although the basic technology of phone lines didn't change much over Switchboard's first few decades, additional tech did come on board. The Minicom system, which we commented on briefly in Chapter 1, is mentioned in the log books at least as early as 1992. A Minicom was a type of landline phone with a small keyboard and screen which allowed deaf users to converse with Switchboard volunteers, the text being sent back and forth down the same phone line as a vocal conversation. The Minicom is an example of Switchboard trying to adapt to the needs of its callers, to make the service more accessible, while also struggling with it due to limited capacity. There was also a lack of will on behalf of the able-bodied (and often ableist) volunteers, which other volunteers took note of:

24 January 1995
Could the Minicom be put on a trolley – I received a call on line 1 today and by the time I'd rushed over and grabbed the Minicom

and set it up the caller had lost patience. There are too many bits to set up fast, on a trolley it could just be whizzed over.

9 April 1995

We appear to have ceased operating a Minicom service. This is a pity and seems very much against the grain of an organisation which purports commitment to, inter alia, those with hearing impairment. Who took the decision? Is it open to negotiations? Is it coming back?

22 April 1995

The phones – the minicom

The Minicom is now back in the phone room. We have to wait an inordinate amount of time to get the new add-on couplers delivered.

Switchboard's service expanded beyond the Minicom and into other technologies to increase the charity's accessibility. Later than the log book period, in 2012, Switchboard launched its service on email and instant messaging, which was especially useful for those without the confidence or ability to call. But back in the days of the Minicom, disabled people never stopped calling. Sometimes they were looking just to converse with a volunteer, and other times calling for advice on where else they could go.

4 March 1999

Just had a call from a man using [an] electronic voice-simulator, looking for friendship and to talk about his speech with a gay organisation. According to our files there are no groups specifically dealing with speech and communication issues, so I suggested ringing his local S/B (Birmingham) who offer befriending. We had quite a long conversation and he may ring again.

In 'looking for friendship', this caller represented millions. Switchboard was a basic technology, really, but it was astonishingly powerful at building the connections the community needed. Even the most basic technology can struggle, though. If you flick through the log books of the eighties you will find a constant hum of irritation and occasional outrage over the quality of the actual phone lines that led to Switchboard:

1 June 1985

7327 is doing odd things, intermittently the bell may not always ring, so watch for the flashing light. 5.45pm.

Volunteers complained constantly to British Telecom about the shoddy lines. At length, they received a letter from M. F. Owen, BT's service manager, dated 29 May 1985, saying that 'as a matter of urgency' the problem had been elevated to 'emergency status' on account of Switchboard 'handling a high percentage of crisis calls from distressed members of the public'.

BT employees like Owen insisted that they were investigating the problems, and yet the issues persisted. Julian Hows was one of the volunteers working on finding a solution, trying to get BT engineers to attend the premises. 'The crazy thing about this whole thing was that if engineers came to the building they only needed to see there was nothing wrong at our end,' he said, recounting the story to us in 2020, glasses perched on the end of his nose and eyebrows raised. Julian even worked for BT at the time, and did what he could to convince his work colleagues to also check the nearby telephone exchange. 'It was almost as if they wouldn't go into their own switch room,' he said. Julian was joined by veteran volunteer David Seligman in the fight with BT. It is in one of David's notes to the other volunteers, in June 1985, that we learnt one reason why the telecom engineers were stalling:

'MULTIPLE PARADOX NET FILES'

Remember that the awarding of emergency engineers status to Gay Switchboard and the commencement of this work is a result of a lot of hard work by members of the Admin Group. (Just 3 months ago we were in a situation where all telephone engineers were banning visits to this building, on the grounds they would catch AIDS by coming here. This was the climax of 11 years of homophobic attitudes by Telecom towards us.)

This was in the terrifying and confusing early days of what became the HIV epidemic. The phone lines were becoming overloaded with panicked callers, and volunteers could not give them the advice and calm words they needed, due to the ignorance of the engineers. Julian explained, 'That is how the twin fears of homosexuality and HIV came together and created a total and mass panic. And also, if they were being nice to these homosexuals, maybe their mates at the telephone exchange might think, "He's one as well."'

When engineers did agree to come to fix the technology, some volunteers advised others to tone down their conversations – the notoriously strait-laced David Seligman asking them 'to refrain from what they rather than us would consider to be outrageous behaviour'. In 1986, on the eve of another visit by engineers, a volunteer in the phone room wrote, 'Let's hope we don't get too many calls about fistfucking.'

A year on, volunteers were irate about the ongoing problem:

28 May 1987 – 3.00 a.m.
The phone system is completely kaput!
Just spoke to a guy who works for a communications company. He said he had all 5 of our lines ringing before I answered. Nothing rang this end! It seems all 5 must be ringing before anyone can get through. He said the only solution is to keep

picking the phone up every 10 seconds to see if anyone is on the line. Sod that!

3.30 – it's completely dead! (Have lost count of the number of times I have tried it).

3.36am – Still dead as a dodo!

And at least once, in April 1988, they had to take out an advert in *Capital Gay* to apologise and explain themselves to the community:

An announcement from
LONDON LESBIAN AND GAY SWITCHBOARD
Sorry folks – there are gremlins at Switchboard. We've been having trouble with our phone system. If you call us and get no answer after 10 rings, hang up and re-dial.
Basically, you will have run a 'ghost' line – there is someone there. Please try again.
We hope the problems will be quickly resolved – in the meantime, please keep dialling.

It's clear from the log books that whatever kind of gremlins haunted Switchboard, people persisted in dialling the number. They still needed help.

Switchboard volunteers had been picking up the phone for twenty-five years already by the time the internet made it into our homes. We were young teenagers when we first went online, when the early internet was a physical thing. We connected to it via chunky tower computers, fat monitors, endless cables, and the same socket in the wall that our home phones used.

Our dial-up modems made the sound of someone scraping in the dirt for gold. After the scratches and swishes came the beeps and the clicks – and Tash knew what to look for. They hungrily logged on to Gaydar Girls. The lime-green homepage promised 'What you want, when you want it'. Tash wanted it, constantly tinkering with their profile, updating their pics, and waiting for a tantalising little pop-up. They were following in the footsteps of those who had used Gingerbeer before, and, before that, the personal ads in gay and lesbian newspapers. Tash surfed for lesbians in the South West with one eye on Gaydar Girls, the other on MSN, an instant messaging network. They were constantly checking to see if their crush from school was online and, when she was, doing absolutely nothing but staring at the screen.

At home in Cleethorpes, Adam made a Geocities website that nobody looked at, and soon began to access porn made in alleys in eastern Europe and dorm rooms in California. Photographs loaded slowly, line by pixelated line; early videos lasted fifteen seconds. He hovered in chat rooms using fake names, making up his ASL (age, sex, location), typing his fantasies, trying to get a wank out before his parents arrived home. The smartphone had not yet been invented; these journeys into what we called cyberspace were grounded in the home computer which, in the 1990s, filled one corner of one room in our homes. We couldn't take it upstairs to our bedrooms or carry it in our pockets to the world outside.

As members of the generation that was both held back by Section 28 and thrust forwards by the internet, when we looked into our collective history as queer people we had to think about the paradox of information. The architects of Section 28 who wanted to stop us seeing a particular storybook probably did not imagine that within a few years we'd be able to access gay porn from home. If we'd have wanted it, even on the early internet we could have found basic support articles about being queer. We were just a few years behind our elders, but we were coming of age in such a different world. 'I remember going to my local library,' remembered Catherine Lee. It was the only place she could think to go, when she was growing up a couple of decades before us, to explore her early lesbian feelings. 'There was a book [of] short stories about coming out . . . I never dared take it out of the library. But I used to go into the library, put it in another book, and literally just read some of these stories and be absolutely thrilled.'

The early, clunking internet that hooked up our homes was not great, then, but it was *something*. And it had become clear to Switchboard's more technically minded volunteers by the mid-nineties that it was going to be a big deal:

> 6 September 1994
> Calling all netties
> Anyone with access to Internet email?
> Send me a message or leave your address in my pigeonhole or log book. Let's start a LLGS net group? Barry.
> [Here another volunteer has responded: 'Barry, you techno-freak, you!']

Barry wasn't the only techno-freak. As the nineties rolled on and more and more personal computers were rolled out, queer people flocked to the internet – just as they had taken to bulletin board systems in the 1980s. In the early days of the internet, it was forums and chat rooms like AOL Chat and Yahoo! Groups that became powerful connectors for trans people such as Steph Fuller. 'Suddenly I started to realise that actually there's quite a network of people that feel like I do,' she said, 'but were entirely underground.'[1] Trans people no longer even had to go through organisations like Switchboard, which were used to referring them to local groups or trans-inclusive night clubs. Instead, trans people (and other queer people) could directly find each other by cruising chat rooms. We couldn't find a hint in the log books that Switchboard thought its days were numbered, but it was clear that its role as a community nexus was going to change.

Online groups were great for sex too, as Harry F. Rey remembered: 'One of my usernames was CyberSpy27, from a long, long, long time ago, so if you ever cyber-sexed with CyberSpy27, then, you know, hello, it was me!'[2] We both giggled at this memory from Harry. Before he went to Glasgow's gay bar Bennets, Harry crossed the queer threshold into the internet, where he had cyber sex with men. 'It was all night spent on the internet,' he remembered. Another contributor, Clare Truscott, connected her body to the internet, too: 'I remember once, with a friend, on our dial-up modem at home, saying "OK, what shall we look for?" and she said, "Er, a naked picture of Catherine Deneuve."' Clare's face broke out into a big smile in front of Tash as she then said, 'It took us twenty minutes to find a rather rubbish picture of Catherine Deneuve in a bikini' – before bursting into laughter.[3]

And the internet immediately benefited those with even more niche tastes. Although Switchboard's log books show how kinky people sought and found each other, the internet brought the benefit of scale. Our interviewee Derek Cohen, who was involved in various online and offline fetish groups from the 1970s, said that people into SM sex were particularly taken with the opportunities of the internet. 'For some reason, SMers tend to be more techies,' he told Adam in 2021, a little bemused by his own observation. 'I dunno if it's because we play with all this gear and stuff, so obviously early adopters getting on this were people who were quite techie, because you had to have a thing that you plugged your phone handset into, and it made lots of noise, and you needed a computer and stuff.'

For Derek, and men like him, the great connector was a live chat system called the Closed User Group, or CUG, which was run on the early internet by employees at British Telecom, then owned by the British government. 'There were a group of people who had the leeway within their department to set this up,' he said. 'So that's my first experience, and it was just text, you typed, and everyone had a little nickname . . . You chatted about sex, and I'm still friends with some of the men I met on the CUG.'[4]

Long before influencers began making us feel pathetic and incels blamed their loneliness on the entirety of womankind, the early internet promised friendly connections like Derek's. People imagined the internet as a kind of utopia, an online society built around the expression of feelings and desires with like-minded people. Like a gay bar, but with emoticons. Just as queer people had built alternative housing models, online they were building alternative, affirming societies. The internet promised a new way to connect, to share time and space, and this empowered kinky and queer people. They even dared to expect that people could be held accountable:

> 6 April 2002
> Caller is looking for a gay internet watchdog, because someone's sending him anonymous emails, telling him he's being slagged off in various chatrooms. What can he do about it? Surely they monitor these chatrooms? I've given him GLAD's number, the gay and lesbian legal advice line, but do they still exist? I suggested he contact the internet providers.

Looking back through the trolling, bullying, fraud, death threats, and doxing that LGBTQ+ people came to experience online, that log book entry seems quaint. The reply from another volunteer is so optimistic that it is charming, as they explain the perceived responsibility of tech companies:

'MULTIPLE PARADOX NET FILES'

If you send an email to 'abuse@' whichever IP the emails are coming from, they will, should be able to help, eg 'abuse@hotmail.com'. It's an offence to send an abusive email.

In any case, before most of the tech industry came to absolve itself of responsibility for abusive content, users were starting to use the internet to run things themselves. Groups got together on forums and email listservs, where members subscribed their email addresses to a group that they could also email themselves. This was a boon to LGBTQ+ people seeking community. In 1995 the Switchboard volunteer Richard Desmond got wind of one such listserv and told fellow volunteers about it. The 'uk-motss' group, i.e. 'for members of the same sex' aka lesbians, gays, and bisexual people, was already up and running. It had over four hundred members, around seventy of whom were active. Posting in the log book about the listserv, Richard described how uk-motss was doing some of the same community work as Switchboard and was therefore an opportunity:

> It is a very useful group. If callers have access to E-Mail (i.e. Students) then it is probably worth mentioning. The E-mail equivalent to 'Coming Out Calls' happen all the time, as do some of the sort of general enquiries we get.

The listserv even provided a check on Switchboard itself, as the charity was still not as inclusive as it should have been. Having read some uk-motss emails, Richard wrote:

> There has been a correspondence recently about LLGS's refusal to accept bisexuals as Vols. It is a closed group and as such I have had to ask the individuals involved for permission to reproduce their correspondence, but a selection from this is on the wall by the Sink.

Two days later, another volunteer thanked Richard for his note. 'Perhaps this will be enough to get us to reexamine our entire policy re. Bisexual volunteers?' he wrote in the log book, suggesting volunteers have a meeting to discuss: 'I'd go!' Switchboard did come to accept bisexual volunteers – just one step of many on its way to striving to become as inclusive as possible. The scrutiny brought by the ability for queer people to connect via the internet was no doubt a part of this reform.

This was not the only way that the internet started to change how Switchboard worked:

> 11 June 1995
>
> I've been asked a number of times for gay email addresses, databases on the internet. If there are any volunteers who understand or know about such things, could they put the details in 'New Info' and could Info Group either start or incorporate a file?

Two decades after Switchboard began, this log book entry reveals the start of a shift in how queer people would try to feel less isolated. The callers referred to in this entry knew that the internet could help them connect to a wider queer world. At this point, they were still calling Switchboard to make the connection, even a connection via the internet. But the writing was on the wall (by the sink!): eventually queer people would use the internet to find places, clubs, information, and even each other. With that log book entry, Switchboard's role as connector started to fray.

> 7 March 2001
>
> Lots of messages in this book about how quiet the phones have become. Maybe in today's much more liberal climate there's just not as much use for Switchboard. Or it could be our profile has

dropped a little. Anyways, I find it nicer these days not to spend a shift doing accommodation call after accommodation call.

Volunteers noticed this shift and, as usual, picked up their pens to debate it in the log books. Another volunteer drew a cartoon of a thinking face and wrote, 'If I wanted to spend an evening sat by a phone that never rang, I would've stayed at home.' The following day, writing in red ink from a different pen, a third volunteer noted: 'Interestingly it is now 8 March and 2 of us did not manage to get a break cos it was so busy!' Clearly there was not a single moment when the service at Switchboard really changed, but change it did. The volunteer above claimed that the accommodation service, which was part of Switchboard's role to share information, was being used less. They didn't say that people were finding housing in different ways, or specifically on the internet, but new methods and alternatives were arising. It was the dot-com era.

Just one year before the log book entry above, three entrepreneurs launched Gumtree, a local listings website. It became popular with people in London looking to rent rooms and flats (and was sold for millions in 2005); in 2004 a site called SpareRoom launched, and it was dedicated to flat-sharing (its founder's precursor business with the same mission having launched in 1999). Google Maps launched in 2005, soon becoming indispensable as a wayfinder, and one that meant users needed less input from other people. In 2007 Apple launched the iPhone, ushering in an era where most people carried a phone that was also a handheld computer with internet access. Even Switchboard itself was on the move: in 2005 volunteers began a project, named after Alan Turing, in collaboration with other helplines. The Turing Project produced a web-based database of venues, organisations, and services for the LGBTQ+ community, and Switchboard volunteers themselves used it to find information to give to callers. The Turing Project was still live when Tash joined in 2012, but by then it was outdated, clunky, and old. Tash and other volunteers were just googling anything they needed. People were using their smartphones to look for gay bars near them, right now. The Turing Project soon withered and was taken offline. Specific requests for information, such as pub recommendations, had fallen away.

―――

When we began writing this history, we thought about the people behind the Turing Project, and about the way that Switchboard's role as a navigator was already ending by the time of the final log book in 2003. We imagined all the volunteer meetings at which people had debated what the internet was going to be used for, and whether people would still need Switchboard at all.

The fact is, though, that as we were doing our work, from 2019 to 2025, the helpline was still in demand. In its fiftieth year, in 2024, volunteers handled over 14,000 contacts. As we interviewed, researched, and wrote, Switchboard volunteers were listening to people who were reaching out for support around relationships, sexuality, mental health, gender identity, and struggles with coming out. The technology had changed, but even the newer, supposedly more reliable phone lines were still going through tricky days. When Tash read the log book entries about old phone lines breaking, they took pictures and sent them straight to the technology team to make them feel better, writing, 'Some things never change!'

In 2003, after handwriting log books for three decades, volunteers had switched to typing call logs into a digital system. But the basic principle from 1974 had survived: two queer people speaking to each other, an essential and often life-saving connection. These connections were still being made as we produced our series, as we interviewed long-retired volunteers and heard from listeners of the podcast. It was remarkable to us that our listeners said similar things about the podcast that callers to Switchboard had said about the phone calls: that it was a lifeline, that it made them feel less isolated, more connected, and that they loved to listen to the voices of their queer family members.

Our podcast is not half as important as Switchboard, of course. The two things are distinct technologies, with distinct purposes. And yet they both managed to connect people. As we thought about this, and about our own early journeys into the internet, we could hear the connections clicking into place. The technology can change, from phone lines to video calls and probably to hologram VR or something else, but the thing that people need is the same as it ever was. No doubt John Lindsay, given a smart and ethical AI-powered database in 1974, would have ditched his index cards in a heartbeat.

Neither of us ever phoned Switchboard, but through making a podcast, we got the connection we'd longed for. We got to meet people like George and Steve, Femi and Diana, Ruth and Richard, sharing space and swapping stories. Through book writing, however, we got something deeper than connection: we got reflection. In researching further and having the time to think, we could see our own histories alongside those of our elders. We could even spot how our lives were lived in parallel and when they were entangled, and what this meant to us. So if Switchboard's volunteers listened to callers, and our podcast followers listened to our contributors, through writing this book we got to listen to ourselves. We've tried to blend all those voices and thoughts together here, so that you, too, can connect with these histories.

THE LOG BOOKS

When Switchboard used log books, volunteers started every shift by flicking back through the current book's previous few pages. They needed to read about the topics that had been coming up on calls, to know the latest updates on nightlife and accommodation, and to review the backstories of recent callers in case they phoned again. After checking the recent entries, the volunteer would be ready to answer the phone that day. We've tried to offer something similar in writing this book. Fifty years since Switchboard's first call, working on this book gave us the chance to review queer life since 1974 and understand our place within it. We've used a unique collection of text and voices that, like a messy web of cables, reveal just how they are all – *we* are all – connected.

9
CONCLUSION

The Power of Listening

We connected with our elders, finally, through the log books. We absorbed their words from the scruffy pages and we heard them tell their stories into our microphones. We also delved into our own histories, to listen to our younger selves, to hear what troubled them. Adam had felt so ashamed to be gay, even as he grew alongside the powerful role model of his proud lesbian sister. Tash, denied a viable model altogether, tore themself up in confusion, scrawling teenage diary entries like this one:

> Something weird is happening to me, there's this girl, I don't know her name or anything but I can't help noticing her + I know she notices me too. There's definitely something between us, I don't know what though. It's not like I fancy her, she's pretty but I know it's not like that. I don't know what it is but I don't want to become friends with her. It's so weird.

We cannot help but wonder how our stories might have turned out differently if we'd been able to talk to our teachers, librarians, and youth workers. But they'd said, *No, I can't listen to you.* As Ruth's colleague told her, *Talking about this is against the law.*

Section 28 and other laws and policies discussed in this book tried to sever the connections between queer people. The fact that homosexuality was considered immoral as a matter of public policy engendered Switchboard with an illegitimate status in the eyes of the state. When people wonder why LGBTQ+ people experience isolation and loneliness at greater rates than others, it is not just that we are small in number; it is also that we have been cut off from finding each other.

Imagine being born into a world where you don't fit in. Some days you contort yourself to fit in, and others you try to break the world. Either option is isolating and painful. Then imagine discovering later in life that all along there'd been a group of people who knew exactly how you felt, because they felt the same, and they could have cared for you as you tried to find your place in the world. It's heartbreaking to know they had been there, out of reach. That is how it felt to us, when we met our queer elders. We collected their stories, making sure that they had our full attention, that the recordings we were making were focused only on them . . . after these sessions we felt our own feelings return – taking the form of relief and grief all at the same time. It's unforgivable that these elders had been held from us.

Working on the podcast was a great unblocking for both of us. It opened our eyes and ears to the stories of our queer elders. And it helped us to see inside ourselves, too. Tash began to allow themself to feel more like their younger self did, the one who sometimes was 'Jase', and in doing so they started to settle into their genderfluid identity, thirty-odd years later. Finally, they learnt how to listen to themself, and they felt a dissolution of the anger they had carried for so long. They began to think about whether it might be possible to forgive their teacher for turning away from them. Adam came to understand the social and political context that influenced his parents' rejection of his sister, but also to see it as an act of emotional violence that they chose to commit against their family. He began to reckon with his compulsion to pour energy into studies and work instead of pursuing the pleasures of his body. As he listened to himself, the

CONCLUSION

more he felt his duty shift away from his parents and towards his queer elders.

This is how working with the log books became such a personal project. We wondered, if this research had had such a big impact on us, how had it affected everyone else?

———

'I think you got out of us a great deal more than we meant to say,' exclaimed Neville, one of our oldest contributors. Tash had interviewed him and his husband James at the same time, about their experiences coming of age in the 1950s, and then seeing so much change in how our country handles gender and sexual difference. James arrived in London in 1969, and fifty years later could still recall the buzz he felt when he passed the Coleherne pub in Earls Court. 'I remember just glancing in, looking across and there were two young men sitting by the bar, and I thought, *Lord, they're gay*, and I looked around the pub and thought, *Heavens, it's gay*.'

As much as we wanted to hear stories like Neville's and James's, we wanted to give folks like them the chance to *tell* their stories. Here were two elderly gay men, born in 1944 and 1940, who had just lived their lives; they were not famous, they hadn't stormed parliament. They'd just built love and friendship and community between queer people. 'I think you made me remember things and think of things that, frankly, were buried so deep in me that I've more or less forgotten about them,' Neville realised some time after his first interview with Tash. 'It was quite astonishing.'

Neville's reflection helped us to understand the power of what we were doing. It also hinted at why we were so drawn to stories like Neville's and James's, why we wanted to listen to them, and why they needed to be heard.

When we speak to people from a different generation to ours, with whom we share identity or experience but not blood, we feel a distinct connection. Our lives are wound tight enough together to enable us to understand each other, but the generation gap requires some work from each speaker. We have to explain ourselves in ways that we're not used to, crossing the chasms of time and culture. Crucially, though, this kind of conversation is underpinned by those bonds of identity and experience. This is how each speaker, no matter their generation nor how wide the gap, learns new things about themselves. Speaking matters. This is how Neville surprised himself in sharing his long-forgotten memory of the Coleherne, and how we realised what queer club nights meant to us.

The more we listened to these people whom we considered our elders, and even our 'ancestors', the more we learnt about ourselves and our community. We were not giving support in the way that Switchboard was, but we were really listening, and this meant as much to our contributors as it meant to us. 'I was just so grateful that you were telling our stories,' Catherine Lee told Adam, 'and that you cared.'

Of course Catherine was paying us a compliment, but she was also getting at something deeper. We'd listened to our elders because we cared, and we cared because . . . perhaps it was because we were so like them? Or maybe it was because, in fact, we were so like all the callers to Switchboard. We needed community and connection. We needed to not feel so isolated. Even though when we made the podcast we were part of strong queer friendships and families, we were still reckoning with the years that we'd been held back from all that. We were the same as the elders whom we were so hungry to hear from; the same as people like Catherine, who had spent years feeling so alone and isolated as a lesbian

CONCLUSION

teacher during the dark years of Section 28. We were the same as Tony and Pete, gay men who had worked as teachers during the years of our education, being made to feel deeply uneasy about themselves in schools. Pete never came out to his colleagues: he told Adam that he felt like he'd been cowardly. Sitting close by, his partner Tony said that they had been forced into that position. Pete then asked Adam, 'Do you feel we've let you down, as gay teachers?'

Catherine only began to reckon with those years and the violence they had done to her and her students when she embarked on her own research project about it (culminating in a PhD). On our episodes that tackled Section 28, Catherine shared her memories of feeling constrained as a teacher, unable to help the young queer women who asked for help, and also enduring horrific homophobia including the word 'DYKE' being graffitied on to her car. Sharing stories can be cathartic. But it took her some time before she had the courage to listen back to the episodes featuring her contributions and hear herself in what she called the 'chain of history'.

When Catherine listened to the podcast, she heard more than she'd bargained for. The noisy stories from lesbian clubs in the seventies, of police raids on gay men, on the messy debates over trans and bisexual inclusion, of runaways and flatmates, of lavender marriages and sperm deliveries – in all of this pandemonium, Catherine heard where she fitted in. 'It wasn't perhaps until then,' she said, of her interview with Adam, '[that] I understood my place in the timeline, which was really quite powerful.'

For other elders, speaking to us was a way of experiencing intimacy with other queer people. When Tash managed to connect to Steve, who'd been so integrated into Switchboard as a volunteer in the eighties, he was living a very isolated life in Neath, a small town in Wales. They spoke online during the 2020 Covid lockdown; Tash was living on their own in London due to a recent breakup, and Steve was isolating due to the impact of HIV on his immune system. On one call Steve broke down, crying at how long it had been since he had felt the touch of another human. Tash welled up with him because they felt the same absence. In that moment, Tash promised Steve that one day, they would visit him and give him the hug that they both so desperately needed. Just as Adam's interview with Catherine had stayed with him, Steve's had stayed with Tash.

Four years after their first call, Tash walked down Neath's boarded-up high street, through an underpass which gave way to a deserted garage whose graffitied walls declared 'poofters and queers go to hell'. Tash's heart sank.

Steve opened the door to his grey pebbledashed terraced house, sockless, in a *Doctor Who* T-shirt, one pair of glasses hanging around his neck and another propped on his nose. He smiled and welcomed Tash in.

Tash watched Steve as he spoke, his mind clouded with the endless medicines he had to take, displayed in their variety of colours and sizes on his coffee table. Tash stayed for hours, drinking Steve's tea, listening to his love of tarot, how lockdown had been for him, and how their conversations had led to a period of deep self-reflection and wondering. He held a lifetime on his shoulders, but they both smiled a lot, especially when Steve told Tash how he had reclaimed the word 'queer' for himself.

As Tash was about to leave for their train, they asked Steve if he remembered that one particular interview in lockdown – how Tash had told him that one day they would come to Neath? Steve nodded, and as he did Tash walked towards him, arms open, and said, 'Well, this is that hug.' As their arms wrapped around each

CONCLUSION

other, they both welled up. Steve gently chastised Tash, 'You are making an old man cry', and they both smiled.

Retracing their steps back to the train station, Tash thought about what had brought them here, that moment of finding the log books in the crawlspace. Tash realised that this journey had been about reaching our queer elders. We all craved human connection. We now understood our elders' stories, we knew them, and finally we could hold each other against the tides of time.

This is how our work reached new depths. The podcast was like journalism, our first draft of history: we had run into the field to grab some facts and quotes. The longer we spent with all that reporting, the more conversations we had with our elders, and the more archives we visited, the more the project became this book – not a definitive account of history but a rich, multilayered tapestry that could be added to by each generation. We'd listened, and then we'd listened harder. Many of our contributors who became part of the project even found that they were listening harder to themselves. Catherine said, 'Ultimately *The Log Books* helped me to look back and forgive those people I felt weren't there for me back in the day.' And Tash understood their teacher Miss Morgan's story too, because of Catherine, who had given them the chance to listen to the other side.

When Catherine reflected on the first time Adam reached out to ask her about the 1980s, she laughed and said, 'I just remember feeling a bit old.' She wasn't our only contributor to be bemused at the idea of being classed as 'history'. Even we were confused about whether to describe this project as 'doing history'. Even though we were using archives and writing about times before we were born, most of our subjects and the issues we were covering were still very much alive. Maybe calling it all history was just a way of convincing people that it was significant. It was the same with memories. Once we'd realised that people's stories are crucial to our understanding of the past, of politics, of freedom, we came to think of them as our shared cultural heritage. We wanted to collect this heritage, our elders' memories, into a kind of archive. Memories are stories that need to be recorded, remembered, retold. And we could only have done that if we listened to them. Doing history, then, was our act of active listening, and in doing so we were creating a new archive, within ourselves and our contributors.

We'd learnt so much from Switchboard.

———

As we listened, we felt ourselves unwinding, creating more space in our lungs with which to breathe. We remembered the log book entry where a volunteer had angrily written, 'Fuck society for twisting people.' This project was our un-twisting, and perhaps it could be for you, too.

We discovered that we felt so different from the parents who raised us, simply because our bodies and minds diverged from theirs; we longed for relationships that sat differently in the home and out in the world. This is how we came to feel more connected to our queer elders. Even when we didn't know it, we wanted to live more similarly to them than to our parents and most of our other blood relatives. Our queer ancestry is stronger.

One day when Adam was talking to his sister Hannah about the way they, and her partner Sam, had created Adam's nephew, Hannah said something about how family works. She said that as two lesbians who'd made a baby using donated sperm from Adam, they had created a new blueprint. The child would have a very different experience of family to what Hannah and Adam had had. His experience of family, with two mummies and a special uncle,

CONCLUSION

sketched out a blueprint for how a family can be made. His friends would see this too. Of course, there was actually nothing novel in this – as we had discovered, lesbians had been intercepting sperm for decades already. But still, somehow, it did feel new, like an idea or a promise.

Section 28 had not actually stopped people from growing up gay or forming families in their own ways, but the fact is that, statistically speaking, Hannah's family was still pretty unusual when her and Sam's baby was born in 2023. We'll never know whether a Britain without Section 28 would have led to more families like theirs. But it became clear that by the 2020s people like Hannah, Sam, and Adam were sketching out a new blueprint that others could see and follow, if they wanted, much like the lesbians who'd lived in squats and the gays who'd adopted children. Tash's niblings have met Tash's girlfriends, drawn rainbow flags together and had chats about whether Tash is a boy or a girl. Tash never got to do these things when they were little, with Great-Uncle Fred or Uncle Quentin.

Every generation has the option of trying to copy the blueprint of the previous one, to preserve and conserve some idea of how things should be done – but that is not the only way to be. The quiet pioneers in this book, the ones who followed their bodies, who heard their hearts, who found the strength to talk, and to listen: they created new blueprints. They said: this is how I do it, and it can be good. They never said that life has to be lived like this; they also want to see us find our own ways. They are our precious elders, because they have shown us what it looks like to live in our own bodies and minds.

We thought we were writing a history book. And we do hope it contains stories that you agree needed to be recorded. It's just taken some time. We are the middle generation who had to find ourselves on the timeline before we could convey the stories from our elders to the younger generation. But we also hope that this book offers a blueprint of sorts. Not a set of instructions for how to live, but a model, let's say – a way of paying attention. A simple suggestion: to listen.

2023
ADAM

There were so many pages that I had to lay them all out on my bedroom floor. I sorted through the sheets, placing them in piles in a taxonomy that worked in my head alone. Some of the pages were stuck together, still damaged by the sewage water that had once flooded George's flat. Some of the pages held stories that were illegible, written when George had lost full control of his poor hands. I sat down among the papers of his life, trying to collect and assemble and process, trying to understand what it all meant.

It was 2023. My friend George had just died. Somehow I had inherited his stories, captured in around twelve hours of audio and a carrier bag filled with scrappy notes. I was holding the grief of losing yet another person whom we had met in making *The Log Books*. But I also found myself carrying the responsibility of having to share George's memories. We had done it already on the podcast – and, in time, thank god, he'd listened back to his own words and felt proud to have been included. The pages and pages of messy notes and stories he'd left me were for a book, his book, a book we had been working on together. But now he'd died, at home, alone, with his beloved Brussels Griffons nudging at him to wake up.

I wondered what to do. Tash and I were already working on this book, and now somehow I was assembling another one. With George gone, I was alone in that project, and it wasn't even my story. I sat among the piles of scrawled notes and yellowed pages that at first glance seemed just like the Switchboard log books that I'd become accustomed to. And I thought about why I was so attracted to all these stories, from the log books, or George's journals, or the countless contributors who'd recorded their memories with us. I guess, sitting among the pages, I was trying to grasp the essence of what I was learning from all these old queer people. Or why I felt the need to convert their stories into work for me to do.

Maybe another way of asking myself these questions was: if all these stories are an archive that I want to get lost in, what am I trying to escape?

When I was little, I would write a newspaper for Mum, Dad and Hannah. I replicated the traditional layout, with columns and pictures and a masthead, black text on white paper, and I always wrote two copies. I pushed one under Hannah's bedroom door and the other under our parents'. I don't remember what stories I wrote, but they weren't about me. There were always more interesting stories to tell, and that the world (that is, 39 Robson Road) needed to know. It's no surprise that I loved English lessons, studying novels, writing stories, learning about how the media worked, and eventually became a journalist. I reported stories in my jobs. As a social media editor, I helped to get them out into the world. In my spare time I made short films and podcasts and tried to get my novels published. I guess I was obsessed. I loved exploring ideas, ways of living, characters and their curiosities. Always other people.

In writing this book, and getting to the end, and wondering what it has all been about, I've realised that even as I made these earlier outputs I wasn't directly accessing *my feelings*. Unlike Tash, I didn't even keep a tortured teenage diary. Absolutely not. Instead, I kept a travel journal filled with wannabe wry observations about the caravan sites where we holidayed because, of course, yes, I thought I'd make a good travel writer. I loved stories. I ate books for breakfast. I watched films before school in twenty-minute sprints, and I adored the musical theatre shows our parents treated us to.

When I was sixteen, I went on a school trip to a serious theatre, probably in Hull or Sheffield, for a production of Arthur Miller's play *A View from the Bridge*. Brooklyn, 1950s, Italian-Americans – what did I know of these? It was all so far away from everything I'd experienced. But with the play I was travelling again, observing, taking notes, and I was pulled in by the tensions dramatised by Miller. I'd been reading the text closely for weeks, quietly amazed that this joy was a formal requirement of my English GCSE. Other kids yawned all the way through those lessons, and saw the theatre trip as just a way to get out of school. I took my seat early and waited for my boisterous classmates to shut up so the performance could begin.

As the story played out, I could feel the strength of the anger that the middle-aged labourer Eddie feels for Rodolpho, this younger, newer type of man who sings and goes on dates with Eddie's niece. Eddie thinks Rodolpho is 'not quite right', and declares him a threat to the family. In featuring a same-sex kiss, *A View from the Bridge* is the kind of text that could have led teachers onto shaky ground in the era of Section 28. Then again, the kiss in question can hardly be seen as promoting the gay life.

In a moment of rage, confusion, and masculine aggression, Eddie kisses Rodolpho, as if to 'prove' something unsaid about Rodolpho. I knew the text well, so I'd been waiting for that moment. It's a real piece of theatre, filled with pure rage. There is no romance in the kiss, no desire. In the show I saw, when Eddie attacked Rodolpho with a kiss, my classmates erupted. All of that drama and tension, which should be a climax for the scene if not the entire play, disappeared. I interpreted Miller's message to be about the destruction wrought by rigid ideas of 'family' and 'masculinity', but I heard this message drown in the fits of laughter and shouts of disgust from the other teenagers in my class. I was pissed off. They'd ruined the play, mocked the performance, disrespected the whole show.

When I remember this theatre trip, I have to wonder why I do. For sure, it could be that it was the first time I'd seen two men's lips meet. But maybe it was what the audience reaction told me: that, in my daily life, I was surrounded by people who would bray at me if I dared to kiss another boy. I now realise my school years were lonely. These people couldn't even respect the theatre! There was no way I could expect them to stop bullying me for being studious or for being what they perceived as a 'puff'. I made school into a scheme: do well so you can get out. My eyes were set – first on college for A levels, then on university. To me, university meant a big city and people who cared about thinking as much as I did. In my family, only Hannah had been to university. Our parents were working-class baby boomers; they'd left school at sixteen and gone to work. They were desperate for us to get a degree. 'No one can ever take it off you,' Mum used to say.

At home my parents celebrated my studiousness, while at school I was tortured for it. I'm sure I was often smug or cocky when I knew the right answer, but the name-calling and the occasional punch still stung. Mum and Dad nurtured my curiosity: museums, theatre, cinema, and they let me load up the caravan with library books before we set off down the road for the summer holiday. The world was open to me. We got a PC with Microsoft Encarta, which was an encyclopedia with a trivia game rolled in. And then: the internet. Learning was my life. School was bearable because I liked the work.

2023 – ADAM

Work was good, I knew. But I had to learn that talking about being gay was not. Since I'd started school, every teacher who'd taught me was subject to Section 28 of the Local Government Act 1988. Some of them probably panicked whenever something gay came up; more than one of them couldn't tell the bullies why it was wrong to say 'puff'; and I'm sure that some of them hid themselves, like our contributors Pete, Ruth, and Catherine. Section 28 poisoned us all, silently, unknowingly. I also had no idea that my parents had voted for the government that brought it in. If I had, maybe I wouldn't have been so surprised when they rejected my sister.

I met George in 2020, when he was aged seventy-one. It was the year my dad Jim would have turned sixty-nine, so he and George were of the same generation, but somehow time is a wormhole and life is confusing. My dad died in 2016, aged sixty-five. I couldn't conceive of George and Jim as being of the same generation; George seemed to me like a grandfather, and yet he also held views that were found among people younger than me. When George was living his best gay life in San Francisco in the 1970s, Jim was getting married to my mum Patsy. When George was nearly dying from AIDS-related illnesses, Jim was driving his young family to the Yorkshire Dales for a half-term holiday. When George was hermitting himself in a basement flat and making survivor art, Jim was working in an office and saving money so his kids could go to university.

George had been privately educated and had made it to university. Jim had quit his state school so he could start paid work to support his single mum in their council house. He always regretted not being able to get a degree, to push his brain like that, and so he was thrilled that Hannah and I belonged to a generation that could. He loved to debate, my dad, and of course, so did I. In one of our exchanges, which crackled a little like an argument but was really an intellectual exercise, we clashed over whether a drummer was right to destroy his drum kit during his act. Dad said it was stupid and a waste. I countered that I thought such destruction could be art, and the act all the better for it. It was silly, really, but we wound each other up like this. I think he liked the fact that I could think, and that I could be independently minded and stubborn. One memory is illustrative. I did my teenage work experience in a factory out of town. When the bus didn't show up one morning, I walked for an hour through some dodgy streets, over a field, and finally through an industrial estate. It was just what I had to do, and when I told my dad, he wept with pride.

The problem with raising your children to be so independent is that they do their own thing, and sometimes this is a thing that you don't like. When Hannah came out as gay, our happy family imploded. Mum and Dad hated the idea. They felt hurt and betrayed. They thought they'd done something wrong to us. For nearly a decade, they kept Hannah at arm's length. And during this time I argued with them. I was in my twenties, educated, trained in seminars, working as a journalist by now, trying to get to the truth, always. (Ironically, I was still hiding my *own* truth from them.) On one evening, Mum was smoking in the kitchen, and I was sitting on the sofa across from Dad, and we got to speaking about my sister again. He put it to me like this: 'Look, if there's a row of trees, and they're all the same species, but one is growing crooked, at a weird angle, something is wrong, it's unnatural, it's not right.'

I could respect the logic, the clarity, the image. But I said, 'If that tree is getting the light and water it needs, who cares?'

Dad shook his head, exasperated. We weren't getting anywhere, and we never would. Instead, we turned to the TV in silence, fizzing. Bizarrely, it was Eurovision that night, and we sat and watched the whole show.

They were born in the early 1950s, my parents, the same generation as many of the LGBTQ+ people whom I would eventually meet when working on *The Log Books*. As heterosexuals, though, my parents were so different to those queer folks. Any time the topic of queerness came up, about Hannah or me or someone else, Mum always just said she never knew anything about it. I know that Dad did, because his old friend told me they'd once been in a pub toilet together when a guy cruised them. The guy told them they looked good, and Dad and his friend didn't even realise that the guy was flirting until later. They laughed it off. Boys will be boys. When Dad's friend told me this story, I'd already made *The Log Books*, learnt about the gay underworld, the cruising, and the cops, and I wondered about that guy, the man who'd cruised my dad. Like the story of a Switchboard caller, his tale is incomplete. Another scrap on the floor of the archive.

Thank god Tash and I did the work to find men like him. Like George, his life was another life that was lived in parallel to my dad's. True parallel. No touching. And I think, now, that this is what drew me to Switchboard's log books. I had always loved stories, always loved putting them together and sharing them. These stories, the stories of the ghosts, the stories of the ancestors who were both not mine and also definitely mine – these stories were really what I wanted all along. When I spoke to people like George, Sali, Julian, Femi, Catherine, Ritu, I heard the stories that I'd unconsciously yearned for. Their words were what was missing; their lives had been kept away from me, censored, withheld, lost.

I was drawn especially to the characters who were like me of course: David Seligman and John Lindsay, who'd brought order and organisation to Switchboard; and to the horny pervs who'd listened to their bodies. I had silenced mine for so long. By the time I was into the log books project I was in full exploration mode, like a twenty-something, enjoying the pleasure, giving in to intimacy. I was well into my thirties and finally living a sex life. The joy of sex matched the thrill of finding stories from the people who I hadn't even known were missing. I was so stimulated by the log books project. The work resonated in me, exorcising a grief that I didn't know I was carrying. It was a grief for the adolescence when I'd felt loved; an adolescence that died when Mum and Dad told Hannah to leave. It was also a grief for an adolescence I'd never had: one in which I had gossiped with friends about the boys I fancied, one with queer elders around me, and with parents who made it known that it would always have been OK to be me, even before I knew who I was. I realised that the queer elders I'd met through this project, not my parents, were the people who made me free.

I loved listening to people like George tell their stories because it gave me the experience of nostalgia: *This life could have been mine.* If only the law had mandated queer-inclusive education instead of banning all things gay. I had long borne some pain about this, even though I couldn't feel it until reading through the log books. The project showed me what I'd been doing for ever: in order to understand and express my feelings, I have to make work out of them. And here we are, here I am, writing it as another story.

Now my story sits in the archive, slotted in among the call logs, the interview transcripts and, of course, George's scruffy notes. We're all connected via these stories, if only we can all listen to each other and give each other what we need.

———

2023 – ADAM

I have a collage by George. It hangs on a wall in my flat, starting conversations. Inside the black plastic frame, George has scattered hundreds of glossy metallic confetti pieces: stars, pumpkins, moons, hearts, numbers, flowers, dinosaurs. It's a messy cacophony of glued-down party-bag glamour, like the multicoloured sugar beads on a child's birthday cake. On top of this chaos, George has laid a cut-out cartoon dog riding a skateboard, giving side-eye and even a bit of tongue. The paper dog has the stiff texture of something that's been glued before; he was probably ripped down from a street poster.

I can't help but love this collage that George made and gave to me. It is a gift from my ancestor, as full of love and mischief as all the memories Tash and I have collected from our elders. George's gorgeous dog is surrounded by shining colours, gliding by on his skateboard with audacity and somewhere to be. He's gaudy and cheap and my flatmates don't like him, but I think he's wonderful. If that sassy hound can keep going, then so can this one.

2023
TASH

'Hello Tash.'

Instantly I recognised the voice on the phone, despite the twenty years that had passed. I felt nervous, like a Switchboard caller who doesn't know what to say.

'Hello,' I replied, before blurting out, 'I don't know what to call you! Miss Smith?'

She chuckled, asking, 'Well, how old are you now, Tash?' I told her I was thirty-eight. 'Then I think Juliet is fine.'

It was a clear sunny day in October 2023 and I was on the phone to one of my old schoolteachers – one of the two whom I had confronted about being gay, all those years before. I was seated at my kitchen table, my sweaty palm pressing my phone to my ear. I didn't know what to expect. I explained to Juliet why I was calling, telling her about the book I was writing and why I thought it was important to speak to my old teachers like her. I had learnt that Juliet had married Miss Morgan, the PE teacher, and it was even more of a surprise when she told me that they now had two teenaged kids and were still teaching at my old school. I asked gently if she, and maybe Miss Morgan, would be open to talking to me. The answer was a vehement yes. 'I'm a history teacher after all,' Juliet said. Though she'd need to check; Miss Morgan had had a harder time of it. Juliet said her wife had come out young and it hadn't been easy. We quickly agreed to set a date and go for a pint.

I put the phone down on the table and felt a swell of emotion rising up in me. The call had lasted only a few minutes, and I was left buzzing with questions. I wondered what Miss Morgan would say. I took some deep breaths, stood up, and tried to capture the moment. Then I burst into tears. Suddenly it felt like I was a teenager again. I picked up my phone to text my friend Ruth about the call. She replied straight away, telling me I was brave, and that she was there if I needed to talk.

The next day Ruth sent me a picture of a postcard. She'd found it being used as a bookmark in one of the old textbooks she'd used as a teacher herself in 1995. The postcard had been produced by Stonewall and it declared 'Support the Sexual Orientation Discrimination Bill', alongside some statistics. Ruth drew my attention to two of the numbers: '8% of lesbians and gays lose their jobs because of their sexuality', and '68% of gays and lesbians are not "out" at work.' She wrote:

> The 8% & 68% are shocking. I was leading an exhausting double life & decided to join S/B [Switchboard] on new years day 1996 after hearing a piece on the radio about it. The bookmark explains why I wasn't out at work & why you had no role models @ secondary Xx

---

It was December by the time I was on a train to my hometown, Plymouth. My parents had recently moved away, but Juliet had invited me for dinner and to stay the night. With a real mix of feelings, I'd said yes.

It was a strange journey as I watched the British countryside whizz by, turning to sea as we entered Devon. I felt like I was going back in time. I hadn't seen my teachers in twenty years. I wondered if they still looked the same, whether they would recognise me, whether they would remember *that* day, the day Miss

2023 – TASH

Morgan had shut me down when I told her I was gay. From the moment she had walked into my school as the new PE teacher when I was in Year 9, I had noticed *something* about her. Something different. The way she held herself. I still couldn't put my finger on it now. Her manner, maybe, the way she walked, the way she used her hands when she talked. Would it be the same? Would she talk to me, this time, now her wife had invited me over?

As the train sped on, I started to think about Ruth and what she had told me for the podcast back a few years ago about her years as a lesbian teacher. 'I was never able to share things that had happened to me,' she'd said. 'It was very oblique. It was like talking to somebody through a pane of glass.'

Until that conversation with Ruth, I'd never thought about what my teachers might have been going through. I had just felt hurt, hurt at the denial of something that seemed so obvious and true. Something that I was trying to own, not deny, not feel shame about. When I told Ruth that I was thinking of reaching out to my old teachers, as I tucked into a cake she'd bought me from Sainsbury's, she nodded and listened to me. She told me to go with care, that it had been a really difficult time for her, and I might not get the response I was looking for. I held those words in my mind, 'go with care', as I stepped off the train and out of the station.

Within seconds I saw a hand waving at me from behind a car's steering wheel. I climbed into the front seat, beaming, and was thrown straight into the midst of Juliet's parent-teacher life. As we drove to their house through the streets I knew so well, she told me we had to stop off at Morrisons to get pizzas for their daughter and her friends. The phone then rang: it was her wife, Miss Morgan, and Juliet answered on speakerphone. 'I'm with Tash!' she shouted, that little bit louder than she needed to, just like my parents do.

'Hi Tash,' Miss Morgan said through the car speakers. I'd forgotten her accent, Welsh, soft, and gentle. She was going to join later when she was back from work.

We arrived at the house. It was a whirlwind: two kids, two working parents, Wilbur the dog, Dexter and Rex the cats. Chaos, but full of warmth. I was offered a drink and a seat at the breakfast bar while Juliet started the cooking. The house was full of life and the rotating door of a family home introduced me to their two teenagers, Nate and Ava. Ava's friends arrived squealing, announcing that they had *so* much to tell her. But, as Juliet muttered, they had seen each other only two hours previously. I'd forgotten what teenagers are like.

Juliet told me how she had gone part-time and was hoping to leave that year, and that Miss Morgan was deputy head and safeguarding lead. She explained that the school had an LGBTQ+ group. They'd just won a Rainbow Flag Award from the Intercom Trust, a community charity supporting inclusion in the South West.

Wow, I thought, *what a different world to the one I came from.*

When Miss Morgan arrived home, she was smaller than I remembered, but her hair was the same, pulled back into a ponytail. We both smiled. And as soon as she was sitting next to me at the breakfast bar, the stories started to surface.

Miss Morgan had grown up in the shadow of domestic violence and abuse. Her parents had found a letter she had written to her first girlfriend when she was fourteen and, in her words, they had said, 'this isn't going to fly'. She put her gayness away. She shut it out until she left home and made it to university.

As I listened to my old teacher tell me, finally, about her private life, I heard shame ringing out under every word she spoke. I could see it in the droop of her shoulders as she unfurled her memories, the weight of her childhood, her young adulthood. So much shame. Before my eyes my old teacher became a human. I thought, *No wonder she couldn't be there for me*. She continued, told me how lost she had been, and how she had created an armour to help her deal with life. She'd had to shield herself from the world.

Miss Morgan was thirty-four when she joined my school as head of PE. It was January 2001, and I had not long turned fifteen. She didn't come out to anyone. Juliet joined at the start of the following school year, September 2001. Miss Morgan remembered that moment clearly, describing Juliet blowing into the staffroom as a twenty-eight-year-old inquisitive kid who had been travelling all over the world, fresh from discovering her bisexuality, and not afraid to share it. Somehow she'd landed in Plymouth, at Devonport High School for Girls.

Their relationship began soon after, but they didn't tell the school until they got engaged in 2006. That was just two years after I had left. They 'came out' together during a morning staff briefing. Half the team were shocked, and the other half thought, *About time*. After they got married, they decided to start trying for kids. Juliet carried them both but with Miss Morgan's egg first, and then hers second. They made me guess who their sperm donor was. Confused, I gasped, 'Who?!'

They replied in unison: 'Mr Med!' – one of the language teachers at the school.

The stories flowed, and I felt like I was catching up with old friends whom I'd known for years, but had never asked all the questions I'd wanted. It was one of the most exhilarating interviews I'd ever done. In fact, by 9 p.m. I still hadn't taken my recorder out. What was stopping me? This was the purpose of my visit; they knew that, and I had asked for it. I had asked to interview them. I interrupted the flow and posed the question. The table was cleared, the recorder placed in the middle, wine poured, and I pushed the button. The red light encircled it. And I was a teenager again, asking my teachers, 'Why didn't you tell me you were gay?'

'I hated denying it,' Juliet answered, shaking her head, 'but I hadn't had permission . . . because the problem is, if I outed myself, which I have no issue with, I would have outed her as well, obviously by association, and I couldn't do that. Because it's not just my story.'

I looked to Miss Morgan, but she said nothing.

Although I appreciated everything Juliet was saying, I needed to hear from Miss Morgan. It was Miss Morgan who was the first gay woman I ever saw. Who walked into my fifteen-year-old world and then turned away from me. Here she was beside me, twenty-four years later, not saying a thing. All these years later she still wasn't able to respond to what I'd said when I was fifteen, when I'd asked if she was gay like me.

I tried again. 'I just, I said it because I was so desperate. I wanted to connect with you. I wanted to . . .' I stuttered. On the tape, my voice struggles but holds the emotion. 'I wanted . . . I wanted this . . . that we're having now. I wanted that.'

Miss Morgan sat next to me, looked at me, her brow furrowed and said, 'I don't remember.'

What she was able to share with me was how exhausted she felt at having to come out throughout her life. 'As a child, you think . . . I'm gonna have to come out once,' she said. 'It's this big thing. But it's bullshit. You come out and you come out and you come out and you come out and I'm so jaded.'

Miss Morgan's exhaustion felt like an invisible wave in the room, crashing out of her body. 'In my fifties I am so bored of coming out to people. It's exhausting. As a gay woman [having] to do it, it's fucking exhausting.'

She told me that she remembered having other conversations like ours throughout her career, where a child had needed to hear her come out, but she couldn't respond. She couldn't even remember the day I'd needed it. Her wife Juliet seemed genuinely shocked by this, but they both agreed Miss Morgan had a terrible memory, maybe to do with the trauma she'd experienced as a kid.

I gently asked whether she could have still been in the depths of denial when I asked her. She wasn't out, so maybe she *couldn't* remember it. We both looked at each other for a moment, her head tilting slightly to the right, her eyebrows raising a little, and she looked up into the air for an answer.

I took a sip of wine, smiled, and the conversation moved on to an email they'd once sent me. They'd written me an apology, but now I was at their table Juliet told me that it was likely just her who had sent it, as it wasn't something Miss Morgan would have done. She said how much she'd hated hiding her sexuality in school. 'It's the wrong thing to do,' she said, tapping her hand on the table, 'because anyone who's asking you' – tap, tap – 'is asking you because they need to know, not just because they want to know.'

Juliet then turned to Miss Morgan to say, 'And that's what I told you all along. We're going to tell people because there will be girls at this school who need to know it's okay to be gay.'

I sat with my old teachers well into the early hours, telling them about my journey, my turbulent teenage years. They told me how they'd learnt that there is no such thing as a difficult kid; there is always something else going on underneath. And I felt grateful that these two people were teaching and looking out for kids at the school I had grown up in.

I saw how hard it had been, and still was, for Miss Morgan. There was something heavy about her that I wanted to help her carry. She sat in her chair with her arms crossed, protecting herself. I told them how angry I had been at them for a long time. That even though my anger was easing, I still felt hurt and sad. The hardest part, I said, was that I hadn't believed them when they'd denied they were gay. Juliet leant across the table and looked me directly in the eyes, 'And you know what?' she said, 'I knew you didn't believe me . . . it was like a dance we had to go through.'

A dance, I thought. I took a deep breath, remembering one of my old diary entries:

Learn your lines, learn the moves. Learn to be not like YOU.

―――――

I woke up early the next morning. I was in the spare room, on a single bed, tucked under a Minions duvet that had once belonged to their kids. I felt tired. I'd slept badly, cursed by strange dreams. In one, I'd needed to use their bathroom but first I had to build it out of the bedroom I was staying in and put it back together myself. Each part of the bathroom was almost too heavy for me to move. I rolled my eyes and thought, *Yes, Tash, your therapist will love this.*

Somehow, I also felt happy.

I left Plymouth to head to my sister's. It was a typically grey morning in the grey seaside town, but as I looked out the window from the train, the sky was breaking into blue smudges, and there was a rainbow appearing in the sky. *God*, I thought, *how predictably basic – it doesn't get gayer than that.*

―――――

2023 – TASH

I started secondary school amid the silence of Section 28. I did not realise it until my thirties, but I am a child of Section 28. When my friend and fellow Switchboard volunteer Ruth first told me about that law, she'd used the word 'pernicious'. I had not heard that word before, and it felt alive in my mouth as I said it back, feeling its slippery, subtle methods on my tongue. *Pernicious*. It took a moment of connection with Ruth to understand how the impact of that pernicious piece of legislation was still burning through me, nearly twenty years later.

Ruth once told me what she loved about being a volunteer at Switchboard:

> There is something magical, some sort of alchemy that happens. It's hard to describe . . . It's an amazing thing. And I hadn't realised how much our callers would become part of me . . .
> I think we've become a product of all the amazing people that we've spoken to over the years . . . being a volunteer is not a one-way exchange. It's such a gift. It's an absolute gift.

As volunteers, both Ruth and I have been shaped by all the people we have spoken to on the phones. But we have also had this opportunity to hold space for each other. Our training, the work we've done, and the friendship we've formed through it all have made Ruth and I a part of each other. We are connected. In fact, Ruth has become the teacher that troubled teen Tash needed. And I am the queer kid she wanted to support at school. She is my queer elder and my guide. Her life resonated with me; her story vibrated through my memory; it brought up my trauma, and taught me how to heal.

I've talked about what Switchboard has taught me, the power of patience and the power of listening. But I actually think that it was Ruth who taught me what it feels like to be *heard*. That power is what has changed me. Like Ruth said, listening is an absolute gift.

The final page of Switchboard's final log book contains the following entries.

27 April 2003
Unfortunately the kettle has broken! As a temporary measure I have taken the one from the smoking room. Both kettles will be replaced by the end of the week. Bryan

30 April 2003
The kettle has been replaced in the phone room and the common room. They are rapid boil kettles!! Enjoy! Bryan

3 May 2003
At the end of my shift, 1pm, all phones are logged out, but phone displays continue to show callers queueing. Graham

3 May 2003
Repeat caller – softly spoken older gay man who begins by saying he's called before and thinks he might be gay. Has had relationships with women, and sex with men. Unsure about starting a relationship with a man – keeps bringing conversation back to 'do you think I'm gay?'
He's very pleasant to talk with but does not seem to move on with his issues at all. He already goes on the scene and to a gay group and has no difficulty meeting men.
But we never get beyond the idea that he might say 'yes' to the offer of a date next time! Helen xx

BIBLIOGRAPHY

Books

Outrageous! by Paul Baker
Against Landlords by Nick Bano
Surviving the Future edited by Shuli Branson, Raven Hudson, and Bry Reed
Women in Law by Julia Anne Brophy
Queer Premises by Ben Campkin
The Apparitional Lesbian: Female Homosexuality and Modern Culture by Terry Castle
Queer Beyond London by Matt Cook and Alison Oram
Queering Psychotherapy by Jane C. Czyzselska
The Transgender Issue by Shon Faye
Blowing the Lid by Stuart Feather
AIDS: Don't Die of Prejudice by Norman Fowler
The End of Innocence by Simon Garfield
The Pink Line by Mark Gevisser
A Short History of Trans Misogyny by Jules Gill-Peterson
Queer Data by Kevin Guyan
Rocking the Cradle: Lesbian Mothers by Gillian E. Hanscombe & Jackie Forster
Before We Were Trans by Kit Heyam
Queer London by Matt Houlbrook
Every Body by Olivia Laing
British Queer History edited by Brian Lewis
Gay Bar by Jeremy Atherton Lin

Making Gay History by Eric Marcus
Out of the Shadows by Walt Odets
Revolutionary Acts by Jason Okundaye
The Hidden Case of Ewan Forbes by Zoë Playdon
The Lesbian Mother's Legal Handbook by the Rights of Women Lesbian Custody Group
Queering Desire edited by Róisín Ryan-Flood and Amy Tooth Murphy
Peace! Books! Freedom! The Secret History of a Radical London Building by Rosa Schling
Bi by Julia Shaw
Straight Jacket by Matthew Todd
Talking about Young Lesbians edited by Lorraine Trenchard, London Gay Teenage Group
Something To Tell You by Lorraine Trenchard and Hugh Warren
Against the Law by Peter Wildeblood

Film

What's Safe, What's Gross, What's Selfish and What's Stupid by Jasmine Johnson

ACKNOWLEDGEMENTS

We'd like to give thanks to so many people for listening to us, caring for us, and helping us to do this work.

To our agent Sophie Lambert who saw this book as we saw it, and has guided it all the way home, along with her assistant Alice Hoskyns.

To our editor Mo Hafeez, whose insights, precision, questions, guidance, and care have made this book the best it could be. To the rest of the team at Faber for all their excellent work.

To everyone who helped with permissions, research questions, connections, and ideas.

For help with our research: the team at Bishopsgate Institute, led by Stefan Dickers, and Victoria Iglikowski-Broad at The National Archives.

To Shiv Dave who co-produced the podcast with us, and the team at Acast who supported us in providing a platform for people to listen.

To Katie Carpenter, Bertie Darrell, Francesca Davey, Robert Haynes, India Latham, Will Nutland, Peter Scalpello, and Amy Spiller for reading various scraps and drafts, and giving us things to reflect on. To Justin Bengry for his deep insight and holding us to account for how we were framing this history.

To our queer families, the constellations of friendships that have held us throughout our lives, and especially those loved ones who trusted us to tell their stories.

Adam wants to thank his sister Hannah for her lifelong support and queer sibling solidarity.

Tash wants to thank their mum Julia and sister Livi, whom Tash is proud to hold as friends too.

We remain in deep gratitude to, and awe of, our contributors. They have opened their hearts, revisited old wounds, shared their stories, and transferred their power to us and, now, you.

We remember especially those who were lost in the years the original log books were written, and those who died after we captured their voices: Judith, James, John, and George.

Finally, to Switchboard's volunteers and staff: the most devoted friends of the LGBTQ+ community in our country. You listen, you care, you love, and we thank you.

IMAGE CREDITS

PAGE 1:

Top left: Tash aged 2.5 years in the summer of 1988, Dartmouth, Devon. Photo courtesy of Tash Walker.

Top right: Adam with his older sister Hannah in their living room, Cleethorpes, 1985. Photo courtesy of Adam Zmith.

Bottom: Tash holding Switchboard's first log book, dated 1975. Photo taken in 2019 at Bishopsgate Institute by Imogen Forte.

PAGE 2:

Gay Switchboard poster advertising the service, c. 1978. Switchboard archive, Bishopsgate Institute.

PAGE 3:

Top left: Switchboard's phone room above Housmans Bookshop, 1984. Photo by Robert Workman.

Top right: Andy Piccos taking a call at Switchboard, c. 1978. Unknown photographer, Switchboard archive, Bishopsgate Institute.

Bottom: Lisa Power and other volunteers taking calls in front of the many files that were used to help callers, 1980s. Unknown photographer, Switchboard archive, Bishopsgate Institute.

PAGE 4:

Top: Switchboard's volunteers at the helpline's 10th birthday celebration, 1984. Photo taken in the garden of the Edward IV Pub by Robert Workman.

Bottom left: Photograph of Denroy, a Switchboard volunteer, posing with the phone in front of the computers in the phone room, c. 1997. Unknown photographer, Switchboard archive, Bishopsgate Institute.

Bottom right: Volunteer morale boosting in Switchboard's phone room, 1984. Photo taken by Robert Workman.

PAGE 5:

David Seligman, Switchboard co-founder, 1982. Photo by Robert Workman.

PAGE 6:

A poster made and distributed by Switchboard to raise awareness about HIV transmission, c. 1991. Switchboard archive, Bishopsgate Institute.

PAGE 7:

Top left: A4 poster for supporting organisations to display, 1985. Switchboard archive, Bishopsgate Institute.

Top right: Leaflet made by Switchboard to raise awareness about HIV among lesbians, c.1986. Switchboard archive, Bishopsgate Institute.

Bottom: Hand-drawn volunteer recruitment leaflet, 1979. Switchboard archive, Bishopsgate Institute.

PAGE 8:

Top: Switchboard volunteers and their banner at Lesbian and Gay Pride in London, 1983. Photo by Robert Workman.

Bottom left: Femi Otitoju, dressed in homage to Grace Jones at London Pride 1985. Unknown photographer, Switchboard archive, Bishopsgate Institute.

Bottom right: Protest at British Home Stores against the sacking of Tony Whitehead, 7 February 1976. Tony holds the 'Equal Rights' sign. Photo by Robert Workman.

NOTES

INTRODUCTION

1. *Daily Mail*, 5 June 1986
2. House of Lords debate, 7 May 1986, in *Hansard* hansard.parliament.uk/Lords/1986-05-07/debates/fb8c411a-d0eb-4050-a05d-e84570ea0d6a/LordsChamber#contribution-8dce7b7a-5f9f-46b7-b77c-b6ebab80f9b6
3. House of Lords debate, 7 May 1986, in *Hansard* hansard.parliament.uk/Lords/1986-05-07/debates/fb8c411a-d0eb-4050-a05d-e84570ea0d6a/LordsChamber#contribution-b9ddf280-f91b-4664-b5fe-50237dd2e9fe
4. Margaret Thatcher's Conservative Party Conference speech, 9 October 1987 margaretthatcher.org/document/106941
5. *Peace! Books! Freedom! The Secret History of a Radical London Building* by Rosa Schling, Housmans Bookshop
6. ibid.
7. *Gay News* 31, 11–24 October 1973
8. *Gay News* 38, 17–30 January 1974
9. *Gay News* 42, 14–27 March 1974

1: 'A BIT CONFUSED, EXCITED . . .'

1. 9th British Social Attitudes Report (1992), 13th British Social Attitudes Report (1996), 16th British Social Attitudes Report (1999) and 17th British Social Attitudes Report (2000)
2. 'In Conversation: Amelia Abraham & Jack Parlett', *Granta*, 26 March 2024 granta.com/in-conversation-abraham-parlett/
3. *The Log Books* podcast, season 3, episode 7 thelogbooks.org/transcript/s3-e7-the-inability-of-others-to-understand-transcript

2: 'HUDDLED TOGETHER IN A CORNER'

1 *The Log Books* podcast, season 3, episode 5 thelogbooks.org/transcript/s3-e5-they-do-mean-us-harm-transcript
2 *Straight Jacket* by Matthew Todd, Bantam Press, 2016, page 11

3: 'TODAY IT'S LOOKING, TOMORROW IT'LL BE THINKING'

1 *The Log Books* podcast, season 1, episode 4 thelogbooks.org/transcript/s1-e4-pretty-policemen-transcript
2 'Lesbianism and Feminist Legislation in 1921: the Age of Consent and "Gross Indecency between Women" by Caroline Derry in *History Workshop Journal* 86 (Autumn 2018) pp. 245–67 oro.open.ac.uk/55535/
3 House of Lords debate, 15 August 1921, in *Hansard* hansard.parliament.uk/Lords/1921-08-15/debates/b1cfe8ab-774e-42d0-a86e-d55a6b58fecc/LordsChamber
4 'Breaking the Silence: Criminalisation of Lesbians and Bisexual Women and its Impacts' by the Human Dignity Trust, 24 September 2024 humandignitytrust.org/wp-content/uploads/resources/Breaking-the-Silence-Criminalisation-of-LB-Women-and-its-Impacts-FINAL.pdf
5 Articles by Research Unit staff in journals, including: 'Indecency Between Males and the Sexual Offences Act 1967' by G. R. Walmsley in *Criminal Law Review*, July 1978, in The National Archives, ref HO 522/7
6 *The Log Books* podcast, season 1, episode 4 thelogbooks.org/transcript/s1-e4-pretty-policemen-transcript
7 Home Office Equality Impact Assessment 2010 assets.publishing.service.gov.uk/government/uploads/system/uploads/attachment_data/file/98420/removal-consensual-gay-sex-eia.pdf
8 Disregard process for convictions for decriminalised sexual offences (consensual gay sex), Home Office, 17 November 2022 gov.uk/government/publications/statistics-on-the-disregard-and-pardon-for-historical-gay-sexual-convictions/statistics-on-disregards-and-pardons-for-historical-gay-sexual-convictions

NOTES

9. Police operations against crime: Metropolitan Police and homosexuals, 1990–1992, files in The National Archives, ref HO 528/54
10. Agents provocateurs: homosexual importuning and entrapment, files in The National Archives, ref HO 287/3533 and Homosexual importuning: entrapment, files in The National Archives, ref HO 287/3549
11. *The Log Books* podcast, season 1, episode 4 thelogbooks.org/transcript/s1-e4-pretty-policemen-transcript
12. Interviewed for the podcast, but this quote was not featured in an episode
13. *The Log Books* podcast, season 3, episode 5 thelogbooks.org/transcript/s3-e5-they-do-mean-us-harm-transcript
14. Galop's statement on institutionalised homophobia and transphobia in the Met Police, 21 March 2023 galop.org.uk/news/galops-statement-on-institutionalised-homophobia-and-transphobia-in-the-met-police/
15. Policing the gay community, 1994–1996, in The National Archives, ref HO 500/165
16. Mr Oke's letter held in The National Archives ref HO 500/165
17. 'The brutal murder of a gay man in Central Park that changed Plymouth forever' by Edd Law, *Plymouth Herald*, 16 September 2007 plymouthherald.co.uk/news/plymouth-news/brutal-murder-gay-man-central-467665

4: 'THIS TROUBLESOME BODY'

1. 'Gay Times', BBC *Panorama*, 27 October 1997 bbc.co.uk/archive/panorama--gay-times/zhqghbk
2. British Social Attitudes report, published by the National Centre for Social Research, September 2023 natcen.ac.uk/news/britains-attitudes-towards-moral-issues-have-become-much-more-liberal
3. We have turned these names into initials for confidentiality
4. Caller's name changed to an initial for confidentiality
5. *For Women Scotland Ltd (Appellant) v. The Scottish Ministers (Respondent)* supremecourt.uk/cases/uksc-2024-0042

6 *Legacy of Kindness* podcast, produced by Lucia Scazzocchio, episode 4 lok.gires.org.uk/exhibition/podcasts/episode-4-policy-over-politics/
7 *Chessington World of Adventures Ltd v. Reed*, 1997 casemine.com/judgement/uk/5a8ff86b60d03e7f57ec0113#:~:
8 *Legacy of Kindness* podcast, produced by Lucia Scazzocchio, episode 2 lok.gires.org.uk/exhibition/podcasts/episode-2-trans-at-work/
9 Home Affairs. Homosexual rights in Great Britain and Europe: part 1, held in The National Archives, ref PREM-49-882
10 *Goodwin & I v. United Kingdom* [2002] 2 FCR 577
11 *The Log Books* podcast, season 1, episode 5 thelogbooks.org/transcript/s1-e5-you-might-well-be-very-angry-transcript
12 'Separatism: A Look Back in Anger' by Janet Dixon, in *Radical Records: Thirty Years of Lesbian and Gay History, 1957–1987*, edited by Bob Cant and Susan Hemmings, Routledge, 1988
13 *Law, State and the Family: The Politics of Child Custody* by Julia Anne Brophy, PhD thesis at the University of Sheffield, 1985 etheses.whiterose.ac.uk/1795/
14 'Lesbian Mothers on Trial: A report on lesbian mothers & child custody' (Rights of Women, 1984), viewed in Bishopsgate Institute, Peter Ashman collection, ref PAMA/2/6
15 *The Log Books* podcast, season 1, episode 5 thelogbooks.org/transcript/s1-e5-you-might-well-be-very-angry-transcript
16 *The Log Books* podcast, season 3, episode 2 thelogbooks.org/transcript/s3-e2-the-little-darlings-transcript
17 *The Log Books* podcast, season 3, episode 1 thelogbooks.org/transcript/s3-e1-multiple-paradox-net-files-transcript
18 'Arrested Development?' (Stonewall report), held in Bishopsgate Institute, Peter Ashman collection, ref PAMA/2/6
19 *The Log Books* podcast, season 3, episode 2 thelogbooks.org/transcript/s3-e2-the-little-darlings-transcript
20 *The Log Books* podcast, season 2, episode 8 thelogbooks.org/transcript/s2-e8-kiss-my-rump-transcript
21 Richard Desmond's case, and the decision of the European Commission of Human Rights, can be read in the Peter Ashman collection at Bishopsgate Institute, ref PAMA 1/11/3
22 *The Log Books* podcast, season 2, episode 8 thelogbooks.org/transcript/s2-e8-kiss-my-rump-transcript

NOTES

23 House of Commons debate on Amendment of Law Relating to Sexual Acts Between Men, 21 February 1994, in *Hansard* hansard.parliament.uk/Commons/1994-02-21/debates/ d4e66c65-098e-4bd3-ad8e-c719e08482ed/NewClause3

24 *Age of Dissent*, directed by Will Parry, Maya Vision, 1994 vimeo.com/120489293

25 House of Commons debate on Amendment of Law Relating to Sexual Acts Between Men, 21 February 1994, in *Hansard* hansard.parliament.uk/Commons/1994-02-21/debates/ d4e66c65-098e-4bd3-ad8e-c719e08482ed/NewClause3

26 Sexual Offences (Amendment) Act 2000 legislation.gov.uk/ ukpga/2000/44/enacted

27 *Minority Stress and Lesbian Women*, Lexington Books, 1981 by Virginia R. Brooks; and 'Minority Stress and Mental Health in Gay Men' by I. H. Meyer, in the *Journal of Health and Social Behaviour*, 1995 pubmed.ncbi.nlm.nih.gov/7738327/

5: 'PLEASE BE GENTLE'

1 *Sun*, 14 October 1985

2 *The Log Books* podcast, season 2, episode 1 thelogbooks.org/ transcript/s2-e1-please-be-gentle-transcript

3 *The Log Books* podcast, season 2, episode 1 thelogbooks.org/ transcript/s2-e1-please-be-gentle-transcript

4 House of Lords debate on the family, 29 November 1989, in *Hansard* hansard.parliament.uk/Lords/1989-11-29/debates/ c49fbfee-46c0-456d-a9f4-8d88e8edd391/TheFamily

5 House of Lords debate on Sexual Offences (Amendment) Bill, April 11th 2000, in *Hansard* hansard.parliament.uk/Lords/2000-04-11/debates/836e9caa-1c02-4bae-8568-15d9cdb47392/ SexualOffences(Amendment)Bill

6 National Health. Acquired Immune Deficiency Syndrome (AIDS): part 1, held at The National Archives ref PREM 19/1863; and 'HIV/AIDS and the LGBTQ+ community: Education, care and support' by Mollie Clark, 21 March 2021 blog.nationalarchives.gov.uk/ hiv-aids-and-the-lgbtq-community-education-care-and-support/

7 'Harwich: Key figure returns to party', *Daily Gazette*, 18 April 2008 gazette-news.co.uk/news/2209390. harwich-key-figure-returns-to-party/
8 A moral framework for sexual education, held in The National Archives, ref ED 269/482
9 'Kemi Badenoch: Some will think the government's guidance on gender in schools is too strong – but WE don't duck the hard questions' by Kemi Badenoch, Mail Online, 19 December 2023 dailymail.co.uk/debate/article-12883171/KEMI-BADENOCH-think-governments-guidance-gender-schools-strong-dont-duck-hard-questions.html
10 'Education Secretary Gillian Keegan says gender identity "should not be taught in schools at any age"' by Claire Gilbody Dickerson, Sky News, 16 May 2024 news.sky.com/story/education-secretary-gillian-keegan-says-gender-identity-shouldnt-be-taught-in-schools-at-any-age-13137110

6: 'WOULD LIKE TO STAY'

1 *The Log Books* podcast, season 1, episode 1 thelogbooks.org/transcript/the-log-books-transcript-s1e1
2 Black Lesbian and Gay Centre Newsletter, April 1987, held at Bishopsgate Institute s3.eu-west-1.amazonaws.com/bishopsgate/1987-04-BLGC-newsletter.pdf?mtime=20221021101832
3 *The Log Books* podcast, season 2, episode 11 thelogbooks.org/transcript/s2-e11-would-like-to-stay-transcript
4 Thatcher years in graphics, BBC News website, 18 November 2005 news.bbc.co.uk/1/hi/in_pictures/4446012.stm
5 'From Right to Buy to Buy to Let' by Tom Copley, Greater London Authority, 2014 assets.londonist.com/uploads/2014/01/from-right-to-buy-to-buy-to-let-jan-2014_5.pdf
6 'Exclusive: Great Tory housing shame: Third of ex-council homes now owned by rich landlords' by Rich Smomerlad, *Mirror*, 5 March 2013 mirror.co.uk/news/uk-news/right-to-buy-housing-shame-third-ex-council-1743338; 'Meet the new class of landlords profiting from Generation Rent' by Patrick Collinson, *Guardian*, 28 June 2013 theguardian.com/money/2013/jun/28/new-class-landlords-profiting-generation-rent

NOTES

7. *On Railton Road* by Ian Giles and Louis Rembges, Polari Press, 2023
8. House price to earning ratio stats published by Building Societies Association, published 2022 bsa.org.uk/getmedia/7b7e8048-12d6-4c47-b321-c22a66ccf7f0/House-price-earning-ratio-PUBLISHED.xls
9. *The Log Books* podcast, season 1, episode 1 thelogbooks.org/transcript/the-log-books-transcript-s1e1
10. 'Separatism: A Look Back in Anger' by Janet Dixon, in *Radical Records: Thirty Years of Lesbian and Gay History, 1957–1987*, edited by Bob Cant and Susan Hemmings, Routledge, 1988
11. *Sisterhood and Squatting in the 1970s: Feminism, Housing and Urban Change in Hackney*, by Christine Wall, History Workshop Journal Issue 83, 2017i
12. ibid.
13. *Black and Gay, Back in the Day* podcast, episode 7, produced by Aunt Nell auntnell.com/episode-7-yvonne-taylor-with-jewel-foster
14. *Peace! Books! Freedom! The Secret History of a Radical London Building* by Rosa Schling, Housmans Bookshop, p.103
15. ibid., p. 104–105
16. Housing costs and income inequality in the UK, Institute for Fiscal Studies, 17 November 2023 ifs.org.uk/publications/housing-costs-and-income-inequality-uk
17. An intergenerational audit for the UK, Resolution Foundation, 13 March, 2023 resolutionfoundation.org/publications/an-intergenerational-audit-for-the-uk-2023/
18. Housing affordability in England and Wales: 2023, Office for National Statistics, 25 March 2024 ons.gov.uk/peoplepopulationandcommunity/housing/bulletins/housingaffordabilityinenglandandwales/2023
19. House price (existing dwellings) to residence-based earnings ratio dataset, Office for National Statistics, 25 March 2024 ons.gov.uk/peoplepopulationandcommunity/housing/bulletins/housingaffordabilityinenglandandwales/2023/relateddata

7: 'FATALLY DISRUPTIVE'

1 House of Lords debate on Local Government Act 1986 (Amendment) Bill, 18 December 1986, in *Hansard* hansard.parliament.uk/lords/1986-12-18/debates/afda921e-413c-46f1-9d08-883838f2367d/LocalGovernmentAct1986(Amendment)BillHl
2 Interviewed for the podcast, but this quote was not featured in an episode.
3 1991 Census: Census topics; household composition analysis; cohabiting couples of same sex, letter in The National Archives, ref RG 19/1144
4 Black Lesbian and Gay Centre Project newsletter, Oct 1990, held in Bishopsgate Institute s3.eu-west-1.amazonaws.com/bishopsgate/1990-10-BLGC-newsletter.pdf?mtime=20221024140113

8: 'MULTIPLE PARADOX NET FILES'

1 *The Log Books* podcast, season 3, episode 1 thelogbooks.org/transcript/s3-e1-multiple-paradox-net-files-transcript
2 ibid.
3 ibid.
4 ibid.

INDEX

2point4 Children (1991–1999), 294–5

ableism, 336–7
Abraham, Amelia, 51–2
abuse, 26, 161, 208, 236–7, 245, 289–90, 374
accessibility of Switchboard, 336–7
accommodation *see* homes and housing
Action for Lesbian Parents, 176
activism, 140, 155–7, 191–3, 201
Adams, Jeremy, 26–7, 44–5, 109, 111–12, 114, 123, 146
Admiral Duncan pub bombing, 1999, 110–12, 113, 145–6
adoption and fostering, 324–7
adult babies, 43
After the Act (theatre production), 52
age of consent, 106, 126–7, 145, 182–7; campaign for equality, 187–90; government policy, 190–4
Age of Dissent (1994), 191–2
Ahmad, Layla, 267, 306–8
Ajamu X, 273
Ambrose King Centre, Royal London Hospital, 216
anal sex, 40
anonymity, 1
Apple, 347
Armatrading, Joan, 88
armed forces, 136–9
Armstrong, Boo, 146
Armstrong, Mrs (letter writer), 159, 188–9
artificial insemination, 293–4, 314–19
asexuality, 68
Ashman, Peter, 186
Ashton, Paul, 200
Asian gay community, 92–4, 96–7
asylum, 267
Athlone Road in Brixton, London, 280–3
audio, 332–4
AZT treatment for HIV, 209, 225

Backstreet, London, 98
Badenoch, Kemi, 247
badges, 81–2, 238
Barbican Centre, London, 20, 21
BBC, 248
BDSM, 44–6, 101–2
Beasley, Sue, 177
Bell, Andy, 105
Bell pub, King's Cross, 109–10
Bethnal Green Working Men's Club, 81
biases, 1–2
Bill, The (1984–2010), 146–7
biphobia, 229–30, 345–6
Birmingham, 92
birth certificates, 169, 172
bisexuality, 47, 59, 229–30, 300, 334, 345–6
Bishop, Timothy, 200
Bishopsgate Institute, London, 1, 18, 20, 28, 82, 117, 177, 187
Black and Gay, Back in the Day podcast, 284
Black Lesbian and Gay Centre, 260, 263–4, 284, 324
Black queer community 52, 216, 284, 308; housing, 260–2, 273; nightlife, 76, 77–8, 92
Blackliners, 284
blackmail, 185
Blair, Tony, 144–5, 150, 151, 171, 193
Blake, Jonathan, 274
Blunkett, David, 170, 235
Body Positive, 214, 241–2
Boothe, Michael, 140
Bornstein, Kate, 168
Bösche, Susanne *see Jenny Lives with Eric and Martin* by Susanne Bösche
Brabazon, Baron, 125
Braham, Laurie, 324
Breach Theatre, 52
Bristol, 102, 267, 306
Bristol Switchboard, 26–7

British Empire, 126
British Home Stores (BHS), 295
British Social Attitudes survey, 37–8, 158–9
British Telecom, 338–40, 344
Brixton, London, 273–5, 280–3, 289
Broadway Market, London, 280, 284
Bronski Beat, 105–6
Brophy, Julia Anne, 177, 180–1
Brown, Ted, 289–90
Brownies Sauna, London, 117–19
Bryan, Roy, 260, 262
Buckmaster, Viscount Martin Stanley, 13, 227
Bucknell, Ali, 21, 335
bullying, 151, 155, 158, 196, 364
butch or femme, 84–5

Caledonian Road, London (home to Switchboard), 17–18, 286–7
Campaign for Homosexual Equality, 22, 186
Campbell, Alastair, 169–70
Capital Gay, 76, 117, 118, 131, 132, 340
care, 233–4, 246–9, 311, 354; HIV/AIDS crisis, 212–13, 216, 221–2, 225; Switchboard volunteers, 220, 241, 243–4
care homes, 288–91
Casey, Louise, 148
Catholicism, 16, 228, 297–8
Cave, Dudley, 313
Census data, 320–4
Chaguaramas bar, West End, 79–80
Challoner, Alan, 229–30
Channel 4, 217
Chapman, Tracy, 73
Charity Commission, 196–200
chat rooms, 341–3
Chessington World of Adventures, 169
children of gay parents, 317–18, 320
Chislett, Leigh, 221–3
Christianity, 236, 259, 301–2, 307, 313
Ciechomski, Suzanne, 83–4, 279–80
citizenship, 263–7
civil partnership, 319–20
Cleethorpes, 11, 41, 217, 282
Clit Club, London, 101
Closed User Group (CUG), 344

Club Kali, London, 92, 94, 96–7
clubs *see* nightlife
codes to indicate sexual preferences, 39, 41–3
Cohen, Derek, 99–101, 343–4
Coleherne pub, Earls Court, 97–8, 353
Collins, Phil, 137–8, 139
colonialism, 126
coming out, 25, 293, 355, 375–6; family reactions, 15, 253–4, 300–1, 303, 306, 366
communes, 280–3; *see also* housing co-ops; lesbian separatists; squatting
community, 96, 99–101, 114–16, 260; *see also* connection and belonging
computers, 335–6, 340–1, 364
confidentiality, 1
connection and belonging, 84, 86–8, 94, 284, 291–2, 338, 349–54; *see also* community
Conservative Family Campaign, 13
Conservative Party, 13, 173, 188, 227, 247, 324, 331
Copeland, David, 111
Copley, Tom, 272
Cornwall County Council, 168
Coronation Street, 63
cottaging *see* cruising and cottaging
council housing, 270–3, 288–9
councils, 11, 13, 14, 99–100, 101, 324–5; *see also* local authorities
Coventry, 279
Covid-19 pandemic, 86, 108, 159, 222, 249, 250, 276, 356
Cox, Baroness Caroline, 12–13
Craftman, Steve, 214–15, 241–3, 250–1, 332, 355–7
Criminal Law Amendment Bill, 1921, 125
criminal records, 130
criminalisation of homosexuality *see* homosexuality and the law; police; Section 28
cruising and cottaging, 47–52, 121–4, 141–2, 367
cultural depictions of LGBTQ+ characters, 25, 63, 146–7, 193–4, 268
cultural heritage, 16–17, 29–32
Currie, Edwina, 190–1
custody cases, 173–81

INDEX

Daily Mail, 12, 185, 247
dancing, 103–4, 107, 115–16
dating apps and websites, 46–7
Dave, Shivani, 28
demonstrations, 140, 155–7, 191–3, 201
Desmond, Richard, 97–9, 112, 183, 185–7, 208–13, 286, 288, 345
dildos, 55, 216
Disability Discrimination Act, 1995, 67
disabled people, 51–2, 64–7, 75, 94–5, 284, 336–7
discrimination, 151, 244–5; gay parents, 319–20; workplace, 295, 372; *see also* employment rights; equality
diversity of volunteers, 165–6, 261, 345–6
Dixon, Janet, 176, 279
DJ Ritu *see* Ritu (DJ)
domestic violence, 308, 374
Donovan, Jason, 38, 309
drag artists, 77, 281
drug use, 50–1
dual prejudice, 66
Dyke Marches, 201

Eaks, Louis, 140
Eclipse, Truro, 73
Ecola, Carla, 305
economic circumstances, 287–91; *see also* housing crisis
education *see* schools; Section 28: education under; sex education; teachers
Education (No 2) Act, 1986, 227
elderly care, 249, 288–91
Ellis, John, 118, 119
email, 337, 344–5, 346
emotion, suppression of, 196–7
employment rights, 168, 169, 244–5, 295, 372
entrapment, 132–4
equality, 25, 145, 150, 182–3, 193, 194
Equality Act, 2010, 67, 180
Erasure, 105
Ewart, Steve, 200

Fairbairn, Nicholas, 191
families: adoption and fostering, 324–7; coming out to, 15, 253–4, 300–1, 303, 306, 366; conventional and unconventional, 293–6, 323, 327–30, 358–9; making babies, 314–19, 327; queer families, 306–11, 313–14, 328–30; rejection by, 276, 303–6, 307–8; role models, 300–1, 359; state homophobia, 301–2, 304, 320–4; support of, 96–7, 115, 153–4, 186, 309; Switchboard family, 311–12, 329–30; *see also* parents, relationships with
fascism, 110, 111
femininity, 84–5
feminism, 40, 57, 308, 315–17
Feminist Self Insemination Group, 315–17
femme or butch, 84–5
fetishes, 43–6, 98–102, 343
Finn (Switchboard caller), 163–4
Fisch, 47, 84, 102
FIST, London, 101
Fitzgerald, Elaine, 87–8, 175–6, 178–80, 181
forums (online), 342–3
fostering *see* adoption and fostering
freedom, 102–3, 115–16
friendship, 306–11, 338; *see also* connection and belonging; queer elders, connection with; queer families
Fright, Martin, 243–4
Fuller, Stephanie, 89–91, 310–11, 342–3
fundraising, 286

Galop, 148–9
Gateways, Chelsea, 87–8
Gau, Justin, 144
Gay and Lesbian Legal Advice line (GLAD), 143–4
Gay Conservative Group, 331
gay identities, 85–6
Gay Liberation Front (GLF), 18, 19, 140, 143, 176, 243, 273, 279
gay liberation movement, 40, 50, 57, 82
Gay Men's Health Project, Southampton, 233
Gay News, 18–20, 23, 44, 76
Gaydar, 46
Gaydar Girls, 46, 341
gender conformity / non-conformity, 283–4, 285; *see also* gender identity
gender dysphoria, 171, 172, 299–300

genderfluid, 156–7, 161, 352
gender identity, 57–62, 149, 245–7, 283–4, 299, 309; *see also* non-binary identity; transgender identity
Gender Identity Research & Education Society (GIRES), 169
Gender Recognition Act, 2004, 172–3
gendersex, 58, 103
general election 1987, 13
generational differences, 287–8, 354, 359, 367
Geocities, 341
Geymonat, Melania, 84
Ghey, Brianna, 155–6
Giles, Ian, 274
Gillespie Sells, Kath, 66–7, 284
Gingerbeer, 46–7, 341
Glynn, Noel, 289–90
Google Maps, 347
Gordon, Arnold, 284
government policy, 151; age of consent, 186–7, 190–4; family, 319–23, 325; HIV/AIDS, 230–1, 239–40; sex education, 227–8, 232–3, 235; trans rights, 169–71, 172–3, 247; *see also* state homophobia; state transphobia
Gow, Ian, 272
Grainger, Dennis, 200
Granta, 51–2
Greenhalgh, Hugo, 188, 190, 191–2
Grey, Anthony, 323
grief, 17, 112–13, 210–12, 225–6, 242–4, 361, 368
Grimsby, 11, 41, 75, 282
Grindr, 46
gross indecency, 118, 123, 125, 126, 127, 153
Gumtree, 347

hanky code, 41–3
Hannah (Adam's sister), 256, 276, 303, 314; coming out, 253–5, 296, 301, 308, 366; parenthood, 318–20, 327–8, 358–9
Haringey, north London, 11, 13
hate crimes, 150–1, 155–6, 269, 280–1; *see also* Admiral Duncan pub bombing, 1999; homophobic attacks
Haworth, Thomas, 200

Hay, Paul, 200
Health Service Journal, 229
healthcare, 216; HIV/AIDS, 211, 213–14, 221–3, 224, 245; pregnancy and parenting, 315, 319; trans community, 160–1, 169, 172
Henry VIII, 125
Herrick, Mrs (Adam's teacher), 217–18, 232
heterosexual callers to Switchboard, 240
Hey, Baby, 104
Hill, Dawn, 284
Hirana, Rita, 92–4, 96–7, 103, 111, 114
historical context, 3
history, recording of, 331–4; *see also* memories, preservation of
HIV/AIDS: discrimination, 244–5; government policy, 230–1, 239–40; healthcare, 221–3; impact on LGBTQ+ community, 203–4, 208–12, 223–6, 304; impact on volunteers, 212–13, 214–15, 241–4; impact on younger generations, 205–7, 216–20, 226–8, 232; loss and grief, 30, 192, 225–6, 242, 243–4; panic and ignorance, 15, 118, 189, 207, 221, 248, 339; public health campaigns, 237–40; survivors, 223–6, 249–51, 288–9; Switchboard calls, 24, 203, 204–5, 208, 211, 213–14, 222, 233, 240, 244–5; women's role, 212, 215–16
Hodson, George, 223–6, 249, 288–9, 314, 332, 361–2, 365–6, 369
Home Office, 129, 130, 132, 225, 266
homelessness, 244–5, 262, 303–5
homes and housing: alternative living arrangements, 269–71, 272–8, 280–3; under attack, 268–9, 280–1; belonging, 256, 260, 284, 291–2; council housing, 270–3; family homes, 253–5; gender non-conformity, 283–4; generational differences and elderly care, 287–91; lesbian separatists, 278–80; living with friends, 255–6; prejudice, 260–2; Switchboard as home, 285–7; Switchboard accommodation service, 256–7, 260–2, 347; *see also* housing crisis; migrants to the UK

INDEX

homesteading schemes, 270
homophobic attacks, 150–1, 155–6, 108–15, 269, 280–1, 355; *see also* Admiral Duncan pub bombing, 1999
homosexuality and the law, 47–9, 67, 97–8, 124–32; *see also* government policy; police
Hoon, Geoff, 170
house parties, 77–8
Housing Act, 1980, 271
housing co-ops, 269–76; *see also* communes; lesbian separatists; squatting
housing crisis, 271–3, 277–8, 287–8
Housmans bookshop, London, 17–18, 19, 166
Hows, Julian, 39, 43, 50, 124, 281–2, 285, 338–9
Hughes-Morgan, Sir David, 119
human rights, 170–1, 172, 186
Human Rights Act, 1998, 145
Hunter, Chryssy, 161, 162

Imaan, 107
immigration, 225, 263–7
imperialism, 126
importuning, 129–30
In Other Words bookshop, Plymouth, 107
inclusivity *see* diversity of volunteers
index cards, 22–3, 334–5
Ingham, Bernard, 230–1
instant messaging, 337, 341
Intercom Trust, 374
internet: early days, 334, 340–1; impact on Switchboard, 342, 346–8, 348; online abuse, 344–5; online connection and belonging, 25, 46–7, 342–3, 344–5; and sex, 46, 343–4
internet generation, 333, 341–2
iPhones, 347
Islam, 307
Islington Gay Housing Co-Op, 270
isolation, 95–6, 298–300, 306, 352, 354–5, 356
Izard, Jonathan, 257–8

James, Diana, 57–60, 164–6, 173, 201, 211–13, 264, 286–7
Jarman, Derek, 192

Jenny Lives with Eric and Martin by Susanne Bösche, 12–13, 107, 174, 206, 227, 255, 301
Jim (Adam's father), 365–7
Johns, Ian, 286
Julia (Tash's mother), 11, 239, 296

Keegan, Gillian, 247
kinks, 43–6, 98–102, 343
Knight, Ralph, 231
Konrath, Tony, 104, 239

L Word, The (2004–2009), 25, 268
Labouchere, Henry, 125
Labour Party, 13, 144–5, 169–70, 196, 231, 247, 301, 324
language and terminology, 2–3, 62–3, 64, 161–2, 171
lavender marriages, 264–7
law *see* homosexuality and the law
leather, 98–9
Lee, Catherine, 268–9, 342, 354–5, 357
Leeds, 82
Lees, Ed, 52, 61, 68
Legacy of Kindness podcast, 168, 169
legal advice, 142–4, 176, 179, 244–5, 263–4
legal history, 124–9
Leicester, 92
Lemon, Denis, 18–19
Leontarakis, Constantinos, 200
Lesbian Custody Group, 177
lesbians: HIV/AIDS crisis, 212, 215–16; hostility and prejudice, 15, 125–6, 267–9; identity, 58–9, 84–5; legal system, 121, 124–5; mothers, 173–81, 293–4, 314–19, 322, 327–8, 358–9, 371, 375; nightlife, 71–2, 76, 78–9, 83–4, 87–8, 92, 93–4, 101; online, 341; separatists, 278–80, 315, 317; sex, 40, 47, 52, 53–5
Lesbian Self Insemination Pamphlet (1980), 315–17
Lesbian Strength Marches, 164, 201
Levy, Ken, 118–19
LGBTQ+ History Month, 28
'LGBTQ+' terminology, 2
Lianna (1983), 268
Liberty, 170–1

399

libraries, 11–12, 14, 301, 342
Lindsay, John, 20–3, 32–3, 333, 335, 349, 367–8
listening, importance of, 25, 348–9, 353–8, 360, 379
listservs, 345
Liverpool, 268
Livi (Tash's sister), 296, 300–1, 328
local authorities, 14, 15, 217, 229, 301; *see also* councils
Local Government Act 1988 *see* Section 28
log books; anonymity and confidentiality, 1; discovery and origins of, 5–7, 17, 22–3; as historical documents, 3, 331–2, 333, 348–51, 357, 380; *see also* Switchboard
Log Books, The podcast, 17, 135, 187, 243, 361; impact of, 106, 159, 349, 355; making of, 28–32, 250, 332–3, 352, 357
London, 308, 353; housing, 256, 257–8, 272, 280, 282, 288, 290
London Assembly, 272
London Gay Men's Chorus, 113
London Gay Teenage Group, 183, 235
London Lesbian and Gay Centre, 92, 99–100, 101
London Lesbian and Gay Switchboard, 26
London Lighthouse, 212
loneliness, 250, 313, 352, 354–5, 356
Longford, Lord Frank Pakenham, 301–2, 304, 328–9
Lorde, Audre, 216
love, 208–10; *see also* care; families; relationships
Lyn (Switchboard caller), 78–9, 87–8

Mackay, Anson, 283
McKellen, Ian, 189
McKerrow, Graham, 275–8
Maclaughlin, Marguerite, 315
McMicholas, James, 200
Major, John, 188, 189, 320, 325
Malin, Alan, 118–19
Man Hunt, 46
Mandelson, Peter, 170
Manning, Lulu, 106

Marlow, Tony, 191
Marquess, Paul, 136, 146–7
marriage, 178, 264–7, 293, 312–13, 319–20, 371
Martin (Tash's father), 138, 296
masculinity, 84–5
May, Lyn, 177
Meakin, William, 200
media, 230–1, 235, 239, 247–8
memories, preservation of, 87, 116, 353, 357–8, 359–62, 368
mental health support, 209, 210–11, 214
Metropolitan Police, 129, 146, 147, 148–50
Michael, George, 121–2, 144
middle generation, 205–6, 213, 226–7, 249, 275, 287–8, 291
migrants to the UK, 263–7, 306–8
Miller, Arthur, 363–4
Minicom, 65, 336–7
minority stress, 201
Moir, Lorraine, 135–6
Moncrieff, Monty, 192
morality, 187, 227–9, 231–2
Morgan, Miss (Tash's teacher), 219–20, 357, 371–8
mpox virus, 234
murder of LGBTQ+ people, 150–1, 155–6
music, 105–7
Muslims, 107

National AIDS Helpline, 241
National Archives, 128–9, 133–4, 149, 152, 159, 169, 189, 195, 233, 320
National Health Service (NHS), 229, 234, 247; *see also* healthcare
National Organisation of Lesbian & Gay Youth & Community Workers, 233
Navy, 137–8
Neighbours, 38, 298
Neville and James (queer elders), 353
New York, 140
NG1, Nottingham, 73
nightlife, 71–4; connection and belonging, 46, 86–8, 94, 114–16, 353; disabled and older people, 94–5; freedom, music and dancing, 102–7, 115–16; hostility and violence, 79–80,

INDEX

81–4, 108–15; leather, SM, BDSM, 98–102; people of colour, 92–4, 96–7; trans community, 89–91; volunteer knowledge, 74–9
NME, 105
non-binary identity, 3, 106, 149, 283; *see also* gender identity
non-judgemental listening, 40, 44–5; *see also* listening, importance of
North, David, 171
nostalgia, 74, 79, 87, 102–3, 368
Not Going into the Care Closet campaign, 290
Nottingham, 73

Odets, Walt, 205
Offenbach, David, 142–3
Office for National Statistics, 287–8
Oke, Mr (letter writer), 150–2, 321
Okundaye, Jason, 273
older Switchboard callers, 95–6
On Railton Road by Ian Giles and Louis Rembges, 274
Opening Doors London, 290
openness, 25
Otitoju, Femi, 40, 53–5, 83, 92, 176, 216, 288, 308
Out and About exhibition, 2023, 20
Outback, The (newsletter), 107
OutRage! 140
Outside Project, 305
Owen, M. F., 338

paedophilia, 184, 195, 198–9
Panda (volunteer), 243–4
Panorama, 158
parents, relationships with, 262–3, 276, 293, 296, 299, 303–6, 308, 365–7; supportive, 96–7, 153–4, 186
Parks, Alex, 73
parliament, 190–4; *see also* government policy
Parry, Will, 188, 191–2
Partridge, Nick, 238, 239
Patsy (Adam's mother), 11, 239, 303, 364–5, 366–7 Payne, John, 141
Phillips, Andrew, 199–200
phone line gremlins, 338–40, 348
Piccos, Andy, 269–71, 272–3

Pink Paper, 76
Pink Singers, 106
Planningtorock, 106
Playdon, Zoë, 168
Plymouth, 11, 46, 74, 80–1, 107, 138, 150–1, 282, 372
podcast *see Log Books, The* podcast
podophiles, 44
police: cruising and cottaging, 47–9, 121–4; improving relations with LGBTQ+ community, 145–6; institutional homophobia, 132–6, 148, 153; persecution of gay community, 126–32, 160, 188; raids and entrapment, 97–8, 117–21, 131–3; Switchboard's relations with, 139–44, 145–6, 264; transphobia, 148–50
Pollack, Joanne, 200
poppers, 50–1, 102
pornography, 341
Power, Lisa, 55, 190, 193, 269, 288; Switchboard veteran, 63–4, 123–4, 165, 178, 185, 260–1, 311–12
pregnancy, 314–19, 327
Prescott, John, 170
Press For Change, 169
Preston Gay Switchboard, 71–2
Pretended by Catherine Lee, 268–9
pretty police, 132
Pride, 18, 53, 67, 146
pronouns, 3, 156–7, 161
protests, 140, 155–7, 191–3, 201
public health campaigns, 237–40
public places, sex in, 47–52
Pulse nightclub shooting, Orlando, Florida, 2016, 112–13

queer ancestry, 16–17, 29–32, 51, 116, 134, 152–3, 181–2; *see also* queer elders, connection with
Queer as Folk (1999–2000), 25, 147, 193–4
queer elders, connection with, 351–8, 367–9, 379; *see also* queer ancestry
queer families, 306–11, 313–14, 328–30
'queer' terminology, 2
Quentin (Tash's uncle), 255–6, 329

racism, 52, 91–4, 111, 213, 260–2

Railton Road in Brixton, London, 273–5
Rainbow Flag Awards, 374
Rao, Maurice, 196–7, 198, 199
Rasmussen, Tom, 106
Reed, Niki, 169
Regard, 66–7, 284
relationships, 208–10, 218, 224–5, 233
religion, 18, 307, 313; *see also* Catholicism; Christianity
Rembges, Louis, 274
Revolutionary Acts by Jason Okundaye, 273
Rey, Harry F., 183, 343
Rights of Women, 176–7
Riposte club, 108
Ritu (DJ), 92–4, 96–7
role models, 219–20, 298–301, 351, 359, 377
Rose, Dinah, 169
Ruby (child of two mums), 317–18, 320
runaways, 262–3

Sadie Masie club, 99, 101
sadomasochism (SM), 85, 99–102, 343
safer sex campaigns, 237–40
Samaritans, 62, 199
saunas, 117–19
schools, 14–15, 30, 151–2, 157–8, 236–7, 281–2, 363–5, 374–5; *see also* sex education; teachers
science curriculum, 228
Scotland, 229
Section 28: censorship, 341; creation of, 13–14, 119, 121; education under, 14, 163–4, 206–7, 216–20, 229, 232, 355, 365, 379; family, 96–7, 208, 295, 301, 324, 359; opposition to, 107, 157; repealed, 2003, 25, 151, 235, 236; social impact of, 14–17, 52–3, 61, 160, 268–9, 351–2; terminology, 3
self-care, 241–3
Seligman, David, 33, 197, 262, 338–9, 367–8
sex acts, talking about, 26
sex clubs, 47, 50
sex discrimination, 168
sex education, 36–7, 40, 144, 206–7, 216–20, 226–9, 232–3, 235, 247
sex questions from callers, 23, 35, 37–8, 67–9; codes and kinks, 39–46; cruising and cottaging, 47–52
sex toys, 55, 67–8
sexism, 83, 109, 125, 126, 135, 174–5
sexual community, 100–1
sexual health campaigns, 237–40
Sexual Offences Act, 1967, 19, 126–7, 128–9, 153, 182
Sexual Offences (Amendment) Act 2000, 194
sexual orientation and identity, 58–62
sexually transmitted infections, 217, 218, 233, 234, 239
SHAKTI, London, 92, 93
shame, 35–8, 40–1, 68; *see also* social stigma
sibling bonds, 308
Sistermatic club night, 284
Sisters Uncut, 308
Sisterwrite bookshop, London, 284
Skinner, Judith, 183
SM *see* sadomasochism (SM)
'Smalltown Boy' by Bronski Beat, 105–6
smartphones, 347–8
Smith, Chris, 133, 191, 225
Smith, Earl F.E., 125
Smith, Juliet, 219–20, 371–8
social attitudes, 158–9
social groups, 107
social media, 113
social stigma, 119, 123, 130, 136, 143–4, 153–4
social workers, 236
soliciting, 132
Somalia, 267, 306, 307–8
Somerville, Jimmy, 105–6
South Asian gay community, 92–4, 96–7
SpareRoom website, 347
sperm donation, 315–19, 375
Spice Girls, 91
squatting, 270, 275, 279–80, 284
Stallard, Lord Albert William, 228
Starmer, Keir, 247
state homophobia, 128–30, 132, 133, 152–3, 159–60; family, 301–2, 304, 319–24, 324–6; *see also* government policy; police; Section 28
state transphobia, 156, 158–9, 247; *see also* trans rights
stereotypes, 295, 298–9

INDEX

Steve (volunteer seeking HIV support) *see* Craftman, Steve
Stewart, Terry, 129–30, 136
stigma *see* social stigma
Stonewall, 184, 188, 189, 194, 372
Stonewall Housing, 262
Stonewall Inn, New York, 140
stories, 7, 16–17, 29–33, 72–3, 120–1, 349, 351–3, 355, 358; *see also* listening, importance of; memories, preservation of; queer ancestry; queer elders, connection with
Straw, Jack, 169–70
Streeting, Wes, 247
suicide, 26, 27, 136, 151, 233
Sun, 12, 207, 230–1
Sunak, Rishi, 247
Sutherland, Euan, 193–4
Swallow, The, Plymouth, 80–1
Swenson, Rebecca, 112, 115, 297–8
Switchboard: archive, 28; charitable status, 195–200; establishment of, 22–6, 334–5; home of, 285–7; origins, 17–22; present and future, 348–9; *see also* log books; volunteering for Switchboard
Switchboard Development Group, 105
Switchboard Information Group, 142
Switchboard Women's Group, 166
symbols to indicate sexual preferences, 39, 41–3

Tatchell, Peter, 131–2, 148
Taylor, Yvonne, 284
teachers, 11–12, 157, 163–4, 237, 268–9, 355, 365; Tash's school teachers, 15, 357, 371–8; *see also* schools; sex education
technologies and communication, 331–4, 336–7; Switchboard phones and computers, 335–6, 338–40, 348; *see also* internet
teddy bears, 39
teenagers, 182–7, 231, 235–6, 262–3, 303–5
television *see* cultural depictions of LGBTQ+ characters
Terrence Higgins Trust (THT), 222, 238, 248
terrorism, 111–13, 145–6

Tesauro, Advocate General Giuseppe, 168
Thailand, 224–5
Thatcher, Margaret, 13, 230, 244, 271, 272
theatre, 363–4
they/them, 156–7
Thompson, Eric J., 322–3
Thompson, Marc, 77–8, 86, 273, 304
Thompson, Ray, 168
Todd, Matthew, 115
Tony and Pete (teachers and fathers), 218–19, 325–7, 355
Tossell, Darren, 200
touch talk, 65
Tower Hamlets Council, 100
toxic masculinity, 282
training for volunteers, 53–5, 63, 336
trans children, 247
Trans Pride, 2023, 155, 156–7, 160, 173
trans rights, 155–7, 158–9, 160, 162, 168–73, 247
transgender identity, 38, 52, 58, 299–300; family, 304–5; language and terminology, 2–3, 62–4, 161–2, 171; legal system, 121; nightlife, 76, 77, 89–91; online connection and belonging, 342–3; queer family, 310–11; Switchboard calls, 160–1, 162–3, 167, 172, 245–6; Switchboard volunteers, 164–8
transphobia, 148–50, 155–6, 158–9, 166, 247, 304–5
'transsexuals', use of term, 63, 149, 162
'transvestites', use of term, 63, 149, 162
Truscott, Clare, 71–2, 73, 85, 86, 184, 290, 343
Turing Project, 347–8
Turner, Ruth, 206–7, 219–20, 302, 312–13, 315–17, 372–3, 379
TV/TS Newsletter, 90
Tyler, Don, 270

uk-motss, 345
university, 306, 309–10, 364, 365–6

Vaults, The, Exeter, 73
vegetarianism, 279
Vicky (letter writer), 320–4

View from the Bridge, A by Arthur Miller, 363–4
violence *see* abuse; bullying; homophobic attacks
voices, 331–4, 349; *see also* listening, importance of; stories
volunteering for Switchboard, 26–7, 29, 285–7, 379; diversity of volunteers, 165–6, 261, 345–6; training, 53–5, 63, 336

Walker, Tash: activism, 155–6; adolescence, 15, 40–1, 107, 158, 164, 171, 268, 351; biases, 1–2; childhood, 11, 14, 38, 138, 150–1, 203, 309; education, 15, 144, 219–20, 232; family, 294, 296, 298, 300–1, 306, 309, 312, 328, 329, 359; gender identity, 156–7, 161, 163, 283, 309, 352; as historian, 332–3, 349–58; homes and housing, 255, 256, 259–60, 271, 280, 282–3, 284, 287, 291; hostility towards, 120, 125–6; log books, 5–7, 28, 38, 244; nightlife, 72–3, 79–81, 88, 102, 104; online life, 341; podcast, 28–32; queer family, 306–7, 312–13, 379; religion, 297–8, 307; reunion with teachers, 371–8; self and identity, 57, 58–9, 60, 69, 85–6, 153; sexual experiences, 35–6, 46, 51, 58–9; volunteering for Switchboard, 26–7, 113, 210, 264, 310–12, 379
Wall, Christine, 280
Walmsley, Roy, 128–9
Walters, Jonathan, 269–70
Warner, Nigel, 186

WayOut Club, London, 90–1, 161
West London Day Centre, 54
Whitehead, Tony, 295
Whitehouse, Mary, 18
Widdecombe, Ann, 158
Wilde, Ralph, 188
Willetts, David, 230
Williams, Martin, 200
Woman's Hour, 239
Woman's Own, 178
women's rights, 176–7
women's role in HIV crisis, 212, 215–16
women's safety, 108–9, 125–6

York, 82
Youth Concern, 37

Zamimass, 216
Zmith, Adam: adolescence, 41, 164, 189, 190, 193–4, 196–7, 226–7, 351, 362–5, 368; biases, 1–2; childhood, 11, 14, 203; education, 15, 144, 217–18, 232, 235; family, 153–4, 253–5, 276, 296, 300–1, 303, 306, 308, 314, 358–9, 365–7; health, 234; as historian, 332–3, 349–58; homes and housing, 253–6, 258–9, 277–8, 282–3, 291; hostility towards, 108; learning and work, 27–8, 362–5, 368; nightlife, 72–3, 80–1, 86, 89, 102, 104; online life, 341; podcast, 28–32; queer family, 309–10, 314, 361–2, 365–9; self and identity, 69, 283–4, 352–3; sexual experiences, 27, 36, 50–1, 56, 100, 368; sperm donation, 318–20, 327–8, 358–9

Switchboard is still open today, operating as the national LGBTQIA+ listening service. Their volunteers are on hand to discuss anything related to sexuality and gender identity. Whether it's sexual health, relationships or your feelings. The service is run by the LGBTQIA+ community, for the LGBTQIA+ community, and is there to provide support to anyone, anywhere in the country, at any point in their journey.

You can contact Switchboard from 10 a.m. to 10 p.m., 365 days a year:

Phone: 0800 0119 100
Email: hello@switchboard.lgbt
Instant Message: switchboard.lgbt

Further details on how to volunteer or support Switchboard through donations can be found at switchboard.lgbt